Lukang

SUNY Series in Chinese Local Studies

Harry J. Lamley, Editor

Lukang

Commerce and Community in a Chinese City

Donald R. DeGlopper

THE STATE UNIVERSITY OF NEW YORK PRESS

Published by
State University of New York Press, Albany

©1995 State University of New York

For information, address State University of New York Press,
State University Plaza, Albany, NY 12246

Production by Laura Starrett
Marketing by Terry Abad Swierzowski

Library of Congress Cataloging-in-Publication Data

DeGlopper, Donald R. (Donald Robert), 1942–
    Lukang, commerce and community in a Chinese city / Donald R.
DeGlopper.
        p.   cm.
    Based on both the author's thesises (Ph. D.) — Cornell University,
1973, and (master's — University of London, 1965)
    Includes bibliographical references (p.) and index.
    ISBN 0–7914–2689–0 (cloth) : $59.50. — ISBN 0–7914–2690–4 (pbk.)
: $19.95
    1. Lu-kang chen (Taiwan) — Social conditions. 2. Lu-kang chen
(Taiwan) —Social life and customs. 3. Lu-kang chen (Taiwan) —
Economic conditions. 4. City and town life Taiwan — Lu-kang chen
I. Title.
HN749.L8D44   1995
306'.095124'9—dc20   95-2525
                                                                CIP

10 9 8 7 6 5 4 3 2 1

Contents

Preface

This volume is the evolutionary descendant of a doctoral dissertation presented to Cornell University in 1973. In places, particularly in chapter 2, it incorporates elements from a master's dissertation presented to the University of London in 1965. I owe a clear debt to my mentors at those institutions, and most especially to the late Maurice Freedman, to G. W. Skinner, to Robert J. Smith, and to Arthur P. Wolf. My initial fieldwork in Taiwan was supported by a fellowship from the then Foreign Area Fellowship Program. A subsequent period of research in Taiwan in 1979, which informs though is not directly represented in these pages, was supported by the Social Science Research Council. The work benefited enormously from my access to the libraries of Cornell University, Yale University, the Australian National University, and to the collections of the Library of Congress.

My single greatest debt is to the many inhabitants of Lukang, who took time from their busy lives to patiently respond to the ill-put questions of a foreign student with an imperfect command of their language. I owe an equally great, if different sort of, debt to my immediate family, to Eva, Jacob, and Peter, who shared the costs, if not the rewards, of this endeavor, and provided assistance ranging from editing to solving software problems. Much of the work was done (if I may echo Johnson) without patronage, and not in the soft obscurities of retirement or under the shelter of academic bowers, which made the forbearance and assistance of my family even more necessary.

The final version of the final chapter was completed while I was enjoying the shelter of the academic bower of the Australian National University's Contemporary China Centre, whose support I gratefully acknowledge. In a manner reminiscent of Dr. Johnson and his *Dictionary*, I have protracted my work till many of those I wished to please have departed this world. Let me here acknowledge the inspiration provided by the work of Maurice Freedman and Barbara E. Ward, and confess my hope that what I have produced might approach the standards of their work, which continues to inspire scholars.

Glossary

This glossary excludes geographical names; terms of extremely local and particular provenance, such as names of Lukang neighborhood temples; personal names; and terms that are, in my judgment, so common as to be known to any reader literate in Chinese, such as *kuan-hsi/guanxi*. I have, however, tried to include characters for all terms originally cited in Hokkien (Taiwanese, Min-nan Hua) romanization (which follows that of N. C. Bodman). Mandarin terms are given in both modified Wade-Giles and pinyin romanization.

ai-mng (H)	隘門
bi-kok-lang (H)	美國人
bi-kok-lang (H)	米國人
bin-cieng (H) min-ch'ing (minqing)	民情
biou-hui (H)	廟會
Ching Yi Yuan (Jingyi Yuan)	敬義園
ch'ing (qing)	情
hang (hang)	行
hap-kang-e (H)	闔港的
hok-cap (H)	複雜
hsiang (xiang)	相
hsin-yung (xinyong)	信用
jen-ch'ing (renqing)	人情

jen-ch'ing-wei (renqing wei)	人情味
kak-thau (H)	角頭
kak-thau-sin (H)	角頭神
kheq-hia:-tu (H)	客兄廚
kuo-hsiang (guoxiang)	過香
lau-ziat (H)	鬧熱
li	理
li	禮
lieng-kam (H) ling-kan (linggan)	靈感
lo-cu (H)	爐主
lo-kha (H)	爐下
lo-mua (H)	鱸鰻
nei-hang jen (neihangren)	內行人
p'ai-hsi (paixi)	派系
pao (bao)	報
shen-shang (shenshang)	紳商
shu (shu)	恕
sia-hue (H)	社會
sieng-li kuan-he (H)	生利關係
thau-ke (H)	頭家
thiau (H)	柱
u lang kong (H)	有人講

Place Names

These are administrative units, ports, and market towns mentioned in the text. Most are in Taiwan; a few are in Fukien's Ch'üan-chou Prefecture.

Chang-chou	彰州
Chang-hua	彰化

Ch'ao-chou	潮州
Ch'ien-chiang	錢江
Chin-chiang	晉江
Cho-shui	濁水
Chu-lo	諸羅
Ch'üan-chou	泉州
Erh-lin	二林
Fan-wa	番控
Han-chiang	蚶江
Hou-lung	後龍
Hsin-hai	潯海
Hu-wei	虎尾
Meng-chia	艋舺
Lu-kang	鹿港
Pei-kang	北港
Pei-tou	北斗
San I	三邑
Ta-tao-ch'eng	大蹈城
Tung-shih-kang	東石港
Wu-ch'i	梧棲
Ya-k'ou	衙口
Yuan-lin	員林

The use of travelling is to regulate the imagination by reality, and instead of thinking how things may be, to see them as they are.

—Samuel Johnson to Mrs. Thrale

Just about the time when . . . one felt he had reached a conclusion, he [Simmel] had a way of raising his right arm and, with three fingers of his hand, turning the imaginary object so as to exhibit still another facet.

—Abraham Flexner, *I Remember: The Autobiography of Abraham Flexner*

Introduction

Some Problems

In April 1967 I moved into Lukang, an old city on the west coast of Taiwan, and spent the next eighteen months watching the people of the city and talking with them. As an anthropologist doing fieldwork my ultimate goal was to discover how the people of Lukang thought about themselves and their society. My more immediate goal was to understand how a Chinese city rather than a village was held together, and to do this I proposed to look at urban businessmen and their social relations. I wanted to concentrate on their ties with people who were not their kinsmen, finding out how they created relations of mutual confidence with people who initially were strangers. I wanted to learn what language they used to describe their social relations and to understand the relation between the concepts of the marketplace and the classic Confucian model of society. In the jargon of the trade, I was interested in personal networks, in voluntary associations, and in contractual relations.

Consequently I spent a lot of time hanging about in shops and asking anyone who would talk with me about such things as go-betweens, sworn brotherhood, what they could expect from their in-laws, and how shopkeepers decided who to extend credit to. I spent even more time in diffuse sociability, chatting with people in my room, at banquets, and on buses. But the more people I talked with and the better my comprehension of the local dialect, the more disquieted I became. I wasn't hearing what I expected to hear.

For one thing, many different people kept repeating the same sorts of statements about Lukang, telling me over and over again that the city was exceptionally old-fashioned, traditional, and refined, and claiming that all of the 28,000 inhabitants shared the same qualities. I regarded such statements as obvious myths, conventional stereotypes, and felt irritated at listening to them over and over. I was eager to get down to cases. This proved difficult. For while people were usually willing enough to give general accounts of such things as rotating credit associations or the way cabinetmakers got jobs, they were very reluctant to give specific details about their own or anyone else's affairs. If specific details of other people's behavior were provided, it was most often in the context of malicious gossip. Cases were hard to collect.

Nor did the attempt to elicit verbal categories and principles for their use, and to discern the inherent logic behind them go as I had hoped. Attempts to specify the meaning and range of application of such common terms as "sentiment" (*kan-ch'ing/ganqing*) or "old friend" were frustrated when people either insisted that such terms weren't relevant to what we were discussing, like buying cloth from wholesalers, or that individual variation made all generalization hopeless. The most common response to my cunningly constructed questions was "it depends" (*pu yi-ting/buyiding*).

As I saw it, the people of Lukang either overgeneralized about the city as a whole, or refused to make any generalizations at all when discussing individual people. Sometimes they described their city as if it were a pure community, an undifferentiated *gemeinschaft* united by common tradition and sentiments. At other times they talked as if it were an aggregation of atomistic individuals, all perfectly free to make or break whatever agreements or contracts with each other that they pleased. They consistently showed a puzzling lack of interest in topics, such as the segmentation of the major descent groups or the criteria for defining neighborhood boundaries, which my training had led me to believe they should be interested in. It looked as if sometimes they'd been reading Durkheim and Robert Redfield, while at others they seemed to have been reading Adam Smith or George Homans. What they hadn't been reading though was Robert Merton, or Radcliffe-Brown, or even Hsun-tsu. I found the way the people of Lukang presented themselves and described their city both incomplete and paradoxical.

When ethnography leads to paradoxes we can assume that the ethnographer hasn't quite understood how the alien culture works. Of course, I did not find life in Lukang either totally opaque or paradoxical, and I have managed to write up several accounts of aspects of that life.[1] But the problem of understanding why so many people had so consistently spoken of themselves as they did continued to bother me. Now, after more than a decade of intermittent thought about Lukang and further acquaintance with other

Chinese communities, I think that I am finally able to make sense of what I was told in the dusty shops and temples of Lukang. I have also come to understand that my difficulties were not peculiar to Lukang or to myself. They are difficulties that confront anyone who attempts to describe, to conceptualize, the ongoing life of a community, a society.

The Plan of This Book

What follows then is a sort of community study. The community in question is Taiwanese, urban, and supported by small-scale commerce and industry. Accounts of modern Chinese cities are relatively rare, and this study is intended as a monographic case study, a contribution to the literature on Chinese urban society. All community studies have a focus, and this one is animated by questions of modes of description and self-description, of the nature of Chinese urban society in both the present and the recent past, and of Chinese personal relations and associations beyond the realm of kinship. Although necessarily much concerned with the specific details of the history, economy, and society of Lukang, its ultimate focus is beyond that particular city. The same questions could be addressed in thousands of other communities, and the goal is ethnography rather than a local chronicle.

I am convinced, however, that our understanding either of the grand categories, like Chinese society, or of more restricted topics like the place of guilds in late traditional Chinese cities or the composition of contemporary local-level Taiwanese political factions can only advance through case studies—detailed studies of particular communities or institutions, carefully placed in their proper historical, regional, or administrative contexts. I attempt to do this for Lukang and would argue that the same approach should be followed for any community. I am also convinced that adequate description of anything so complex as a contemporary Taiwanese community demands multiple perspectives, each of which, like the microbiologist's choice of stains, highlights different substructures.

In this study the two initial chapters set out the general problems that will underlie and guide the choice of topics in the historical and ethnographic chapters that follow. Each of those chapters approaches Lukang from a different perspective, cuts through the community along a different analytical axis. Chapter 3 provides a relatively brief introduction to the city of Lukang, attempting to convey basic information with a minimum of analysis and comment. Chapters 4 and 5 place Lukang in its relevant contexts and approach it from an outside, detached, and "objective" perspective. To do this they discuss the geography, history, economics, and politics of the island of Taiwan. The assumption here is that the character of Lukang has been to a large extent determined by these larger economic and political systems, and that if one wants to understand the city as it is now, one must understand the causally prior systems that underlie its existence and historical career. The overall theme of chapter 5 is the changing relation between Lukang's local elite, a primarily mercantile one, and the states that have governed the city. Chapter 6 looks inside Lukang, presenting an account of the major components of its social structure in the past. It is an ahistorical, synchronic exposition of a static structure, providing a model of urban social structure intended to facilitate comparison with other cities. It does not however attempt to explain why that structure was as it was.

Chapters 7 and 8 are in some ways the heart of the study and the place where the theoretical themes introduced in the first two chapters are the most evident. Based on field work in 1967–1968, these chapters look at Lukang from the inside and try to show how the people of the city describe themselves and their community. They attempt to use and refine the concepts of "native models" of society, arguing that the self-presentation of the city's inhabitants appears inconsistent and self-contradictory. Chapter 9, a short analytical chapter, steps back outside Lukang and tries to explain why its people describe themselves as they do. It attempts to put the pieces together and to relate what at first may appear quite distinct and unrelated institutions and structures. Finally, chapter 10, a brief concluding chapter, refers back to the questions raised in the initial two chapters and sums up the analytical lessons of the study.

This work is based on eighteen months' fieldwork in Lukang from April 1967 to October 1968, which was funded by the then Foreign Area Fellowship Foundation. A grant from the Social Science Research Council permitted me to return to Taiwan for six months in 1979, when I made several visits to Lukang. I was able to return to Lukang for two days in April 1992. While I employed a number of research techniques in Lukang, ranging from a shop census to formal interviews, the most productive method was simply talking with people in a wide variety of circumstances and attempting to steer the conversation in the direction of my interests. While residing in Lukang and after my return to the United

States I consulted a variety of Chinese-language published materials, ranging from reprints of eighteenth- and nineteenth-century local histories to collections of essays by natives of the city. All research was done in either Mandarin or Taiwanese (Hokkien or Min-nan) and the translations from Chinese written sources are my own.

The concern with such issues as personal networks and connections (*kuan-hsi/guanxi*) or the way the inhabitants of a certain sort of community describe that community means that information gathered in 1967–1968, the ethnographic present of this study, remains relevant. That Lukang, not to mention Taiwan as a whole, has changed since 1968 is obvious, but that process, amply described by other pens, is not the focus of this work. My feeling is that to the extent that what I report is accurate, it is either still significant or provides a baseline for appraising the present. My return visits to Lukang in 1979 and 1992 gave me no reason to alter the analysis presented here.

Choices, Methods, and Exposition

Although this work is now presented to the world at large, people who read through it before publication severally raised some issues that should be addressed. These revolve around the lag between the field research and the publication of the monograph, a period of rather more than two decades; the use or non-use of various academic forms of terminology, frames of reference, modes of analysis, or "theoretical paradigms"; and my use of the present tense to describe a place that is most certainly not that way now.

When, many years ago, I began graduate studies in the anthropology of China, my mentor, the late Maurice Freedman, assigned me the task of reviewing for our seminar a recently published book. The book, published in 1963 or 1962, reported on Professor Charles Osgood's truncated field research in a village in Yunnan in 1941. I then, with youthful arrogance, found the publication of twenty-year-old research rather risible. Now, demonstrating the irony of life and the correction of youth by age, I find myself publishing research even older than Professor Osgood's. Doing so, and doing so in the form this work takes, represents several related choices and decisions.

Having decided to publish rather than allow the manuscript to rest in the drawer to which it had been consigned, I faced the choice of how extensively to revise and "update" the text. After a good deal of thought and several essays at revision I decided to submit it with only minimal attempts to reflect the time it was published in. The bulk of the work was composed in 1977–1978 and represented a decade's rumination over and analysis of material I gathered in Taiwan in 1967–1968. Much subsequent revision consisted of deleting extraneous detail or references to now justly forgotten academic trends or debates, along with the recasting of sentences and paragraphs. In my view, the work cannot but reflect the time and place of its composition, or the theoretical perspective and model ethnographies that guided the choice of topics for fieldwork. Efforts to provide some sort of intellectual face lift or to camouflage the book as one by a recent Ph.D cannot succeed. It has an integrity of its own, and while the same material could be used to produce a different book, I am not sure it would necessarily be a better book.

As I see it, many academics overvalue being up-to-date, *au courant*, and in tune with fashion. My intention here is scholarship rather than fashion or journalism. Anyone who has been reading the productions of academics for a decade or two knows how quickly intellectual fashions change and new waves are succeeded by yet newer waves. In this work I have taken some pains to avoid being caught in that toil, and to rely, rather, on the strengths of argument, description, and of English prose.

As the bibliography demonstrates, this work has not been produced in intellectual isolation or in ignorance of research on aspects of Chinese society. It is my hope that much of what is said here will prove relevant to that research. That I do not make more extensive reference to such monuments of scholarship as historian William Rowe's two books on the city of Hankow or anthropologist John Shepherd's magisterial tome on *Statecraft and Political Economy on the Taiwan Frontier* reflects my decision to keep a strong focus on Lukang. The issue is length and focus. I myself find that the chapter I usually skip in most monographs is the literature review, and to do justice to a careful comparison of my material on Lukang with that contained in the work of Rowe, Shepherd, and others of equal quality would necessitate yet another complete volume. No one book can do everything, and this one is held together by its repeated efforts to analyze one city in Taiwan from different perspectives.

Some readers were disquieted by my use of the present tense to describe the Lukang of 1967–1968. My response is that, first, the use of the ethnographic present is an accepted convention in the writing of ethnographies. After all, every ethnographic account is an account of a no longer extant society. As soon as the ethnographer departs the field site those field notes become historical documents and the ethnographer's memories begin to fade and be reshaped. None of this is hard to understand. Whether six months, one year, or twenty years, the principle is the same. It would be very difficult to write and probably impossible to read an account that scrupulously dated every observation and that therefore would make generalization of any sort difficult.

Besides which, there are sound intellectual reasons for the use of the present tense in ethnographic writing. One of the goals of such analysis is to try to elucidate how things fit together (or don't), how apparently disparate elements are related. One looks for, or claims, systemic relations. For doing this in written English the present tense is the tense of choice. The analysis may be unconvincing, or a bit off, or even dead wrong, but trying to rephrase it in the past tense won't help. I assume that my readers will realize that things have changed since 1968, and that if they are primarily interested in this month's Taiwan, or west-central Taiwan, or even Lukang, this work is not the one to consult.

I spent two days in Lukang in April 1992 and even physically it is a very different place than the one I observed in the late 1960s. There are traffic lights, seven- and eight-story buildings, and many many factories that do, contrary to the past, overshadow the temples. But none of this affects the validity of my analysis of that city as I found it in 1968. To repeat, although this book contains a great deal of detail about Lukang between the 1760s and the 1960s, it is not in the last analysis about Lukang. It is about patterns of Chinese society and of thought about that society. It is about culture and distinctively Chinese patterns of culture, and about what we, as outsiders, see when we look at that culture. Maurice Freedman, speaking in one of his formal guises (but also, I think, from the heart), said that a purpose of universities is to produce intellectual pleasure, and went on to discuss the "many pleasures" of anthropology.[2] I would hope that, had he lived, he would have derived some intellectual pleasure from this work.

Notes

1. Donald R. DeGlopper, "Doing Business in Lukang," in W. E. Willmott, ed., *Economic Organization in Chinese Society* (Stanford: Stanford University Press, 1972). See also, DeGlopper, "Religion and Ritual in Lukang," in A. P. Wolf, ed., *Religion and Ritual*

in Chinese Society (Stanford: Stanford University Press, 1974); DeGlopper, "Social Structure in a Nineteenth-Century Taiwanese Port City," in G. W. Skinner, ed., *The City in Late Imperial China* (Stanford: Stanford University Press, 1977); DeGlopper, "Artisan Life and Work in Taiwan," *Modern China*, vol. 5, 3 (July 1979); and DeGlopper, "Lu-kang: A City and Its Trading System," in R. G. Knapp, ed., *China's Island Frontier: Studies in the Historical Geography of Taiwan* (Honolulu: The University Press of Hawaii, 1980).

2. Maurice Freedman, "Rites and Duties, or Chinese Marriage," *in* G. W. Skinner, ed., *The Study of Chinese Society: Essays by Maurice Freedman* (Stanford: Stanford University Press, 1979), pp. 256–257.

Chapter 1

Some Chinese Puzzles

Looking at China

From Marco Polo to the present, Occidentals have been fascinated by China. Why this should be so is not entirely clear, for there are after all many other societies just as, if not more, exotic than China. Perhaps China has been alien enough to serve as foil to Europe but not so alien as to be totally incommensurable or incomprehensible.[1] For centuries China has connoted reversal and opposition, an extreme and limiting case of whatever quality (from effective public administration, to gastronomy, to patience, to revolutionary purity) the Occidentals happen to be concerned with. In popular thought the Chinese have a reputation for doing everything backwards, from writing to serving the soup course. Many travelers' accounts, from Marco Polo to the visitors to the People's Republic in the 1970s, have had a through-the-looking-glass quality, which no doubt helps account for their enduring attraction.

In such accounts, as well of those of such foreign residents as missionaries, the Chinese are presented not only as a mirror-people doing everything backwards but as possessing a paradoxical mixture of opposing and mutually contradictory qualities. One of the best examples of the genre, the Reverend Arthur Smith's *Chinese Characteristics,* bears such chapter titles as "Flexible Inflexibility," "The Talent for Misunderstanding," and "Mutual Suspicion." Part of the charm and value of Smith's work, which is the product of a very acute and profoundly ambivalent observer of Chinese life, lies in his constant playing with contradiction and paradox, so that his portrait of the Chinese character gains in depth and nuance what it loses in simple directness. In the chapter on "Mutual Suspicion" (which follows that on "Mutual Responsibility") he says that "while the Chinese are gifted with a capacity for combination which at times seems to suggest the union of chemical atoms, it is easy to ascertain by careful inquiry at the proper sources and proper times that the Chinese do not by any means trust one another in the implicit way which the external phenomena might imply."[2]

Smith never really faces up to the question of how any people who are so deficient in public spirit, sincerity, or sympathy, and whose relations with each other are marked by the extreme degree of mutual suspicion that he attributes to them can possibly live together at all, far less exhibit "a capacity for combination which at times seems to suggest the union of chemical atoms." But he is hardly alone in this regard, for contradictory images of Chinese society run through almost all the Western literature on China. On the one hand, the Chinese are seen as excessively "group-oriented," with all individuals so thoroughly socialized as to be "submerged," in their tight little groups. As a people they are familistic, clannish, and tend to form guilds, tongs, secret societies, and communes, all of which function smoothly and efficiently. On the other hand, the Chinese are also portrayed as an aggregation of undisciplined, anarchic individuals. They won't queue up, refuse to commit themselves to churches or to armies, haggle over every least thing, refuse to rescue drowning people, and generally carry on in a perpetual Chinese fire drill. Each characterization can be supported by examples, illustrations, and anecdotes, and further reading (or experience) only leads us further into paradox.

The Anthropological Perspective

One way out of this intellectual mire comes with the realization that such labels as "group-oriented" or "undisciplined" always assume an implicit comparison with some other group, usually that of the observer. Making the standards explicit helps a great deal, for all that the labels are usually saying is that neither Chinese family members nor, for a typical example of anarchy, crowds waiting for a ship, train, or bus, behave as the foreign observer thinks families or crowds behave in his own society. The labels, so full of terms like "absence of" or "excess of" are no more than a crude, initial notation of cultural difference and an expression of puzzlement. As such they may serve as a useful start in the attempt to understand the foreign culture. This is the purpose of many of Arthur Smith's bald (and, to contemporary sensibilities, outrageous) chapter titles and initial sentences, which are subsequently modified and qualified as Smith attempts, with varying success, to explain the reasons for the initially baffling behavior. But if, as is all too often the case, the labels are taken for explanatory principles rather than observations of cultural difference, then they become obstacles to further understanding. And the Chinese are rendered, in Frederick Gearing's apt term, "unbelievable," and we are further estranged from them.[3]

The next step out of the blind alley of describing other cultures either by listing what they are not (a procedure that Gearing condemns as nondescription because it renders the people so characterized inconceivable and, in a way, nonhuman), or as tissues of contradictions is provided by some fairly simple notions that have been the core of cultural anthropology for the past half century. They come down to looking at behavior in its proper context (explanation, it has been said, is putting things in context) and finding out what the behavior that seems puzzling means to the people doing it. One tries to elucidate the goals of the actors and the way the alien culture assigns meaning to the goals and acts.

Doing this is not necessarily easy, in part because in any culture much of the pattern that lies behind or guides the motivation of actors is implicit and taken for granted. It must be inferred, usually by a detached external observer. The usual illustration of this point is the grammar or phonological structure of a language, which shapes the utterances of native speakers even if they are quite unaware of it. This is elementary, and another elementary notion, dating back to Durkheim and other early-twentieth-century French sociologists, argues that every society has ways of symbolizing or representing itself, and that people everywhere have ways of describing and thinking about their own society, even if they lack sociology. Ritual is often interpreted in this way, as providing, among other things, a sort of folk sociology, a way of symbolically presenting social structure, cohesion and conflict.

We thus come to the idea of a "native model" of, along with other things, society. In small-scale, relatively undifferentiated societies the "native model" is often expressed primarily or only through ritual, which expresses themes of social solidarity, exchange, and reciprocity. Rituals are interpreted by the outside observer by being translated into statements, propositions, or exhortations about social relations. Textbook examples are ancestor cults and wedding and funeral rituals, which involve the definition and reassignment of social statuses. In more complex societies or civilizations (usually defined as those with cities, money, writing, a formal state, and extensive division of labor) the "native model" of the society can be expected to be more explicit and elaborated, as well as more detached from the realm of ritual and religion. It may be found in written documents such as treatises on government or in legal codes.

Confucianism as Sociology

The most obvious place to look for an explicit and elaborated "native model" of Chinese society is Confucianism. Confucianism, in all its schools and over two millennia, takes the proper ordering of society and human relations as its main subject. It is essentially a prescription for a harmonious and orderly society. It contains a theory of human nature, of learning and social influence, and of social structure. In the past, foreigners, struggling to fit Chinese culture into their own categories, sometimes argued whether Confucianism was a religion or a philosophy. I see it as, among other things, a sociology, one that can with relative ease be translated into the language of Western sociology. But, as a complete guide to or model of Chinese society, it is inadequate.

The Sung Neo-Confucianism that served as the officially sponsored orthodoxy in the Ch'ing dynasty saw man and society as integral parts of the larger cosmic order. That natural order, summed up as the Tao and described as a network of principles or regularities called li, included ethics and social hierarchies. In the Neo-Confucian system, that trees bud in the spring and water runs downhill were descriptive statements of natural regularities in the same way as statements that sons are filial and rulers are superior to ministers. The social order, everything from the rules of kinship, to the structure of the state, to the etiquette of funerals, was an aspect of the natural order.

Societies commonly justify their internal arrangements and hierarchies by asserting them to be reflections or consequences of a larger natural or supernatural system, and in this sense there is nothing unusual about the Chinese case. But the way that natural order is conceptualized and described clearly makes a difference. A. C. Graham speaks of the Chinese tendency to think in terms of the interdependent rather than the isolated; of wholes divisible in various ways rather than collections of units; of opposites as complementary rather than contradictory; and of the changing (but in cycles rather than developing) rather than the static.[4] The natural order is always thought of as a system, whose component parts and subsystems relate to each other through subtle gradations of mutual influence. The ultimate order, the Tao, is constantly changing, as are the relations between the constituent parts. Rather than the characteristically Occidental images of geometrical forms or molds and templates, the metaphor for the Tao would be a mobile, slowly rotating, or perhaps a fractal orrery. It follows therefore that human society is always thought of as a system and man always seen in a social context. Confucian thinkers do not begin with atomistic individuals and then have to worry about how to create society; they assume society. Nor do they worry themselves about the relation between the individual and society, for they do not use such polar terms. Humans are by definition always involved in society and interacting with others. All discussions of human nature assume a continual, reciprocal process of action and reaction between any one person and all others in the vicinity. Characteristically Confucian terms include *Hsiang*, mutuality and *Shu*, reciprocity or empathy, a key term in the *Analects*. In Confucian discourse these are given ethical weight, as principles of social life that should be recognized and guide action. On a less idealistic level there is *Pao*, strict reciprocity.[5]

Subject to the influence of other people, humans are malleable. They may be educated, developed, and cultivated as well as led astray and corrupted by bad company. Although early Confucians disagreed about whether humans' "original nature" was good, bad, or neutral, all agreed that it could be improved by education and exposure to good examples. Hence the great attention Confucianists pay to education, socialization, and all processes of social influence. In the Confucian system man is not born free; rather, he is born raw or unformed, becoming truly human only through education and contact with society.

Even though Confucian thought stresses the systemic quality of the natural and hence the social order, and considers the social order prior to the individual, who is socialized into the only possible society for human beings, it does not necessarily follow that humans are seen as totally passive, entirely the creatures of their environment, or that the particular social arrangements found at any distinct time or place necessarily represent the best of all possible worlds. With its bias toward organic wholeness and conflation of social norms with natural laws the Neo-Confucian system has some intellectual problems coping with social disorder, conflict, and evil.[6] Nevertheless it recognizes them, makes clear distinctions between good and bad social arrangements and individual conduct, and recognizes a human capacity for choice and free will. Any concrete society is seen as the consequence of human choices. If people, educated in the principles of human society, choose the proper definition of roles and hierarchies the result is a peaceful and harmonious society, but if they choose improperly or refuse to follow the "natural" principles the result is disorder, conflict, and chaos.

Confucianists desire harmony, but this is not to be achieved by doing away with all distinctions. Just as the skillful farmer takes into account the proper times of planting and harvest and the varieties of crops, so the social engineer takes into account the variable qualities of human beings and the necessary differentiation of society. Confucian harmony is seen in terms of differentiated social units and individuals, all cooperating for the common good.

As a sociology, Confucianism contains the elements of a theory of roles and the division of labor, although these notions are not elaborated very much beyond the family or the gross distinction between ruler and ruled. What we now speak of as roles and role-sets, Confucianism discusses as *li*. *Li*, a semantically complex term, is difficult to translate directly. It is most often glossed as "propriety," but this is inadequate. The term originally referred to the code of etiquette and conduct of the nobility of the Chou dynasty, which included the conduct of rites and rules of politesse. In Confucian hands the canons of feudal etiquette were moralized and their meaning extended and redefined.

In general *li* refer to the customary definition of social roles and the approved patterns of behavior between individuals standing in definite relations to each other, as father and son or husband and wife. Three related ideas are subsumed. *Li* are an ordering of society so that each individual knows his place and hence his rights and duties; *li* are a code of morality, acting not so much through external sanctions as through the individual conscience; and *li* are an ideal of social harmony, emphasizing the reciprocal obligations that tie men together.[7]

Li are rules for one's behavior toward specific other people. They are norms for particularistic, dyadic relationships. *Li* grade off in intensity and precision of definition from the family out to total strangers. Like most moral prescriptions they are not precisely defined. Mothers-in-law are "tender" and daughters-in-law are "dutiful." *Li* are norms for relations that are, in our own terminology, functionally diffuse or multiplex, that involve the whole person over an extended period of time. *Li* define the most important social relationships, those common to all people. These are the classical Five Relationships: father-son; ruler-subject; brother-brother; husband-wife; friend-friend. Three of these are kinship roles, obtaining within a single family, and four of the five are hierarchical. Sons submit to fathers; subjects to rulers; younger brothers to their elders; and wives to husbands. Harmony is assured by the obedience of the subordinates. The key relationships can be arranged in order of precedence. A man's father comes before his brother and his brother before his wife. The priority of the political relation is ambiguous and a source of continual tension within the Confucian system. In expositions such as the eighteenth-century colloquial version of the *Sacred Edict*, the first two relationships, father-son and ruler-subject, receive the most attention, and the final one, friend-friend, not only comes in last place but is little discussed. The single relation between equals, and the only one to be created by the choice of the parties to it, is acknowledged but no more.

If one reads the Confucian Classics and such moralistic but widely disseminated tracts as the colloquial version of the *Sacred Edict* (composed in the early eighteenth century by Wang Yu-p'u, salt commissioner in Shensi) one gets a good idea of the way kinship and families were supposed to be ("mothers-in-law are tender") as well as the way (the Way?) the empire was supposed to be governed. But between the family and the empire the social terrain is vague. It was assumed that there was a link, for in the famous chain-stitch reasoning of the *Ta Hsueh* if all the families were at peace with themselves, then the empire would surely be at peace, but the nature of the link or synapse between families and the empire is never really discussed. And although Confucians were quite sensitive to social learning and to reference groups, the composition of such reference groups as villages is never spelled out.

One might expect a guide to the correct ordering of society to devote some attention to the communities in which people live, are socialized, and act as social beings, influencing and being influenced. But this aspect of Chinese society, which has been a part of that society for as long as there has been anything that could be called Chinese society, is glossed over in the Confucian schema. Chapter 3 of the *Sacred Edict* begins by asking, "What are those things we call local communities (*hsiang-tang*)?" It answers that it is the people, the inhabitants of villages, hamlets, neighborhoods, and streets. "Their fields adjoin; their houses touch; they meet as they go out and come in; they hear each other's cocks and dogs; they marry each other; they help each other in case of fire, flood or theft."[8] A community is those individual people who interact frequently, but instead of drawing lines and discussing stations and duties within the village in the spirit of the ancient sages who instituted *Li*, the author stresses village or neighborhood solidarity and plays down distinctions. "Although some are close (agnates) and some more distant, some are in-laws (*ch'in-ch'i*, that is, matrilaterals and affines) pulled in from elsewhere, and some are just friends who've been together for a long time, still, in all (you should) treat them all kindly and warmly." "If people would only consider everyone in the community as one corporate body (*ch'eng yi-ke jen*)"[9]

Although villages and Chinese communities are known to have been internally differentiated along lines of patrilineal descent, neighborhood, wealth, and length of residence in the community, the colloquial version of the *Sacred Edict* stresses only community solidarity, describing the community as an undifferentiated skein of personal ties. Given that the immediate purpose of the text is to discourage strife and contention, the stress on an imputed community solidarity is rhetorically appropriate. But, it also highlights one of the shortcomings of Confucianism as a sociology and as a model of Chinese society. The argument, which is repeated in chapter after chapter of the text, is to first show that two contending parties belong to the same category, such as agnate, villager, or member of the same occupation. It is then asserted that all members of this category must have common interests, and that any internal contention or dispute is therefore foolish and an example of narrow selfishness rather than concern for the common welfare. The category, whether all descendants in the male line of a man who died four generations ago, or all cobblers, is assumed to be a group, an organic whole. Principles appropriate to one relationship are extended to others. Filial piety covers all members of a lineage, and it is argued, in contradiction to the idea, common in exposition of the *li*, of graded differentiation that the relation with a distant agnate is at bottom "the same" as that with one's own uterine brother. The assumption of complete unity of interest on the basis of sharing one of a great many possible features is good rhetoric but poor logic.

More to the point, this way of talking about, and perhaps of thinking about, society does not lead one to consider the possibility of conflicts of interest between groups, or of membership in more than one group, or of the possibilities of individuals' having multiple and overlapping memberships and allegiances. As long as one stays within the field of the Five Relationships, roles are so defined and priorities so set that (except for priority on loyalty to the ruler or to one's father or son) role conflict is rendered nearly impossible as long as everyone plays his part. The possibility of tension or disharmony between obligations to one group, such as an extended family, and obligations to another group, such as an occupational association is not even entertained.

The colloquial version of the *Sacred Edict* is, to be sure, special pleading and its clear purpose was indoctrination and not abstract social science. But then the Classics themselves were intended to be used as guides for action, and they share with the *Sacred Edict* the goal of a stable society. In the forms of argument it employs and its preference for lumping rather than splitting, the colloquial *Sacred Edict* is representative of much Confucian writing. To the extent that Confucianism provided the major categories that people in Chinese culture and society used to apprehend their own society and to conceptualize their own lives in that society, the adequacy of those categories for the description of that society is a topic of some significance. This is the reason for considering Confucianism as a sociology.

As sociologies go, Confucianism is quite a respectable one, of the structuralist-functionalist variety. It begins with the idea of a social system, considers shared value orientations the foundation of social solidarity, contains a well-articulated functionalist theory of ritual, and an initially clear concept of roles and role-sets. It appreciates the importance of the proper performance of roles and of the distinctions between roles and the actors playing or occupying them—a king is a king because he acts like a proper king, not because his father was king before him. It is also strong in what we might call social psychology and small group studies, devoting much attention to socialization, mutual influence, and the way attitudes are reinforced and changed by group pressures. One could make a case for the Chinese invention of sociology and of functionalism, along with the better known inventions such as paper, printing, and gunpowder. But, although a respectable sociology, Confucianism was not a perfect one. Some of its weaknesses, like its difficulty in handling conflict or change, are common to all varieties of structural-functionalism, while others, such as its failure to include most roles outside the ascribed and hierarchical bounds of kinship, are peculiar to itself. A consequence of this is that Confucianism, in and of itself, never gave a very accurate or complete picture or model of Chinese society.

Confucianism thinks of society largely in terms of dyadic relations. (Recall the "definition" of the local community given in the

Sacred Edict.) Such dyadic ties are not those freely established by isolated individuals; rather, they occur within pre-existing, highly corporate groups, such as the extended family or the ruler's court and administration. Confucianists seem to see their society as composed of an indefinite number of identically organized kinship units, each with a clear boundary and a neat internal hierarchy based on sex and age. The topics of concern are the internal structure of such social segments and the way they define their boundaries and maintain themselves over time (hence fathers, sons, and funerals). The relations between segments are not a matter of concern and, save for the assumption that all segments are subject to a common ruler, the topic is not discussed. Confucians take kinship seriously, but they are descent theorists, not alliance theorists.[10] No wonder Radcliffe-Brown was so fond of quoting Hsun-tze and other Confucian sages!

Confucians are more interested in what men have in common than in how they differ, and are more taken with sharing than with exchange. So, although they recognize a functional distinction between the rulers and the ruled, they only grudgingly acknowledge the existence of artisans and merchants, and rank them below scholars and farmers. They do not develop the idea of division of labor and of organic solidarity. Nor, in spite of their concern for mutuality and reciprocity do they make very much of exchange. Confucianism thus lacks a model of any sort of limited, functionally specific, contractual social relation. It also lacks a model of any sort of social group other than such ascriptive, corporate, and primary ones as families or perhaps small and isolated hamlets. This means that it is impossible to use Confucian concepts or terminology to talk about a marketplace, a city, a wholesaler and his customers, a formal association, or a rotating credit society.

When one thinks about it, this seems rather odd. It is not surprising that the social theory of an elite should describe that classes own practices as "natural" or that it should value social harmony, stability, and tradition, which in practice means peasants who accept their station and pay their rent and taxes on time. Nor is it surprising that the ideology of a class of bureaucrats and landowners should deprecate trade and urban life, or that it should do so by holding up as an ideal a mythical and archaic rural gemeinschaft. What is surprising about the Confucian model is its success, given the lack of fit and extreme variance between it and the realities of Chinese society.

The picture of society one gets in Confucian writing and argumentation is one of people living in small, self-sufficient communities where kinship is the main principle of social structure and where there is little or no commerce or state regulation. This would seem to describe the non-Chinese "barbarian" communities of the southern mountains or perhaps the northern steppes far better than the society of imperial China. Confucianism provides a vocabulary and set of concepts for describing the sorts of small-scale "tribal" societies often studied by anthropologists. It would work for discussing the Tallensi, the Iroquois, or the Baganda, where there is little division of labor save by age and sex, where kinship does regulate most of social life, where settlements are largely self-sufficient, ritual looms large in community life, and rulers have to depend to a large degree on consensus and moral example.

But, Chinese society has been for the past two millennia or so a large complex one, with a monetary economy, elaborate and very rational (in Weber's sense of the term) state structures, cities, and a network of communication that tied together an entire subcontinent. Confucianism perversely seems to ignore precisely those institutions that held China together and made it an integrated society rather than an aggregate of self-sufficient villages. A problem thus emerges. If there was a native model of Chinese society, a set of terms and concepts that members of that society used to conceptualize it and describe themselves to themselves, then that model, those concepts, included something other than the Confucianism of the classical texts. What that model was, how it is to be found and articulated, and how it relates to Confucianism remains open.

Any system of thought that lasted as long as Confucianism did must have been doing something right, but just what that was is not immediately clear. The assumption thus far has been that because people in late traditional China considered Confucianism to be of supreme importance and because the content of Confucian thought overlapped with much of Western sociology, the way to begin was to translate Confucianism into the vocabulary of Western sociology. Explicating Confucianism as a sociology is worth doing, but it does not provide a guide to Chinese society and does not solve the basic question of cross-cultural comprehension. Instead it sets new problems. But these problems have the advantage of being grounded in that particular culture and can be used as starting points for further investigation and research. To me, this represents a step toward eventual understanding of the ways Chinese describe their own society to themselves.

Confucianism and Culture

I think that the immediate way out of the paradox of the manifest unsuitability of Confucianism for the description of Chinese society is to argue that I have taken it out of context, and that after all the average mandarin who had received a Confucian education had also learned a great many other things about how his society operated and how to operate within it. Confucianism is not wrong, or irrelevant, or nothing but a "false consciousness," but it is only one part of a culture. I doubt that my hypothetical mandarin who lived for at least part of his life in a city, had a good grasp of finance, routinely established relations of mutual confidence with people who were not his kinsmen, was a member of several limited-purpose associations, and had a brother who was a successful rice merchant, was aware that those aspects of his life were not covered by Confucian terminology. Nor did he perceive any major disjunction between those aspects of his life that fell within the ambit of Confucian categories and those that lay beyond it.

The problem for an outsider trying to understand Chinese culture is that one part of the native model has been written down and made much of, while others, equally important for guiding and understanding actual behavior, are not usually written down and are not made the objects of conscious attention. Apprehending that or any alien culture is thus like looking at a raised relief in strong side illumination. Some features of the design will be brightly illuminated and stand out while others remain in deep shadow. Those parts of the culture that correspond to the design elements in the shadow zone are learned through normal, diffuse socialization rather than through memorization of a text and are taken for granted by members of the culture as perfectly "natural" ways to behave.

I am arguing that the written text alone is not enough, something that should be clear to anyone who has ever tried to cook or work on an automobile with only a book for a guide. Some anthropologists speak of culture as something like a computer program and consider the task of the ethnographer to be the elucidation of the program. Others in a similar line of reasoning build on Durkheim's notion of culture as prior to and outside individuals, and as carried or coded in rituals or significant symbols that are, as Geertz puts it, "as public as marriage, as observable as agriculture."[11] The problem here is that the other culture's programs or symbols, and even its written texts, which are meant to guide members of that culture, always take a very great deal for granted. They never begin to attain the length and painful explicitness that marks a real computer program, or, to use another metaphor for culture, a piece of the genetic code. It follows then that if we try to analyze the supposed program or code outside of its proper social context we are liable to misinterpret it. Here I am reminded of a quite original dissertation that demonstrates the difficulty of writing a "program" or "ethnoscientific" description of so seemingly straightforward a set of rules as those used by a Japanese cabinetmaker to choose wood.[12]

In late traditional China, Confucianism was but one part of a cultural field; it was one set of answers to unspoken questions, and we cannot understand what it meant to the members of that society unless we know what they saw as alternatives and what sorts of behavior they took for granted as normal and natural. Confucianism was nothing if not formal, explicit, and articulate. In an obvious way it was opposed to those elements of the culture that were heterodox, deviant, and expressive of the interests of the lower depths rather than the commanding heights. But, in a less obvious way, it was also by its very explicitness in contrast to the informal and inarticulate assumptions about what sorts of behavior were normal and natural and therefore not worthy of comment and attention. The only way to learn about those sides of Chinese society that fall outside the Confucian framework is through fieldwork or through careful analysis of such written materials as contracts or guild constitutions. And the prerequisite for either endeavor is conceptual clarity.

The Convergence of Confucianism and Academic Sociology and Anthropology

In the Chinese case we want to know about how people established relations of mutual trust with those not their kinsmen; how they organized formal associations; how commerce was conducted; and how urban society was structured. All of these strike me as reasonable topics for inquiry, but there is less literature on them than one might expect. We know a good deal about some aspects of Chinese life, such as the families of farmers, and very little about others, such as cities. Our picture of Chinese society and life is marked by a high degree of chiaroscuro. One reason for this uneven illumination and knowledge is, I think, the congruity and mutual reinforcement between the Chinese conscious model and the theoretical assumptions of academic, usually foreign, anthropologists.

The Chinese, as Confucians, picked certain aspects of their own society to focus their attention on and were consequently quite aware of them and ready to discuss them. The prime example here is the family. The foreigners, as anthropologists (in Chinese studies the distinction between anthropology and sociology has never been terribly strong) were generally trained as functionalists and were professionally competent at the analysis of families, kinship, villages, and ritual, all topics dear to the Confucian heart. Standard anthropological theory and techniques seemed to work quite well for analyzing Chinese society. In the hands of my late mentor Maurice Freedman, anthropological models developed in the Sudan and the northern Gold Coast (Evans-Pritchard and Meyer Fortes) proved remarkably helpful for understanding the lineages and ancestor cults of southeastern China, while an argument developed to explain why the Zande of the Sudan and Uganda believe in witchcraft served to illuminate the theory and practice of Chinese geomancy.[13] Young Chinese intellectuals took to sociology and anthropology with relative ease, and by 1937 sociology—which included the village studies of such sociologists/anthropologists as Fei Hsiao-t'ung, Lin Yueh-hua, Hsu Langkuang (Francis L. K. Hsu) and Martin Yang—was flourishing in China.[14] Some very good fieldwork was done in China even during the Second World War, and when I had occasion to go over such English-language journals as the *Chinese Social and Political Science Review* and the *Yenching Journal of Social Studies* for the late 1930s and the 1940s I was very impressed at the high quality of the work, most all of which was done on a shoestring in the middle of a war.

For China then, the gap between the native model and the outside observer's "scientific" model was smaller than it sometimes is. After all, structural-functionalism *was* the native model. To the extent that it has been possible for studies of Chinese kinship and marriage, lineage and ancestors to attain a high degree of sophistication, and for the conclusions of such studies to enter the anthropological literature fairly readily, this has been a good thing. Families, villages, lineages, and ancestors are all well worth studying, and anthropological models really do illuminate their working and make those aspects of Chinese life intelligible. I found that undergraduates in anthropology courses were able to grasp the logic of Chinese marriage and even such esoterica as ghost marriage with relative ease.

But, to the extent that the powerful combination of the articulate Chinese model of their society and the theoretical bent of foreign scholars has acted to turn our attention away from some aspects of Chinese society, the theoretical convergence has not been a good thing. All too often foreign observers have taken the Confucian picture of what should be for a description of what is. Or, in a more sophisticated error, they have accepted the Confucian definition of what is most significant. This applies for obvious reasons to travelers and such foreign residents as missionaries who are content to accept what their Chinese hosts tell them. It also applies to serious scholars, for whom the years of toil necessary for an outsider to master written Chinese and grasp Chinese categories may lead to a degree of acculturation.

This issue is touched on in an instructive essay on the comparison of Chinese and Islamic societies by Ira Lapidus, a historian specializing in the Islamic Middle East.[15] He is concerned with "the basic assumptions and explicit or implicit paradigms by which historians of China conceive Chinese culture." He finds a set of ordered antinomies, such as: Confucian/Legalist; bureaucrat/local notable; central/local; public/private; and administrative, imposed structures/natural, self-generated structures. All the potentially contradictory elements were balanced and the whole society represented an example of balanced tension. "It is generally assumed that China is an integrated, well-ordered, and fundamentally harmonious society." "The image of Chinese society which emerges in the historiography is not quite an architectural pile, but rather one of Calder's mobiles with well-fashioned pieces trembling in balance or swinging in circles. . . . Yet, though in constant movement the mobile as a whole floats gracefully, a complete form, a harmonious totality assuming innumerable variant configurations without loss of its inherent unity. It moves in eternity. This, I think, is the historians' implicit image of China. It may be China's image of itself."

"The hierarchical and dialectic view of Chinese society corresponds to one of the traditional Chinese ways of seeing the world. In a similar way, the network view accords with the conceptual world of Islamic culture. . . . Thus the preferred metaphors of Chinese and Islamic historians are not accidental. They correspond to the cultural style and the world view of each civilization—and in fact may derive from the historians' familiarity with the societies they study."

If we continue with Lapidus' elegant metaphor of China as a mobile, then Confucianism is one of the "well-fashioned pieces." But if it is taken out of the mobile, analyzed as a free-standing structure, or taken for the master plan or armature of a single structure, then it is misread. I think this has often been done, and the consequence has been to obscure our understanding of Chinese society. One of the cliches of Western description of China is that the Chinese are deficient in individuality, that they are excessively absorbed or submerged in their group. This picture of Chinese man corresponds very nicely with the "oversocialized conception of man" that Dennis Wrong attributed to the dominant American structuralist-functionalist sociology of the 1950s.[16] Confucian man is indeed oversocialized, but he never existed in the real world any more than the actors of Parsons' Social System who go about trying their best to meet each other's expectations. Both Confucian man and Parsonian man (who would get along with each other quite well) are models, sketches, ways to direct our attention to one aspect of social life.

Confucianists made much of family and kinship, and their moralistic stress accords with the common tendency to label the Chinese as "familistic." We often see such statements as "In China the family is the foundation of society." Mr. Lapidus, who was certainly a good student of the English-language literature on China, speaks of "the basic framework of society-family kinship, lineage, and clan association. Local communities were based on lineage."[17] I would not characterize the basic framework of Chinese society in this way. Although as a social anthropologist I cannot but be aware of the significance of kinship, I have never quite understood what statements such as "the family is the foundation of the social order" are supposed to mean. To be sure, most people in China belonged to families and family membership was a very significant aspect of every person's identity, but I fail to see what is so distinctively Chinese about this. Most human beings after all belong to families, and the families usually loom large in people's lives. Families are about as close to a human universal as one is liable to find, and in that sense they are like breathing or elbows— very important and fundamental, but not something the possession or practice of which distinguishes one human society from all others.

"Familistic" is not a term of art in social anthropology, and the application of such a label to the Chinese seems to depend on an implicit comparison with some other society, presumably one's own. What the term seems to mean is that the Chinese, in some undefined way, pay more attention to or take more seriously their families than we do. Maybe, but one would have to be a lot more specific about just what is meant by "takes more seriously" or "pays more attention to" or "we." American undergraduates confidently asserted that the Chinese were more familistic than they, while ignoring their own financial dependence on their families at an age when most Chinese were supporting themselves. They also ignored matters such as that many of them were present at the university only because their parents could pay the tuition, could afford to reside in the right secondary school districts, or that they were admitted only because their parents or grandparents were alumni. It was not good manners to discuss these matters in public at American universities, but it is hard to see why they are any less evidence of familism than inheriting rice fields or preferring arranged marriages. The evidence for Chinese familism seems to come down to the importance of inherited property, the prevalence of arranged marriages, the frequent conjunction of family and enterprise, and postmarital residence in the parental household, but these are hardly habits peculiar to China.

In a comparative, cross-cultural perspective there is little if anything that is unique or distinctive about Chinese family structure or kinship, which is a fairly common patrilineal type. Chinese families have a great deal in common with Hindu and Arab families, but we never seem to label those societies as familistic even though Saudi Arabia is governed by a lineage and three generations of one family served as prime ministers of the Republic of India. If I wanted to choose a distinctively "Chinese" feature of that society, the family is the last place I'd look.

It is sometimes asserted that the family and kinship are of especial importance in China because many other sorts of relationships or social institutions are modeled on the family or represent the extension of kinship norms and forms. It is true that Chinese villagers commonly addressed each other by kinship terms; Chinese sometimes form sworn brotherhoods and sisterhoods; and imperial spokesmen made fairly labored arguments that filial piety should be extended to the emperor. But otherwise, I see little evidence that such common Chinese sorts of relationships as those between landlords and tenants, creditors and debtors, partners in a business, masters and apprentices, or allies in a faction were modeled on kinship. Nor, so far as I can tell, did such common Chinese associations as irrigation associations, temple cults, rotating credit associations, guilds, same-place associations, or even surname associations resemble families in any significant way.[18] These matters will be discussed throughout the remainder of this work, but if I may anticipate my conclusions I will say that many common Chinese associations and relations shared the same form and might be considered to reflect the same model, but that model was not kinship.

The unintended consequence of taking Confucianism too literally and of concentrating on topics most amenable to anthropological analysis has been to mislead even such sensitive and well-read students of things Chinese as Mr. Lapidus. To be sure, he does not entirely accept the sinologists' picture of China and he suggests that we might profit from looking at China with a perspective similar to that developed for the study of Islamic society, which stresses the importance of *ad-hoc* relations between individuals and groups and of temporary networks linking component groups.[19] In Firth's terms, it might be enlightening to look at Chinese social organization as well as at social structure.[20] Doing this would also help to correct the schizoid views of the Chinese as either excessively socialized or totally anarchical, for a careful look at such matters as behavior in the marketplace or in the city, or in factional contests should, as a matter of anthropological faith and first principles, reveal such behavior to be patterned and orderly, even if not directly explicable in terms of the Confucian model. The following chapters look at precisely such topics in the ethnographic context of a Taiwanese city.

Notes

1. This point is made provocatively, if not entirely convincingly, in Andrew March, *The Idea of China* (New York: Praeger, 1974). The topic is also discussed in William Appleton, *A Cycle of Cathay* (New York: Columbia University Press, 1951); in Raymond Dawson, *The Chinese Chameleon* (London: Oxford University Press, 1967); and in Michael Edwardes, *East-West Passage* (New York: Taplinger, 1971).

2. Arthur H. Smith, *Chinese Characteristics* (New York: Fleming E. Revell, 1884), p. 246.

3. Frederick O. Gearing, *The Face of the Fox* (Chicago: Aldine, 1970), pp. 109–110.

4. A. C. Graham, *Two Chinese Philosophers: Ch'eng Ming-tao and Ch'eng Yi-ch'uan* (London: Lund Humphries, 1958), p. ix.

5. See Yang Lien-sheng, "The Concept of 'Pao' as a Basis for Social Relations in China," in J. K. Fairbank, ed., *Chinese Thought and Institutions* (Chicago: University of Chicago Press, 1957).

6. On this, see Thomas A. Metzger, *Escape from Predicament: Neo-Confucianism and China's Evolving Political Culture* (New York, Colombia University Press, 1977), pp. 108–113.

7. See Sybille van der Sprenkel, *Legal Institutions in Manchu China* (London: London School of Economics Monographs in Social Anthropology, No. 24, 1962), pp. 30–33.

8. Ibid., p. 29.

9. Ibid., pp. 31, 37.

10. On the distinction between descent theory and alliance theory in the study of kinship, see David M. Schneider. "Some Muddles in the Models: or How the System Really Works," in Michael Banton, ed., *The Relevance of Models for Social Anthropology* (Association of Social Anthropologists Monograph No. 1) (London: Tavistock, 1965), pp. 25–85.

11. Clifford Geertz, "Religion as a Cultural System," in Michael Banton, ed., *Anthropological Approaches to the Study of Religion* (Association of Social Anthropologists Monograph No. 3) (London: Tavistock, 1968), p. 5.

12. Carol A. A. Link, *Japanese Cabinetmaking: A Dynamic System of Decision and Interactions in a Technical Context.* Unpublished Ph.D. dissertation, University of Illinois, 1975.

13. Maurice Freedman, *Lineage Organization in Southeastern China* (London School of Economics Monographs on Social Anthropology, No. 18) (London: Athlone Press, 1958); Maurice Freedman, *Chinese Lineage and Society: Fukien and Kwangtung* (London School of Economics Monographs on Social Anthropology, No. 33) (London: Athlone Press, 1966).

14. Ambrose Y. King, "The Development and Death of Chinese Academic Sociology," *Modern Asian Studies* 12, 1 (Feb. 1978), pp. 37–58.

15. Ira M. Lapidus, "Hierarchies and Networks: A Comparison of Chinese and Islamic Societies," in Frederic Wakeman and

Carolyn Grant, eds. *Conflict and Control in Late Imperial China* (Berkeley: University of California Press, 1975), pp. 26–42.

16. Dennis Wrong, "The Oversocialized Concept of Man in Modern Sociology," *American Sociological Review* 26 (April 1961), pp. 183–193. Reprinted in Dennis Wrong, *Skeptical Sociology* (New York: Columbia University Press, 1976).

17. Lapidus, 1975, p. 29.

18. Morton Fried made this point at some length in 1953 in *The Fabric of Chinese Society* but it seems necessary to keep on repeating it.

19. Lapidus, 1975, p. 42.

20. Raymond Firth, "Social Organization and Social Change," *Journal of the Royal Anthropological Institute* 84, 1954, pp. 1–20. Reprinted in Firth, *Essays on Social Organization and Values* (London School of Economics Monographs on Social Anthropology, No. 28) (London: Athlone Press, 1964).

Chapter 2

In the Shadow Zone: Chinese Personal Relations, Associations, and Cities

We begin with two questions. Outside the brilliantly illuminated area of kinsmen and kinship groups that is the core of the Confucian model, what sorts of personal relations and associations are found in Chinese society? How do people establish ties of mutual confidence with strangers, or at least with acquaintances who are not kinsmen? And, of equal interest, how are such relations described and conceptualized? If, as we assume, there was a Chinese "native model" for such personal ties and associations, then what was it and how did it relate to the explicit if inadequate Confucian model?

Morton Fried began the study of what he chose to call "non-kin" relations with his 1953 monograph on Ch'uhsien, a small city in Anhwei Province in east central China. He concludes that: "It is apparent that the citizen of all classes in Ch'uhsien lives much of his life beyond the orbit of relationships provided either by his family or the kinship system in which he is involved. On the basis of the field data we have concluded that most of the extra-kin contacts and associations do not repeat familistic organization or familial functions."[1] Fried devoted much of the book to pointing out what should have been obvious but was not; namely that Chinese society was a large-scale society that had for centuries rested on an extensive division of labor and a monetary economy, and that the "fabric" of that society contained many strands beyond that of kinship. He paid special attention to the sort of dyadic relation that his informants described as involving *kan-ch'ing* or "sentiment," a personalistic and ultimately instrumental tie that cut across class lines and which Fried suggested might operate in much the same way as *compadre* ties in Latin America.[2]

Fried's book was a pioneering effort that, in my opinion, was never adequately followed up. With the advantage of several decades' hindsight, it seems that "non-kin" was an unfortunate term, being what Gearing calls "nondescription" (saying what something is not rather than what it is) and conveying a rather negative tone to the discussion. It implies that kinship-based ties are somehow the norm or the standard, and that those he is discussing represent a deviant subset. The sorts of relations Fried labelled as "non-kin" may have had little in common save that they were not based on kinship. (Intellectually this is rather like putting humans, giant squids, and owls together in a category of "non-quadrupeds.") The anthropological vocabulary available in 1953 for discussing the sorts of relations Fried was interested in, such as those between landlords and tenants, shopowners and clerks, and men active in local politics, was generally inadequate. Even today when anthropologists can throw around such terms as personal networks, brokers, quasi-groups or relational contracting, and can speak of doing processual analysis or using generative models the situation is far from perfect, and it remains a lot easier to be clear and precise when speaking of lineages or marriage systems. We still have no good or commonly accepted vocabulary for describing, far less discussing, some of the most significant sorts of personal relations in Chinese society. They remain, if not totally in the dark, at least in the shadows, and I myself have been approaching them by first setting out the (relatively) clear and well-defined Confucian model.

Interpersonal Relations

After Fried, the topic of culturally specific patterns of personal relations in Chinese society was investigated by a number of anthropologists, most of whom concentrated on business relations.[3] Although based on fieldwork in different countries and different circumstances and spanning at least thirty years, all these studies agree on certain points. Chinese do not trust strangers and prefer not to deal with them. (This proposition does have a certain tautologous air, in so far as the concept of trust implies discrimination, but one must begin somewhere.) There are, however, culturally specific ways Chinese use to convert strangers to trusted associates. The most common way is through introduction by a trusted common acquaintance. As I see it, this means that a great many Chinese social ties are not so much dyadic as triadic, with the third person serving as introducer, go-between, mediator, and sometimes as guarantor. In some circumstances go-betweens may be cantilevered on top of go-betweens, so that chains of friends of friends are made up for some specific purpose. Once a third person has made the introduction, the two parties test each others' reliability though a series of progressively larger and more important transactions until they achieve a bond of mutual trust. If they have a dispute the third person who introduced them may be called in to serve as mediator. In my unpublished M.A. dissertation on Chinese dispute resolution I argued that disputes where a neutral third party who is trusted by both sides can be found will usually be settled peacefully, while those, as within a single family or between two lineages, where no suitable third party exists will either fester unresolved or be settled through violence.

With or without a third person to introduce them, two people who belong to the same culturally defined category will find it easier to establish a bond of mutual trust. The most frequently recognized categories are common place of origin (*t'ung hsiang*), common surname (*t'ung hsing*), graduation from the same school or university (*t'ung hsueh*), or common place of employment or occupation (*t'ung shih, t'ung pan*). Membership in the same category does not, in and of itself, automatically guarantee intimacy and mutual trust, but it does provide a ground on which to begin to develop a relationship.

People who trust each other will usually describe their relation as one of "sentiment" or *ch'ing*. This term, which Fried discussed as *kan-ch'ing*, is a protean and flexible one. Usually it refers to a relationship which is less intense or more shallow than that described as one of "friendship," but the distinction is not sharp. Ch'ing occurs most commonly in the compound term kan-ch'ing, which I glossed in my paper on doing business in Lukang as referring to the affective, variable component of any two person relation. (It may also be used to refer to romantic attachments. In Buddhist and some Neo-Confucian texts it is best translated as "desire.") It is always achieved or built up, never ascribed or given; and is essentially a variable term. Kan-ch'ing can be strengthened or lost, one has more or less of it, it is good, very good, not bad, or absent. There are specific terms for many subtypes of ch'ing, such as *ai-ch'ing*, sentiments of love; *en-ch'ing*, sentiments of gratitude for extraordinary benevolence; *sz-ch'ing*, private sentiments, usually referring to an illicit and secret bond, as between a corrupt official and a businessman or a gangster, or between partners in adultery; and *jen-ch'ing*, human sentiments, which in my experience refers to a more narrowly instrumental and restricted exchange of favors than kan-ch'ing. Businessmen commonly speak of each other's *hsin-yung*, which refers to their reliability, their reputation for meeting their obligations, their credit ratings. One may speak of all these personal relations as involving *kuan-hsi (guanxi)*, a Chinese word that means simply "relations." During the 1980s the term guanxi somehow made its way out of the limited world of sinological social science and into the larger ambit of journalism and semi-popular writing about Chinese society. It's a better term than "non-kin" but using it in the middle of English sentences with the assumptions that either it is perfectly clear or that it is mysteriously "untranslatable" does not really help us to understand the content or significance of "relationships."

There does seem to be a common Chinese vocabulary for discussing at least some sorts of personal relations, a vocabulary that combines notions of sentiment and affect (rather than duty and obligation) with ratings of reliability and likelihood of expectations being met. Young, following the mid–1960s fashion for collecting lists of foreign terms and arranging them in hierarchical boxes, presents a set of ch'ing terms (in Cantonese) that he heard in the market town of Yuen Long in Hong Kong's New Territories.[4] To me, what we need is not taxonomies but careful accounts of just how such terms are used in living contexts. It should come as no surprise that these flexible, rather broad terms are used differently in different places. Kan-ch'ing is as vague in Chinese as "good relationship" is in English. It does not and cannot have as precise a meaning as "father's elder brother" or "lienholder to the field identified in the land register of deeds as . . ." Differences in the use and situational meaning of such broad terms may well prove to be sensitive indicators of differences in social organization. There is a minor disagreement in the literature over whether or not kan-ch'ing can be used to refer to relations within a family, as between brothers. The point is not what the word really, essentially means; it is that relations within families and between brothers can differ and can be conceptualized in different ways, and that both the relations and the conceptualizations of them may vary systematically between different communities.

Interpersonal relations can also be described in Chinese in terms of "face." According to Ambrose Yeo-chi King, Professor of Sociology at the Chinese University of Hong Kong, "It is no exaggeration to say that *kuan-hsi, jen-ch'ing,* and *mien-tsu* [face] are key sociocultural concepts to the understanding of Chinese social structure. Indeed, these sociocultural concepts are part of the essential "stock knowledge," to use Alfred Schutz's terminology, of Chinese adults in their management of everyday life."[5] Face is another shadowy concept, whose use is not entirely clear. From my reading of what strike me as the two best sources on face in China, face seems to be a way of talking about the opinion significant others hold of an individual's overall character and reliability.[6] Hu Hsien-chin says that a serious infraction of the moral code, *once come to attention of the public*, is a blemish on the character of the individual (emphasis mine). She speaks of the consciousness that an amorphous public is, so to say, supervising the conduct of the individual, relentlessly condemning every breach of morals and punishing with ridicule. That the public that watches and condemns is really "amorphous" seems unlikely, for Martin Yang makes it clear that one gains or loses face only in relation to a narrowly defined audience. He says that the question of losing or not losing face is based on the anticipation of the effect on a third party. "If the indignity has not been witnessed or is certain to remain unknown to anyone else, then bitterness may be roused, but not the sense of losing face. When one does something wrong but keeps it secret, he does not feel embarrassed before other people. Whenever the secrecy is violated, he will lose face."[7] Face is defined by reference to a particular set of others. It does not operate if the third person is very intimate. There is no face within the family. Nor does face apply before complete strangers. Yang says that when a man lives in a completely strange society there is no question of face, for no one knows him. He can visit disreputable places or commit an immoral act without uneasiness, as long as he can keep it from reaching the attention of his friends or the people at home. In the same way, strangers have no face. The field of face is limited in yet another way. Hu discusses face in terms of mutual trust and obligation, with an implicit reliance on the sanction of reciprocity. Reciprocity however operates best between equals, and many relations in Chinese society were between unequals. Face does not operate if the gap in status between two people is large. Yang points out that if a "village gentleman" is defeated by a junior village official he loses more face than if it were done by a man of his own class. "But if his opponent were only a plain peasant or a person considered ignorant and mean, the gentleman would lose no face at all." On the other hand, when a plain villager is scolded or injured by a gentleman he may resent it but will not lose face.[8]

The concept of face, which corresponds with a zone of significant acquaintances and equals, thus belongs in the same semantic field as concepts of some sorts of ch'ing and judgements of degrees of reliability, of *hsin-yung* (trustworthiness). It may also be seen to be congruent with the Confucian stress on the importance of public opinion and mutual influence, and with the Confucian definition of man as essentially social and existing in a social context. Face is a moral field, but that field seems to be a restricted one. It seems to operate in small groups, such as villages, where everyone knows everyone else and the opinions of one's fellows are of some importance, since they can refuse to cooperate. Differences of power and status, however, override face, and there would seem to be problems not only in dealing with strangers but with those both more and less powerful than one's self. The assertion of the solidarity of all those belonging to the same category and the careful cultivation of bonds of kan-ch'ing and kuan-hsi (which can and do cross status lines) can be interpreted as ways to create trustworthy bonds that extend beyond small circles of equals and link people of different status.

Another way of understanding what people have in mind when they speak of relations based on or involving "sentiment" is to try to find out what they contrast sentiment with. I believe that they contrast ties based on ch'ing with a category of relations based on what we might call "principle" or "rationality." Here I am on less certain ground than in the discussion of kan-ch'ing and face, where what I said could be backed up with a fair amount of ethnography. I take the contrast between ch'ing, "sentiment," and *li*, "reason" from two quite independent sources. The first is an ethnographic description of a Chinese (Teochiu) village in Malaya, William Newell's *Treacherous River*. The second is a fairly obscure book on Chinese culture by Ch'eng T'ien-hsi, a Chinese jurist.[9]

Ch'ing and li are polar terms. Li connotes reason, regularity, equity, and strict impartiality. Ideally the bureaucrat and the shopkeeper follow li, as does anyone who goes by the book and follows general, codified principles. A relation or transaction governed by an explicit written document or contract, which were common in late traditional China, is a clear example of li.[10] Li may be translated as Weberian rationality.[11] If I buy something in a shop, paying the fixed price to the clerk behind the counter, then I am following li. But if I have been trading there for some time, or my brother-in-law is a member of the same volunteer fire company as the clerk, and in consequence I may get an extra quantity or be able to buy on credit, then ch'ing has entered the picture. While li implies following the rules, which are the same for everybody, ch'ing implies evaluating another as an individual and a total person. It is associated with notions of trust and long-term reciprocity, and with mutual support in a wide and undefined range of contexts. Precise calculation of rights and obligations is contrary to the spirit of ch'ing, as is any expression of the relation in terms of cold cash. Ch'ing implies being flexible, not going to the limit, taking human feelings and a wide social context into account. Cheng Tien-hsi explains that ch'ing is a desirable companion to, or the better half of, reason. He claims that the average Chinese is more likely to be swayed by appeal to ch'ing than to li, and is proud of this, for it makes him more human. In a disagreement one appeals to the other, *liu ch'ing*, leave me some ch'ing, have a heart. As I see it the concepts of ch'ing and li also provide a way to understand the form of Chinese associations, and I now turn to associations.

Associations

Writing in the *Yale Review* in 1892, Frederick Wells Williams remarked that "where a handful of Chinamen are gathered together there will be found among them one or more guilds."[12] Maurice Freedman's statement that "the society built up by the overseas Chinese in Southeast Asia has always been remarkable for its wealth of voluntary associations" might with only minor qualifications be extended to Chinese society in general.[13] I prefer to avoid the term voluntary associations, for membership in many associations was not really voluntary and my interest is in the internal structure of associations rather than motivation for joining them. Formal associations, of varying degrees of corporateness, have been key elements of Chinese social structure, in China as well as overseas, in the countryside and in the cities, and in the past as well as the present.

Every ethnographic account of a Chinese village refers, if only briefly, to a number of associations. This is as true of the single-surname villages of southeastern China which were often dominated by large corporate lineages as it is of the majority of Chinese villages in which no strong lineages were found. Villages commonly had home guard or village militia units; crop watching associations; irrigation associations; temple associations or cults to particular deities; school associations; burial societies; village bands and marching associations; and rotating credit associations. We know far less about Chinese cities than villages, and the best accounts of Chinese urban life refer to overseas Chinese settlements rather than to cities in China itself. Nevertheless, it is clear that formal associations were found in Chinese cities, although there are many unanswered questions about participation and the scope of such associations. In Chinese cities one would expect to find some sort of neighborhood or street association; temple associations; commercial or occupational associations; associations of people from the same native place or old home; charitable or benevolent associations; surname associations; sworn brotherhoods; alumni associations; poetry circles; rotating credit associations; and probably both sectarian religious associations and secret societies as well. In spite of the undoubted importance of formal associations (as well as of informal ones) in China, there are no good accounts of the internal structure of any single association, or the recruitment of members, or of the relations of associations either to other associations or to the social structure in general.[14] It is therefore difficult to say much about the functions of associations, which were usually multiple, or the sociological preconditions for the existence of any specific sort of association. Suffice it to say that, at least during the past century, every adult Chinese male was likely to be a member of at least one formal association. Furthermore, most men probably belonged to more than one, and the higher a man's status the more likely he was to belong to many associations and to play an active part in managing those associations.

From what I can tell, Chinese associations show a surprising uniformity in their formal structure. I see two main types of Chinese association, one based on li or reason, and the other based on ch'ing, sentiment. Here I want to present each as an ideal type.

The first type, the li-based, quintessentially formal association has a name, a defined set of members, officers who direct the association, and some clear, often written, statement of goals. It has a formal meeting place, often in a temple, and holds scheduled meetings. The holders of its offices derive their authority from the office, and not from their personal standing. The association is run by a committee, rather than by a single leader or the consensus of all members. Members of the managing committee are either elected or chosen by lot. They serve for a definite term, often a year, and may be replaced by others. If the group is small enough offices may rotate automatically and all members will hold office at some time. Financial matters are open and explicit. Members contribute and receive set amounts and careful accounts are kept and made publicly available. A code of members' rights, duties, and privileges exists, often in written form, and standardized punishments are meted out to those who break the rules. All members come together at least once a year for a formal banquet of meat and wine, which may be accompanied by professional entertainment (music, drama), commensality symbolizing and sealing corporate unity. In the past at least such groups usually possessed a patron deity and were thus, among other things, a religious cult, a group united by common worship.

Examples of such groups are provided by village irrigation associations, temple associations, lineages, defense leagues, same-place associations, guilds, and sectarian religious associations.[15] Note that in this perspective lineages are not a model for anything else; they are simply one more example of a common Chinese form of corporate group.

The extreme formality and rationality of such associations is impressive. The members seem to be thought of in terms of formally defined and fixed statuses; they are considered functionally equal and interchangeable persona. The association rules always aim at strict impartiality, and a variety of organizational devices from strict rotation in office to public posting of all accounts are used to minimize private or partial relations between members. Guild constitutions, some of which are available in English translation (in a later chapter I will give an English version of the constitution of Lukang's Ch'uan-chou Guild), provide the best examples of the spirit of extreme rationality and formality.[16] The preamble to the constitution of the Shantung Guild at Ningpo notes of the guild rules that: "To be equitable and conform to men's feelings they should be as even as a balance, as uniform as the waveless ocean, and observed with a punctuality as sure as the unerring tides, in order that confidence may be maintained."[17] The funds for one guild were raised by a levy of one-tenth of one percent of all profits. This was collected monthly, and each month two clerks audited the books of each establishment to ensure compliance. The clerks came from two different firms each month, and the firms provided auditing clerks in strict rotation.

Bureaucracy is a Chinese invention. Examples could be multiplied but the theme of rationality and formality should be clear. The stress put on impartiality and on the roles of members as organization men is impressive. But, I do not think it is convincing.

They protest too much. Guild constitutions and association by-laws are, like Confucian precepts, statements of how associations should be organized and operate, not descriptions of how they do operate. There are good reasons for supposing that Chinese formal associations never operated as smoothly or rationally as their constitutions or descriptions of their formal structure might suggest.

For one thing, such associations as guilds seem to have broken up fairly often, only to be reorganized with a new set of regulations. The preambles to guild constitutions with their flowery expressions of common interest tend to begin with the observation that prior to the current draft of the rules, formerly excellent rules had fallen into desuetude or were no longer being followed. I have taken much of my information on guilds from an article published in 1886, and the oldest guild mentioned in the article dated back only to the Ch'ien-lung period (1736–1796) and had been reorganized several times. Burgess, writing on guilds in Peking in the early 1920s notes the organization of new guilds as well as the dissolution of old ones.[18] Donald Willmott's account of the Chinese community of Semarang, in Java, comments on the weak solidarity of Chinese commercial and community organizations, which tended to lapse into desuetude except in times of crisis. "In 1927 and 1929 for several months no one could be found to accept the position of chairman of the Chinese Chamber of Commerce."[19]

Acquaintance with the by now considerable literature on formal organizations teaches one to be wary of tables of organization and strict job definitions, and to look for the covert, informal organization lurking behind the facade of formal hierarchy and regulations. In a well-known essay, Eric Wolf argued that: "the anthropologist's study of complex societies receives its major justification from the fact that such societies are not as well organized and tightly knit as their spokesmen would on occasion like to make people believe." He urges anthropologists to direct their attention to informal structures that are "interstitial, supplementary and parallel."[20] On general principles then one might expect to find Chinese formal associations, no matter how strongly they extol strict impartiality and dedication to the written rules, to be the hosts of informal, more or less covert, structures based on personal ties and loyalties.

This brings us to the second type of association—that based on personal, particularistic bonds and taking the form of a network of variable dyadic relations. This is a group or a network based on ch'ing. In the contemporary People's Republic of China such groups are often called kuan-hsi nets or webs. If "rational" and "formal" relations are best thought of in terms of narrowly defined rights and duties, sanctioned by an association and its code of rules, then "informal" "affective" relations are best thought of in terms of sociograms, networks of personal ties, and diffuse sanctions of general reciprocity. They are expressed in personal influence, mutual favors, and special concessions, which may either go beyond or contravene legal stipulations or associational regulations. Although such "informal" relations might be described in terms of relative functional diffuseness and particularism, it is important to keep in mind that they are limited and ultimately instrumental ties, based on long-term but very real reciprocity and mutual benefit. Personal relations described as based on ch'ing rather than li are especially important in economic and political affairs.

A group based on ch'ing stands in polar opposition to one based on li. It has no name, no single purpose, and no precise structure. It is simply a group of people, all of whom know and, to some extent, trust each other and who interact fairly frequently. There is no set of rules, no membership list or membership dues, and no precise accounting, whether of money or anything else. Such a group consists of a web of interpersonal ties and relies on the diffuse sanctions of reciprocity and face. A ch'ing group may be a number of farmers who exchange labor on one another's fields; it may be a coterie of drunken poets; it may be the village women who gossip while scrubbing clothes and loan each other money; or it may be a faction within the central state bureaucracy. Such groups may be difficult to label and categorize and their members may not publicly acknowledge their existence, but they are nonetheless quite real, and may be the focus of considerable power.

We have then two ideal types of association in Chinese society: one based on rationality and equity, the other on sentiment and special, personalistic relations. The two principles of association might be considered as offering or reflecting two models of association, two ways to bring people together. The first stresses common identity and common interests and considers members faceless and equivalent persona. The second stresses specific identity and unique personal qualities. In Chinese culture both models, though apparently antithetical, are legitimate and both are valued. As anyone familiar with Chinese metaphysics would expect (recall ordered antimonies, balanced tension, and complementarity) ch'ing and li should ideally reinforce each other, and social life should reflect a due proportion of both. In Taiwan today people speak of the best solution to a problem or a dispute as one that is "consonant with both reason and sentiment" (*ho ch'ing ho li*). Economic court judges in the People's Republic of China in the 1980s tried to decide cases by citing the old principle of "*ho ch'ing, ho li, ho fa,*" that is, according to the feelings of the people, congruent with natural reason and according to the law.[21] Balanced or not, there is in good Chinese fashion a tension between the principles or models of society. Overly strict adherence to either is bad, for li carried too far results in legalism, formalism, and inflexible devotion to abstract rules at the expense of human beings, while ch'ing taken too far leads to favoritism, factionalism, and corruption.

The distinction between the two types of association, as represented by an irrigation association and a neighborhood clique, should in theory be quite clear. In practice of course things are not that simple. Every formal association, from a guild to a temple association, can be thought of as having two components, one based on rationality, the other on sentiment. There is a potential contradiction between the two principles or forms. It is in everyone's long term interest to have an explicit set of rules or constitution, but on the other hand what's a constitution between friends? What at first glance impresses as excessive formality and rationality, everything from elaborate schemes for rotation in office to frequent ritual celebration of internal solidarity, may be interpreted as attempts to minimize the potentially disruptive forces of individual interests and informal personal ties.

How one interprets the unstable combination of rational and equitable formal associations with variable and specific personal relations will depend on one's initial perspective. If one takes common interests as paramount and assumes agreement on the goals and functions of associations, then one will condemn ties based on sentiment and try to expunge them or minimize them, labelling them as corruption and selfishness. In this view of life the group or association comes first, and individuals conform and submerge themselves for the common good. If, on the other hand, one takes individuals and their personal welfare as paramount, one will consider groups and associations as means, to be used or not as individuals calculate their own best interests. Two studies of social relations in overseas Chinese communities in Saigon and New York treat formal associations primarily as providing opportunities for individuals to extend their personal networks of kuan-hsi, based on kan-ch'ing and jen-ch'ing.[22] The same individual might express one perspective and standard of judgement on one occasion and the other on another occasion, or one to one person and the other to someone else. If either perspective is elaborated one will wind up with a full-blown social theory.

Guilds and other formal associations were founded and maintained because of men's recognition of their common interests and problems, and their recognition that joint action was more effective than individual action. The constitution of the Ningpo Guild at Wenchow says: "Here at Wenchow we find ourselves isolated; mountains and sea separate us from Ningpo, and when we trade we excite envy on the part of the Wenchow men and suffer insult and injury for which we have no adequate redress. Mercantile firms, each caring only for itself, experience disgrace and loss—the natural result of isolated and individual resistance. It is this that imposes on us the duty of establishing a guild." Guild constitutions also state that equitable rules serve to make unity possible and permit members to fully trust each other. The Amoy subguild of the Fukien Guild at Ningpo begins its constitution by saying: "It is said that well-conducted commerce yields three-fold profits and that the promise of a man of his word is worth three thousand taels. . . . Commerce has its laws founded on reason [li?] which conduce to concord." Another Amoy guild noted that: "In prosperous ports profits are trebled, but to that end truthfulness and sincerity are indispensable."[23] The point of the explicit rules is to permit the members to associate with complete confidence and to preclude dissension and distrust. The rules usually present long lists of forbidden practices, such as delaying payment of debts, giving false weight, dealing with non-guild enterprises and so on. The establishment of formal, li-based associations may be taken as evidence of the recognition that networks of personal relations based on "sentiment" are not enough.

On the other hand, guilds and other formal associations were composed of economically self-supporting and independent members who were theoretically equal and who had united out of recognition of common interests and the logic of collective action.[24] For guilds, the members were, at least in a short-term perspective, potential if not actual competitors. If enlightened self-interest motivated them to join together in formal associations, that same self-interest might well motivate them to evade or break the guild regulations. Besides this, while the theory of a li-based group assumes that the members are equal and interchangeable with no social identity save their membership in the group, in fact every member of a formal association is also the center of a personal network and is bound to certain other members of the association and to some outsiders by ties of sentiment and mutual obligation, which provide him with both immediate advantage and a certain degree of long term security. Such ties might well take precedence over association rules, for ch'ing as well as li is a valued and legitimate principle of social relations. Whether an action merits praise or blame depends on whose perspective one takes, for one man's corruption is another man's evidence of human feeling.

One can consider Chinese formal associations then as inherently unstable structures, coalitions of autonomous actors who, in spite of the rhetoric of mutual solidarity, do not commit themselves totally to the group. Given such a perspective, one can think of the principles of rationality and sentiment as operating, over time, in a dialectical and complementary fashion. Groups are formed out of recognition of common interests and goals, are torn apart by special favors and individual self-interest, and then are reformulated when the long-term inadequacy of narrow self-interest is demonstrated yet again. One can think of formal associations as sometimes crystallizing out of the indeterminate substratum of personal relations and sometimes dissolving back into that substratum. The factors influencing the longevity and solidarity of any particular association would be specific to a time and place, although it does seem that a common estate, as with a lineage, would serve to maintain an association, as would either support by or a moderate degree of opposition from an outside force, such as a government or an equivalent association. But by the time one begins asking about relations between formal associations, about personal links between members of different associations and about the relation between associations and governments, one is already talking about larger issues of social structure, and since my topic is Chinese urban social structure, it is time to turn to cities.

Cities

In Occidental thought "city" and "country" are, as Raymond Williams has said, "very powerful words," for "a contrast between country and city, as fundamental ways of life, reaches back into classical times."[25] Williams has written a book exploring the use of this contrast in English literature, and one could write many other books on the uses of these powerful and very complex words in Western history, religion, and social thought. Civilization after all presumes a *civis*; civil society is the good society; pagan and heathen, originally labels for rustics, have acquired other meanings; and the Occidental God dwells in the Heavenly City.

China has had cities, complete with walls, gates, palaces, markets, paved streets, and all the urban trimmings, since the second millennium B.C., and for considerable periods of time the world's largest cities have been Chinese. Chinese thought has certainly shown a marked propensity for dichotomous classifications—yin/yang; inner/outer; name/reality; center/periphery; and so on—and for balanced opposition in exposition and argument. But city/country has never been a significant Chinese distinction. Pastoral is not a Chinese genre; Chinese pilgrims climb mountains rather than trekking to cities; and, in China, Heaven is an empire rather than a city.

By not making much of the distinction the Chinese doubtless spared themselves much of the confusion that the superficially self-evident distinct between rural and urban has bred in the Western mind and in the minds of Western sociologists and anthropologists. Williams points out that at different times city and country have connoted very different qualities and that: "People have often said 'the city' when they meant capitalism or bureaucracy or centralized power, while 'the country' has at times meant everything from independence to deprivation, and from the powers of an active imagination to a form of release from consciousness."[26] Redfield's notion of the rural-urban continuum has been criticized as overly idealistic and Realist, as ahistorical, as insensitive to issues of class and power, and as of little use in guiding actual research.[27] Field research has produced scores of counter examples, and at least some rural sociologists have pointed out that they study not a special kind of community or way of life but a distinct occupation—farming.[28] There must be almost as many definitions of "urbanism" as of "culture," and attempts to draw precise lines between "urban" and "rural" places or institutions or modes of life have met with so little success and led to such confusion as to suggest that the wrong questions are being asked. G. W. Skinner, the editor and chief contributor to the largest and best book yet produced on Chinese cities, gently but firmly dismisses most of the general sociological literature on urbanism as of little use to students of Chinese cities.[29] But if Chinese thinkers avoided much of the obfuscation generated by the Western distinction between city and country as opposed ways of life, they themselves, their writing shaped by the Confucian model of society, paid little conscious attention to the cities that most of them, for at least part of their lives, lived in. They did not produce detailed or lucid accounts of Chinese cities. For a society as well documented as China and one whose intellectuals were so concerned with the structure of society and with public administration, our knowledge of cities and urban life is surprisingly vague. We know very little indeed about urban society in China, past or present.[30]

Given our present ignorance of many of the most simple facts about life in Chinese cities, many generalizations about Chinese urban life represent no more than the logical consequences of the writers' prior assumptions about the nature of Chinese society or civilization. If one sees China in terms of a despotic and all-embracing state, one will see cities as artifacts of that state, as administrative centers. If one thinks of China as composed, at bottom, of peasants and their landlords, one will see cities as parasites on the countryside. If one sees China as dominated by a class of landholding bureaucrats, one will point to the absence in China of a self-conscious urban bourgeois on the European or perhaps the Japanese pattern, and attribute this to the weight of the landed official class that either squeezed the life out of would-be capitalists or caused the successful merchants to abandon trade and settle down in a rural seat and groom their sons for entry to the Mandarinate. If one sees China as victim of imperialist aggression, one will see only such cities as the Treaty Ports like Shanghai, creations of the foreign imperialists and their Chinese collaborators. If one looks through Confucian spectacles, one will idealize the thrifty peasant and the cultivated gentleman and overlook cities entirely, feeling that the sage is to be found either in the heights of the mountains or the depths of the countryside. If, like Marion J. Levy, one sees Chinese society as an exemplar of an ideal-typical "traditional society," mired in familism and particularism and on the wrong side of every Parsonian pattern variable, then one will take the supposedly self-sufficient peasant family and that of its landlord as models for the whole society, and note cities, in passing, primarily as sites of social breakdown and "Westernization." If Chinese society is thought of, perhaps because of the influence of the Confucian model, as composed of highly particularistic and functionally diffuse little groups whose members are recruited largely through birth or marriage, then urban society will be described as an aggregation of such groups, each serving its members as a surrogate for the clan they left behind in the countryside.

For thinking about cities, I prefer to begin with the general perspective of G. W. Skinner. Beginning with central place theory, a theory developed by economic geographers to account for the spatial distribution of settlements and such economic institutions as retail shops, he concentrates on the functions of cities and their places in regional systems.[31] Such a perspective has many advantages. The city is seen primarily as a site of specialized roles and of processing and conversion functions, the home of brokers, moneychangers, specialized craftsmen, and of administrators (who process information). In this view, urban is an adjective rather than an essence, and settlements can be more or less urban. One thinks in terms of a hierarchy of urban places that begins with periodic markets and works up in a systematic fashion to such great metropolises as Canton or Shanghai. Such an approach demonstrates the futility of looking for a single sharp boundary between city and country, and forces one to see the city as part of a large-scale system. It also leads one to speak of "natural" cities, which exist because they are located at a certain place in a particular landscape and serve the needs of the local and regional economy. Cities are just as "natural" as villages.

All cities serve multiple functions, and it is not helpful to categorize some as administrative cities, others as ceremonial centers, and still others as commercial cities. Pushed to the point of caricature, the point of view that stresses the importance of the state in founding and maintaining cities would see them as artificial, exogenous constructions, administrative wens on the agrarian face of the countryside. If one accepts the administrative city definition, one will expect urban populations to consist of officials, troops, and those who serve their needs. If one accepts the natural city definition, then one will see officials as just one of a number of specialized and powerful groups within the population, and one's model of urban society will be much more complex.

Thinking of a hierarchy of settlements or a regional system of cities also helps avoid the profitless search for some essential Chinese city or urban social structure, which would have to be defined by contrast with an equally static and idealized Western City or Japanese City or rural social structure. As Skinner says:

> The Chinese city is no less a constructed ideal type than the "preindustrial" or the "Oriental" city. And when we survey the range of premodern Chinese cites from imperial capitals to lowly prefectural seats on remote frontiers; from great commercial emporia such as Soochow, Canton and Hankow to central market towns; from the relatively spacious cities of the Lower Yangtze to the congested cities of the Lingnan region,* where intramural areas were on

---

*Lingnan is a physiographic region defined by Skinner, which corresponds roughly to the provinces of Kwangtung and Kwangsi.

average one-sixth as large—when we comprehend this varied array, we run into the same difficulties that beset generalizations about more inclusive constructed types.[32]

Useful though Skinner's approach is, it has little to say about the internal structure of Chinese cities, except that such structure will most probably vary with a city's position in the regional system. The regional systems approach, in which the primary factors considered are sheer topography, population density, production of and demand for goods and services, and transport efficiency, is culture free and could be applied to India, Nigeria, or Brazil as easily as to China. Any picture of the internal structure of Chinese cities must depend on ethnographic and historical information.

We do have some idea of the elements of urban social structure, but no very clear idea of how to put the pieces together. We know that in the nineteenth- and early-twentieth-century Chinese cities one could expect to find guilds, which might but need not have to have been composed of men from the same native place. One could also expect to find some sort of neighborhood or street association, often organized as a religious cult. Urban temples, like their rural counterparts, had territories or catchment areas that celebrated an annual festival with public entertainment, processions, and domestic banquets. Secret societies seem to have been recruited largely from unattached, lower class men and thus to have been located in cities, as well as along waterways and in frontier districts where gangs of miners congregated. Apart from their criminal role, in extortion, gambling, and prostitution, they seem to have controlled or "policed" markets, and to have played an important role in organizing and controlling unskilled labor, thus incorporating the city's poorest inhabitants into an organization that related them, in some behind-the-scenes fashion, to the urban elite. By the mid or late Ch'ing period many cities had charitable or benevolent societies that performed some of the housekeeping tasks of municipal government, such as providing fire companies and poor relief. In at least some cities, confederations of guilds or same-place associations played some part in urban administration, under the supervision of or in collaboration with the resident imperial officials.[33]

Skinner, in a logical extension and elaboration of his concern with regional systems, has devoted some attention to what he calls sojourning. Sojourning is a special subtype of migration in which particular localities cultivated specific occupational skills for export, usually to some more urbanized central place. The sojourners went as single men, leaving their families behind them and intending to return some day when they had made good. When they reached their destination they joined their fellows from their native place and followed whatever calling their group specialized in. Sojourning was what most of the Chinese migrants to Southeast Asia and North America in the nineteenth and first half of the twentieth centuries were doing, and men in China itself did the same thing. Thus, as is often reported from overseas Chinese settlements (which are overwhelmingly urban) and cities in China itself, it was common for, say, all wine shop owners to come from place A, while bankers come from place B, and positions as clerks in local government bureaus are monopolized by men from place C. Membership in the category of "native of the same place" and in the associations formed by such men (*hui-kuan, t'ung-hsiang hui*) permitted the growth of those networks of mutual confidence and communication that were necessary for long-distance, inter-urban commerce. And within a given city even such lowly or unskilled trades as barbering or unloading ships might be monopolized by those from a certain, often nearby, locality. Skinner links division of labor to locality specialization, so that the more extensive the division of labor in a given city the more localities its population recognizes as their native places and the greater the number of native-place associations in the city. In many Chinese cities, Skinner argues, a considerable proportion of the population consisted of sojourners. Merchants, artisans, and unskilled workers flocked to cities that were prospering, like Shanghai in the second half of the nineteenth century, so that a high proportion of the population of such cities consisted of sojourners, while cities on the way down had fewer sojourners.[34]

Skinner's treatment of sojourning is both eminently logical and supported by his citation of many examples. While it certainly serves to help illuminate some of the mechanisms of large-scale economic and even social integration of Chinese society, there do remain some unanswered questions. He concentrates on sojourning as it looks from the perspective of the locality sending out talent, and points out the efficiency for inter-urban trade of having, say, Cantonese firms in one city deal with Cantonese firms in three or four cities of the region. What is less clear is exactly how any given city was structured. That is to say, if we look at sojourning from the perspective of the city receiving sojourners, what structure emerges? What were the nature of the relations between groups of sojourners from different native places, and to what extent did membership in a native place category or group, significant though it was, determine all of men's social relations?

Let us begin with commercial relations. The advantages of dealing with one's fellows from the old home are, as Skinner points out, very great. But, for most lines of trade, at some point one will also have to deal with either the natives of the city, if any, or with sojourners from other places. The point of sojourning after all is to earn money selling goods or services to people who are not one's fellow localites. A Shensi banker in one city could, with confidence, remit funds to a Shensi banker in a distant city, but if all the Shensi men in a given city were bankers, then they had to seek customers from outside their native-place group, and had to have ways to decide which non-Shensi people were trustworthy enough to loan money to. A Cantonese merchant in the Lower Yangtze region would certainly import his pottery and "mixed goods" from a firm in Canton or Hong Kong, but at some point in the distribution network the Cantonese wholesaler or even retailer would have to deal with and repose some degree of confidence in a non-Cantonese. Skinner speaks, perfectly accurately I'm convinced, of local systems competing for control of occupational niches in cities, and there is ample evidence of speech-group competition for control of trades among the overseas Chinese in the cities of southeast Asia. But such competition was, one assumes, usually limited in some way, and may have demanded the formation of coalitions with other native-place groups or the cultivation of special relations with whoever governed the city. While Skinner has explicated the internal structure of sojourning groups, the nature of the relations between such groups remains obscure.

If one pushes Skinner's image of the Chinese city as consisting largely of men from somewhere else further than he takes it, one ends up with a model of urban society that contains some unlikely features. If nearly everyone in a city is a sojourner, there to make money and go back home with it, it follows that very few of the people residing in a city will consider it their permanent home. The Chinese city would then resemble a boarding house, full of unattached individuals who are transients. The component elements of urban society, those same-place and occupational groups, would have little to do with each other and would represent closed, socially self-sufficient groups, interacting only in the market place, and exchanging only money. The Chinese city could then be thought of as rather like the downtown business section of an Occidental city, a place that people come to for work and trade, but leave for their home communities when not on duty. It would differ primarily in frequency of commuting, for while workers in Western cities usually commute home every day, their counterparts in traditional Chinese cities would get back only a few times each year, or once every few years. The only permanent members of the city would be those unfortunates who had no native place to return to, a group composed perhaps of the descendants of failed sojourners, and perhaps earning its living by running the boarding houses, restaurants, laundries, and brothels patronized by the sojourners. When one reflects a moment, this resembles the model of "The City" employed by the pioneering Chicago sociologists in the 1920's. That view of the city, which reflected the experience of a rapidly growing city, one that had added, primarily through migration, half a million people per decade for three decades, stressed the diversity of ethnic groups and consequently the problem of coordinating their activities in the absence of common values and norms.[35]

Granted that a considerable proportion of the population of a Chinese city was liable to consist of sojourners from elsewhere, all of them pursuing a locality-specific occupation, one can still ask how all-embracing or salient native-place identification was for individuals. Were 90 percent of an urban resident's social relations with others from the same local system, or were 50 percent or only 20 percent? Did he spend most of his time with people from the same native place or did he only see them on the first and third Tuesdays of the month? Peter Golas in a paper on early Ch'ing guilds argues that most members probably had little connection with the guild outside of special occasions and that, even in the minority of guilds that had their own guildhalls, the hall does not seem to have served as a social center.[36] Presumably the same-place associations and guilds were dominated by the richest and most successful members of the community. But, if we may apply the argument from Skinner's studies of overseas Chinese leadership, these men were most likely to have the most to do with members of other native-place associations or with the locals (if any), either speaking the local language or a *lingua franca* and participating in banquets and perhaps the board of directors of a city-wide charitable association along with the wealthy and successful leaders of the other sets of sojourners.[37] One can imagine the wealthy former head of the X native place association in Shanghai talking frequently at banquets in the best restaurants of the metropolis about the simple joys of life in his old home, and one can imagine him returning home for a brief visit at New Year's or Ch'ing Ming, but it is harder to imagine him actually settling down to retirement in an out-of-the-way village in the hills or in a minor river port.

The question here is one of the nature of such urban groups as same-place associations, the degree to which they were bounded and closed-off groups, and of the content of the relations between such groups. The more one thinks of them as closed corporate sub-communities, interacting only in the market, the more significant and problematic become the nature of those transactions in the market, and the more puzzling the mechanisms that sanction those exchanges. There is also an uneasy feeling that such a picture of urban society has somehow reinvented the notion of the closed-off corporate community, which we know does not adequately describe Chinese villages and so seems unlikely to serve to describe cities. My opinion is that sojourning and same-place associations were major elements in urban social life, but that there were other sorts of groupings and social relations as well. To find out what they were, we have to look at specific cities, and I now intend to turn to the Chinese city I know best—Lukang.

Notes

1. Morton H. Fried, *Fabric of Chinese Society: A Study of the Social Life of a Chinese County Seat* (New York: Praeger, 1953) (Reprint, New York: Octagon Press, 1969).

2. Fried. p. 227.

3. Major anthropological studies of Chinese personal and business relations include, in chronological order:

T'ien Ju-kang. 1953. *The Chinese of Sarawak: A Study of Social Structure* (London School of Economics Monographs on Social Anthropology, No. 12). London: Athlone Press.

Ward, Barbara E., 1960. "Cash or Credit Crops? An Examination of Some Implications of Peasant Commercial Production with Special Reference to the Multiplicity of Traders and Middlemen," *Economic Development and Cultural Change* 8, 2 (January 1960).

Ryan, Edward, 1961. *The Value System of a Chinese Community in Java.* Unpublished Ph.D. Dissertation, Harvard University.

Silin, Robert, 1964. *Trust and Confidence in a Hong Kong Wholesale Vegetable Market.* Unpublished M.A. Dissertation, University of Hawaii.

———, 1972. "Marketing and Credit in a Hong Kong Wholesale Market," in W. E. Willmott, ed., *Economic Organization in Chinese Society*. Stanford: Stanford University Press.

———, 1976. *Leadership and Values: The Organization of Taiwanese Large-Scale Enterprises*. Cambridge: Harvard University Press.

DeGlopper, Donald R., 1972. "Doing Business in Lukang," in W. E. Willmott, ed., *Economic Organization in Chinese Society*. Stanford: Stanford University Press.

Young, John A., 1974. *Business and Sentiment in a Chinese Market Town*. Taipei: Asian Folklore and Social Life Monograph, No. 60.

Barton, Clifton G., 1977. *Credit and Commercial Control: The Strategies and Methods of Chinese Businessmen in South Vietnam*. Unpublished Ph.D. Dissertation, Cornell University.

———, "Trust and Credit: Some Observations Regarding Business Strategies of Overseas Chinese Traders in South Vietnam," in L. A. Peter Gosling and Linda Y. C. Lim, eds. *The Chinese in Southeast Asia*, vol. 1, *Ethnicity and Economic Activity*. Singapore: Maruzen Asia, 1983. pp. 46–64.

Menkhoff, Thomas. "Xinyong or How to trust Trust? Chinese Non-Contractual Business Relations and Social Structure:The Singapore Case." *Internationales Asienforum*. 23, 1–2, pp.261–288 (November 1992).

Oxfeld, Ellen. "Individualism, Holism and the Market Mentality: Notes on the Recollections of a Chinese Entrepreneur" *Cultural Anthropology* 7, 3, pp.267–300, (August 1992).

Yang, Mayfair Mei-hui. *Gifts, Favors and Banquets: The Art of Social Relationships in China*. Ithaca: Cornell University Press, 1994.

4. Young, 1974, pp. 50–51.

5. Ambrose Yeo-chi King, "Kuan-hsi and Network Building: A Sociological Interpretation," *Daedalus: Journal of the American Academy of Arts and Sciences* 120, 2 (Spring 1991), p. 63.

6. These are: Hu Hsien-chin, "The Chinese Concepts of 'Face'," *American Anthropologist*, 46, 1 (1944), pp. 46–65; and Martin M. C. Yang, *A Chinese Village: Taitou, Shantung Province*. (New York: Columbia University Press, 1945). pp. 168–172.

7. Yang, 1945, p. 168.

8. Yang, 1945, p. 196.

9. William H. Newell, *Treacherous River: A Study of Rural Chinese in North Malaya* (Kuala Lumpur: University of Malaya Press, 1962), pp. 165–174; Ch'eng Tien-hsi, *China, Moulded by Confucius* (London: Stevens and Sons, 1946).

10. On sales contracts in late-nineteenth-century Taiwan, see Rosser H. Brockman, "Commercial Contract Law in Late Nineteenth-Century Taiwan," in Jerome A. Cohen, R. Randle Edwards, and Fu-mei Chang Chen, eds., *Essays on China's Legal Tradition* (Princeton: Princeton University Press, 1980), pp. 103–136. Brockman quotes, from the Japanese compilation Taiwan's Private Law (*Taiwan Shihō*, 1910), the Taiwan adage "the officials have their regulations; the people have private contracts" (*kuan yu cheng-t'iao; min yu ssu-yüeh*). Myron Cohen notes the widespread use of written contracts in late traditional China in "The Role of Contract in Traditional Chinese Social Organization," in *Proceedings of the VIIIth International Congress of Anthropological and Ethnological Sciences, 1968, Tokyo and Kyoto*, vol. 2, *Ethnology* (Tokyo: Science Council of Japan, 1969), pp. 130–32; and gives examples from the contemporary People's Republic of China in "Family Management and Family Division in Contemporary Rural China" *The China Quarterly* 130 (June 1992), pp. 373–377.

11. Commercial contracts in nineteenth-century Taiwan has been described by a Western scholar as "very sophisticated and well-adapted to the uses they secured." They were used even though there was no written commercial law or system of courts to enforce contracts. Although in legal terms such contracts are described as "self-enforcing," as social scientists we are interested in the social mechanisms and relations that made the use of such effective and highly developed contracts possible. See Rosser H. Brockman. "Commercial Contract Law in Late Nineteenth-Century Taiwan," in Jerome A. Cohen, R. Randle Edwards, and Fu-mei Chang Chen, eds., *Essays on China's Legal Tradition* (Princeton: Princeton University Press, 1980), pp. 76–136, especially pp. 83, 103, 127.

12. Frederick W. Williams, "Chinese and Medieval Guilds," *Yale Review* (August 1892), p. 207.

13. Maurice Freedman, "Immigrants and Associations: Chi-

nese in Nineteenth-Century Singapore," *Comparative Studies in Society and History* 3, 3 (April 1961), p. 289.

14. The best studies of overseas Chinese associations, and exceptions to my generalizations, are: G. W. Skinner, *Leadership and Power in the Chinese Community of Thailand* (Ithaca: Cornell University Press, 1958); W. E. Willmott, *The Political Structure of the Chinese Community in Cambodia* (London School of Economics Monographs on Social Anthropology, No. 42) (London: Athlone Press, 1970); Cheng, Lim-Keak, *Social Change and the Chinese in Singapore: A Socio-Economic Geography with Special Reference to Bang Structure* (Singapore: Singapore University Press, 1985).

15. There is a nice account of an irrigation association in Fei Hsiao-t'ung, *Peasant Life in China* (London: Routledge and Kegan Paul, 1939), pp. 172–173. A fairly thorough account of village associations is provided in Daniel H. Kulp, *Country Life in South China* (New York: Teacher's College, Columbia University, 1925).

For lineages, apart from Maurice Freedman's work, see Hu Hsien-chin, *The Common Descent Group in China and Its Functions* (New York: Viking Fund Publications in Anthropology, No. 10, 1948); and Hugh Baker, *A Chinese Lineage Village: Sheung Shui* (Stanford: Stanford University Press, 1968).

Martin Yang's (1945) *A Chinese Village* has a good account of a village defense corps, while militia groups' are discussed in Philip A. Kuhn, *Rebellion and Its Enemies in Late Imperial China* (Cambridge: Harvard University Press, 1970).

For same-place associations, see any good account of an overseas Chinese community, such as Skinner on Bangkok or Willmott on the Chinese Community in Cambodia. Same-place associations and guilds are described in Hosea B. Morse, *The Guilds of China* (London: Longmans Green and Co., 1909) (Reprint, Taipei: Cheng-wen, 1966); and in John S. Burgess, *The Guilds of Peking* (New York: Columbia University Press, 1928) (Reprint, Taipei: Cheng-wen, 1966). An exceptionally useful source on guilds is D. J. McGowan, "Chinese Chambers of Commerce and Trades Union," *Journal of the North China Branch of the Royal Asiatic Society*, 21 (1886), pp. 133–192.

For sectarian religion, see J. C. De Korne, *The Fellowship of Goodness (T'ung Shan She)* (Grand Rapids, Michigan, 1941); and M. Topley, "The Great Way of Former Heaven," *Bulletin of the School of Oriental and African Studies* (London, 1963).

16. See McGowan, 1886.

17. Ibid.

18. Burgess, 1928.

19. Donald E. Willmott, *The Chinese of Semarang* (Ithaca: Cornell University Press, 1960), p. 60.

20. Eric Wolf, "Kinship, Friendship, and Patron-Client Relations in Complex Societies," in Michael Banton, ed., *The Anthropology of Complex Societies* (London: Tavistock, 1966), p. 2.

21. Lucie Cheng and Arthur Rosett, "Contract with a Chinese Face: Socially Embedded Factors in the Transformation from Hierarchy to Market, 1978–1989." *Journal of Chinese Law* 5, 2 (Fall 1991), pp. 224–226, 231.

22. Barton (1977); and Bernard Wong (1974), *Patronage, Brokerage, Entrepreneurship and the Chinese Community of New York*. Unpublished Ph.D. dissertation, University of Wisconsin.

23. McGowan, 1886.

24. On the logic of collective action, see Mancur Olson, *The Logic of Collective Action: Public Goods and the Theory of Groups* (Cambridge: Harvard University Press, 1965); and Mancur Olson and David A. Reisman, *Theories of Collective Action* (New York: St. Martins Press, 1990).

25. Raymond Williams, *The Country and the City* (London: Oxford University Press, 1973), p. 1.

26. Williams, 1973, p. 291.

27. Francisco Benet, "Sociology Uncertain: The Ideology of the Rural-Urban Continuum," *Comparative Studies in Society and History*, 6, 1 (1963).

28. Benet quotes I. Reiss, "Rural-Urban and Status Differences in Interpersonal Contacts," *American Journal of Sociology*, 65, 2 (1959). Reiss in turn is quoting Pitrim Sorokin and C. C. Zimmerman, *Principles of Rural-Urban Sociology* (New York: Henry Holt and Co., 1929), p. 16.

29. G. William Skinner, "Introduction: Urban Development in China," in G. W. Skinner. ed., *The City in Late Imperial China* (Stanford: Stanford University Press, 1977), pp. 4, 264–265.

30. This paragraph does not take account of William T. Rowe's two monographs on the city of Hankow in the nineteenth

century, *Hankow: Commerce and Society in a Chinese City, 1796–1889* (Stanford: Stanford University Press, 1984) and *Hankow: Conflict and Community in a Chinese City, 1796–1895* (Stanford: Stanford University Press, 1989). They do not mandate major revision of my line of argument, and full consideration of their ethnographic detail would lengthen an already lengthy chapter, the purpose of which is to set out terms and categories for the subsequent analysis of Lukang.

31. G. W. Skinner, 1977, "Cities and the Hierarchy of Local Systems."

32. G. W. Skinner, 1977, p. 5.

33. See Skinner, 1977., pp. 521–553. For secret societies, see Jean Chesneaux, ed., *Popular Movements and Secret Societies in China, 1840–1950* (Stanford: Stanford University Press, 1972).

34. G. W. Skinner, "Mobility Strategies in Late Imperial China: A Regional Systems Analysis," in Carol A. Smith, ed., *Regional Analysis,* vol. 1, *Economic Systems* (New York: Academic Press, 1976), pp. 327–364; and Skinner (1977), pp. 265–266, 270–272, 538–546.

35. See Maurice R. Stein, *The Eclipse of Community: An Interpretation of American Studies* (Princeton: Princeton University Press, 1960).

36. Peter J. Golas, "Early Ch'ing Guilds," in Skinner, ed., 1977, p. 580.

37. G. W. Skinner, "Overseas Chinese Leadership: Paradigm for a Paradox," in Gehan Wijeyewardena, ed., *Leadership and Authority* (Singapore: Singapore University Press, 1968), pp. 191–207.

Chapter 3

The City of Lukang

Lukang is (as of 1968) a city of some 28,000 people located on the west coast of central Taiwan. It stands at the northern end of the plain that runs along the southern two-thirds of Taiwan's west coast. The land around the city is intensively cultivated and densely populated, with a rural population density of about 2,100 people per square mile (around 900 people per square kilometer). Almost all the land is irrigated and produces two rice crops a year, with a third cash crop of wheat, vegetables, flax, or rape in the winter. Lukang is a retailing center serving some 100,000 villagers. It is also a center of handicraft and light industry, the site of several hundred small factories, some of which produce goods for export. Administratively it is the seat of Lukang *chen*, a third-level administrative unit of 65,000 people. The *chen*, or administrative township, is one of the twenty-six lowest-level administrative units (*hsiang* and *chen*) that make up Changhua county (*hsien*). Changhua county, with a 1968 population of 990,000 people, is one of the twenty-one counties and cities (*shih*) into which the island of Taiwan is divided. Lukang is the third-largest city in Changhua county, and a paved road and a narrow-gauge railroad connect it with the county seat, Changhua City, which lies twelve kilometers further inland. From Lukang dirt roads run to the villages and to the major market towns of northern and central Changhua county.

Lukang is a compact settlement of low red brick buildings that huddle together along narrow lanes. They turn inward toward the market and the shops that line the three-kilometer main street, and away from the rice fields that are planted up to their blank rear ·
walls. It is a city of foregrounds, of walls, facades, and alleys that

Just down the alleys off the market square are basket shops, peanut oil presses, blacksmiths, and two coffin shops.

twist and suddenly open on dusty temples, racks of noodles drying in the sun, or a pile of newly made barrels. In the center of the city stands the market, a labyrinthine jumble of small stalls under a great covering roof. Townspeople and farmers jostle amid piles of fresh vegetables, displays of cheap crockery, pig carcasses, and brightly colored cloth. The paved square in front of the market is wet underfoot, littered with cabbage leaves, fish scales, and banana peels, and clogged with people, bicycles, and wheeled soup stands. Its margins are occupied by peddlers of fresh fish, betel nut, plastic sandals, and bamboo carrying poles. Itinerant traders tout plastic raincapes, rat traps, live ducklings, and patent medicines. The three sides of the market square are occupied by substantial shops, their interiors crammed to the ceiling with soap, canned food, thermos bottles, Chinese drugs, and miscellaneous plumbing fixtures. The food stalls inside the market sell such local specialties as oyster omelets, fried eels, and noodles with freshwater clams. Just down the alleys off the square are basket shops, peanut oil presses, blacksmiths, and two coffin shops. People, goods, and services are concentrated in the narrow space of the market in an implosion of commercial and social interaction, of sights, sounds, smells, and tastes.

Outside the market square the streets of Lukang are relatively quiet, given over to children, gossiping neighbors, the odd water buffalo cart, and the ubiquitous chickens. Each has its own sights, sounds, and smells, its own variation on the general Lukang pattern of rose brick and narrow lane. The sound of power saws and the smell of freshly cut wood distinguish the "End of the Street" where the carpenters live and work. Nets and piles of oyster shells, and a fishy smell overlaid by the choking smoke from the lime works are characteristic of the "North End," home of oystermen and fishermen. Bright blue and yellow skeins of yarn in the dyer's yard, the background rattle of the textile mill and the snuffling of hogs, along with the acidic smell of the electroplaters identify a specific place at the south edge of the city, the "Channel Bank." The beginning of Ch'uan-chou Street is marked by the oversweet smell of the incense makers and by the bright paper fans drying on notched bamboo poles on the sunny side of the street. The other end of Ch'uan-chou Street is, like the rest of Lukang's periphery, inhabited primarily by farmers, their courtyards piled with rice straw and separated from the fish ponds by a rutted path.

On the other side of the fish ponds the rice fields begin, sweeping in a green carpet from the edge of the sea to the first, abrupt range of hills, fifteen kilometers inland. In the fields windbreaks of bamboo, pine, and coarse grass are planted about every hundred yards, limiting the view to rice and windbreak in any direction. The pattern of enclosures and foregrounds that characterizes urban Lukang is repeated in the countryside on a larger and more monochromatic scale. The countryside is quiet, the creak of bamboo and cries of cicadas being its usual sounds, and often the only movement is the rice rippling in the breeze and a hawk spiraling high above.

The involuted, repetitive pattern of enclosures that marks the city and the fields ceases at the shore. Rice is planted up to a low mud dike, topped with stunted pines whose limbs are twisted back by the constant wind of winter. On the other side of the dike an expanse of sand and mud stretches off to the faint line of surf on the horizon. The flats extend six or seven kilometers out. In the summer they are a space of silence, glaring light, and mirages. In the winter the north wind howls in, blowing over open water all the way from Manchuria and Korea. Lukang is famous for its wind, and from late October through March its people shutter their houses and go to sleep soon after sunset, while the wind rattles windows, shutters, and shop signs, blows dust into houses, peels paper posters from walls, and polishes the patina on brick and tile. Beyond the dike and the tide flats is the Taiwan Straits, and beyond that the forbidden coast of China. For the people of Lukang the shore is an edge, a margin beyond which there is nothing and from which nothing comes. The city looks inward, and beyond itself it looks inland to Changhua City and to the railroad and the main highway that connect Changhua with Taipei and with the rest of Taiwan.

From Lukang it is not difficult to reach Changhua City. Buses leave every ten minutes throughout the day, and the trip takes twenty to twenty-five minutes. On an average day the bus company sells about 1,100 tickets to Changhua City. One can also hire a taxi for the same trip. In Changhua City the buses pull in next to the railroad station, and from there the diesel express train takes two and a half hours to reach Taipei. It is equally easy to get to Lukang, and a casual observer who stepped off a bus on Lukang's main street would find little that was unfamiliar or different from any other small city in Taiwan. The people would be dressed as they are in other places; the same sorts of shops would be selling the same sorts of staple and mass-produced articles; the usual patriotic slogans and advertising posters would be decorating the walls; the children would be wearing the standard khaki school uniforms; and the temples would look much like the temples in other settlements.

Lukang today is one of the scores of market towns and small cities that dot the plains of Taiwan. Communications with the rest of the island are good, and the city is firmly integrated into the islandwide economic and administrative structure. When compared with other towns of Taiwan and seen in an outside "objective" perspective, Lukang is not very different from most other settlements that are neither villages nor major metropolises.

Education is a very serious business in Taiwan, and Lukang's schools provide an index to the city's place in its region. There are three six-year primary schools, which are operated by the national government. They teach a standard curriculum in Mandarin, the "National Language," and are free. Practically all children attend. There is a six-year middle school, which is operated by the Changhua county government. Before 1968 it was necessary to pass an entrance examination for junior middle school, and both that and the fairly low fees the school charged caused many children to leave school after primary education. In 1968 the national government extended its support to junior middle schools, trying to provide nine years of free public education, and a new junior middle school was built in Lukang. Secondary schools in Taiwan are ranked, primarily in terms of the percentage of their graduates who pass the standard university entrance examination. In these terms the Lukang middle school is a low-ranked, second choice school, as only 3 percent of its graduates go on to university. The secondary school that most Lukang parents who are seriously concerned about their childrens', and especially their sons', education aim for is the Provincial Changhua Middle School in Changhua City, some 80 percent of whose graduates go on to higher education. Every day about 1,000 middle school students ride the buses between Lukang and Changhua City at special student fares. Some of these are Lukang students on their way to school in Changhua City and Taichung City, which lies 15 kilometers beyond Changhua. Some are students from Changhua City and the villages scattered near the highway who attend Lukang Middle School only because they failed to get into a more desirable school. Secondary education, which is seen in Taiwan as the primary avenue of social mobility, thus draws the brightest and most ambitious youth of Lukang out of the community and into the larger world of central Taiwan. Few of those selected at age twelve or thirteen for mobility up and out are expected to return.

Most people enter and leave the city by bus, bicycle or motorcycle, or taxi. Most goods are delivered to and leave Lukang by truck or small three-wheeled motorized carts. The widespread use of motorized transport in all its various forms, from large trucks through ox carts pulled by power tillers, has had major consequences for Lukang's economy. Farmers who once had to walk to Lukang and so seldom came can now ride the bus or their very own motor scooter or power tiller. Their wives and daughters can also come to Lukang, and they do. This increases the business of Lukang's retailers and of such specialists as those who repair motorcycles and power tillers and the two midwives who operate lying-in hospitals. On the other hand, the farmers may also, if they wish, continue on through Lukang and turn onto the road for Changhua City, which, with over 100,000 inhabitants, offers more specialized shops and more specialists than Lukang. The natives of Lukang itself, especially those with a little extra money to spend, can easily go to Changhua City or to Taichung City, which has 350,000 people. It is generally accepted in Lukang that better doctors, hospitals, restaurants, films, and hostesses are found in Changhua and Taichung Cities, while those of Lukang itself are described as fit for rustics perhaps but not for the sophisticated, middle class natives of the city. Lukang thus tends to serve as a retailing and service center for the surrounding rural population and for its own lower income group, while its own people go on to the higher-order central places of Changhua City and Taichung City.

Lukang is a retailing center for the villages but it is not, today, a marketing center. Most of the region's agricultural produce is not marketed through Lukang, but goes directly to the major cities or to processing factories. This obviates any substantial brokerage role for the businessmen of the town. Farmers sell their crops for cash, some of which is spent in Lukang, but they do not rely to any great extent on credit from Lukang merchants or shops. Since Lukang is still the center of the local road network it is possible to watch trucks loaded with vegetables or peanuts drive into Lukang from the south and continue on without stopping, bound for Changhua City and the island's main highway. The oysters cultivated on the tidal flats are brought into Lukang on carts pulled by the oystermen. The oystermen's families then shell them, pack them in plastic bags, and send them off to the central market in Taichung City in the trunks of taxis.

The development of efficient motorized transport in Taiwan, most of which has taken place since 1950, has served to undercut Lukang's central-place functions and role as a market town. But the same efficient transport has made it possible for Lukang, which is not on the main railroad line, to become a center of light industry. The city is the site of some 500 small factories and handicraft enterprises. Some of them produce things like bricks, plows, or coffins, which are consumed within the city or its retail service area. Others produce articles for the islandwide or the international market. Small factories turn out hinges, twine, razors, motorcycle reflectors, motorcycle rear view mirrors, wooden barrels and tubs, for sale in Taipei or anywhere else in Taiwan. Others manufacture such things as scissors, toy parasols, or screwdrivers, which are then shipped to Thailand, Zambia, and the United States. Living costs are lower in Lukang than in Taiwan's major cities, and this, along with the ability of small trucks to go anywhere there is a road, is usually cited as the main reason for the recent growth of industry in Lukang.

The economy of the city is characterized by a very large number of very small businesses, and by extensive specialization and division of labor. Apart from the 500 factories and workshops, a count of shops and street stalls made in November 1967 showed 811 shops, 234 market and street stalls, and 129 street peddlers. The none-too-accurate business registration statistics of the Changhua county government listed 1,083 registered businesses in the city. Roughly then, Lukang has one retailer of goods or services for every fourteen adults, a shop or stall for every five households, and one registered business for every seven males above the age of fourteen. There is only one large factory, a textile mill employing about 200 workers, and most manufacturing or craft firms have fewer than ten employees. Almost all retail shops are family businesses, employing only the owner and his household or run by the wife or grandparents to supplement family income. The streets of the city are lined with many small and totally independent businesses, often selling or manufacturing the same thing. There are, for example, twenty-nine grocery stores, twenty-one Chinese drug stores, nineteen furniture enterprises, which both manufacture and sell furniture, and nine photographers.

The multiplicity of small units that marks the city's economy is also found in its religious life. There are thirty-nine temples, probably a larger number of minor shrines dedicated to the bones of the unknown dead, and an unknowable number of private religious cults that unite a few households in the common worship of a deity. There are four small Christian churches: one Roman Catholic; one Presbyterian; one Baptist; and one True Jesus. The Catholic church is led by an American missionary priest, the city's only foreign resident, while the Presbyterian and Baptist churches are led by Taiwanese pastors from other parts of the island. The True Jesus church, a pentecostal church that practices faith healing and speaking in tongues, draws most of its congregation from the coastal villages to the north of Lukang.

Administratively the city is both firmly integrated with the national political and administrative structure, and internally divided. In Lukang, as everywhere else in Taiwan, the authority of the central government is never publicly questioned. The government controls all public media, and in Lukang as elsewhere a surprising number of surfaces, such as walls, buses, matchbooks, and medicine wrappers bear such slogans as "Build Up Taiwan—Gloriously Recover the Mainland" or "Eradicate the Ten-Thousand-Evil Mao Bandits." Every male serves three years in the military and a small garrison is stationed in Lukang. The Kuomintang, the ruling political party, has a branch in Lukang, as it does in almost every other community. It operates a Service Center for the citizens and conducts an annual Winter Relief drive to aid registered paupers.

Lukang has no municipal government as such. Many of the functions of a municipal government are divided among various bodies. The schools are financed and operated by the national and the county governments. The police are controlled by the Taiwan Provincial government, and all are outsiders, many from the mainland. The fire brigade is a branch of the Provincial Police, although there is a volunteer auxiliary composed of Lukang men. The city has no public water or sewer system, households relying on wells, septic systems, and regular nightsoil collection. The lowest unit of local administration, Lukang *chen*, takes in both the city and a large rural area to the north, with the rural population forming a slight majority. The *chen* has a mayor and town council, all elected by universal suffrage. The powers of the town government are quite limited. Its budget is determined by the county government and it has no power to tax. The mayor is responsible for supervising the work of the town office. The town office administers the market, the town slaughterhouse and the public health station. It handles population registration and conscription, and manages local public works, such as road construction and maintenance. The town council meets every three months, and may pass the town budget and communicate officially with appropriate bureaus of the county government. About half the budget of the town government goes for the salaries of public employees and for administrative expenses, while the rest is spent on public works and the health station.

There is also a Lukang *chen* Farmers' Association. The Farmers' association is a quasi-governmental association, whose form and procedures are set by the Taiwan Provincial Assembly and whose operations are supervised by the Provincial government's Bureau of Agriculture. Membership is restricted to, and in practice compulsory for, farmers. Those who are not farmers may join as nonvoting associate members. Farmers elect representatives, who in turn elect a supervisory board and a general manager. The general manager, who need not himself be a farmer but must be at least a secondary school graduate, then hires all the full-time employees of the association. The Farmers' Association is responsible for collecting the land tax, in rice, and for arranging the compulsory sale of (an additional quota of) rice at a low fixed price to the government. It provides fertilizer in exchange for rice, at a rate favoring the government, which imports most fertilizer and controls the supply. Farmers' Associations operate warehouses where rice may be stored, and have marketing bureaus that help market cash crops. The marketing bureau gives contracts for such crops as mushrooms or asparagus and guarantees a supply to processing factories. The Farmers' Association has an agricultural extension division which attempts to promote and disseminate modern farm technology. It employs several veterinary medics, who spend most of their time inoculating hogs. The Association also operates a credit bureau that makes low-interest loans to farmers and provides savings and checking accounts. The Farmers' Association employs more people than the town office and has a larger budget. It employs only local people and its general manager, a native of Lukang, has the power to hire, fire and promote all the employees. The town government and the Farmers' Association together make up that sphere of local administration that is staffed by local people, and in the countryside the Farmer's Association, which is involved with tax collection, marketing and credit, is of more importance than the town government.

Just as there is a Farmers' Association for farmers, so there is a trade association for every trade. The unit of membership is the individual shop or enterprise. The trade associations are imposed by the central government and membership is, in practical terms, obligatory. The territorial base of the trade associations is the county rather than the city or town. There is no Lukang branch of the druggists' association; the local druggists are simply members of the Changhua County Druggists' Association. In Lukang such trade associations are almost universally regarded as something imposed from the outside for the benefit of the government rather than the members. The associations each hold an annual meeting in Changhua City and many members do not bother to attend. The usual response to questions about the functions of trade associations is a laugh and the comment that they don't do anything. Trade associations in Lukang do not regulate prices, control entry to the trade, or settle disputes between members. In some trades, such as motorcycle repair, the trade association sets the two days a month on which all the constituent businesses close. Within Lukang only the barbers and the butchers are said to have effective organizations. Both are regarded as trades with an unusually high degree of solidarity, and butchers are said to have a secret code for discussing prices in front of outsiders. The Lukang butchers have an annual banquet to which they invite people from the town office, the public health bureau, the manager of the municipal food market and the local police chief. The butchers' work brings them into close contact with the town office, which collects the slaughter tax on behalf of the Provincial government, manages the slaughterhouse and the food market, reports the price of pork, the staple meat, to the Provincial government, and is responsible for enforcing health and sanitary regulations. In nineteenth-century Taiwan both barbers and butchers were regarded as members of despised occupations, although I heard no overt expression of such an attitude in Lukang. Lukang has no chamber of commerce, and no formal association unites all of the city's businesses. To the extent that the trade associations imposed by the central government have any effectiveness, they serve to divide the city's inhabitants from one another.

In Lukang one does not find that plethora of overlapping formal associations that characterizes overseas Chinese urban communities. There are no same-place associations, no guilds, no school associations, no benevolent associations, and no chamber of commerce. Many things that in the past or among overseas Chinese were handled by formal associations are in Taiwan today the responsibility of the government. The central government supervises and coordinates many associations such as the Irrigation Associations, which were founded as privately controlled bodies in the mid or late Ch'ing dynasty and first subjected to close government control by the Japanese colonial administration. The central government, considering itself in a state of war and concerned with national unity, discourages the free formation of associations and gives city and county administrations the right to supervise and register all associations. As a result, the sorts of large associations with important economic and political functions that existed in the cities of late imperial China (including Lukang) and among overseas Chinese are not to be found in contemporary Taiwanese communities.

If Lukang is compared with the other small cities of central Taiwan in the late 1960s, it does not stand out in any obvious way. In terms of all available statistical indices the differences between it and other towns are either marginal or can easily be explained as consequences of its role as a center of diversified light industry. Its vital rates and population structure are in no way unusual, and its literacy rates and the educational level of its population are much the same as those of the nearby towns of Yuanlin and Peitou. It differs from other Taiwanese cities and market towns primarily in matters of proportion, distribution, and degree. These can be set out in tables and charts, but it is impossible to say at what point quantitative differences become qualitative differences.

Its population does differ from that of most other towns of the area in one significant way, but that difference is not apparent from the common compilations of local statistics. Practically all of Lukang's population was born in the city. A very great many of the people who live and work in modern Taiwanese cities are recent immigrants from the countryside, or from the Chinese mainland, and many maintain ties with their rural native places. The only outsiders in Lukang are policemen and schoolteachers, along with a few wives from elsewhere. Not only were most of Lukang's people born there, but so were their fathers and often their grandfathers as well. Many natives leave Lukang to seek opportunity in such major cities as Taipei, Kaohsiung, and Taichung, but no one moves into Lukang. When farmers from the villages around Lukang, such as the nearby village of Hsin Hsing where the anthropologist Bernard Gallin has done fieldwork since the late 1950s, leave home to seek work they go directly to Taipei.[1] Lukang is a city with an unusually homogenous population and a high emigration rate.

The unusual homogeneity of Lukang's population and the high emigration rate, which are in a fairly obvious way but two aspects of the same condition, have been characteristic of the city since the 1880s. They can be understood only when we look at the city's economy and population in a wider perspective, which takes in the entire island of Taiwan and the past two hundred and fifty years of its history. Before turning to the nature of social organization in Lukang and the ways its people describe their own society, it is necessary to put the city in its proper place and to see it in space and time.

Notes

1. Bernard Gallin, *Hsin Hsing, Taiwan: A Chinese Village in Change* (Berkeley: University of California Press, 1966); and Bernard Gallin and Rita S. Gallin, "The Integration of Village Migrants in Taipei," in Mark Elvin and G. W. Skinner, eds., *The Chinese City Between Two Worlds.* (Stanford: Stanford University Press, 1974).

Chapter 4

Lukang in Space and Time

Although Lukang is now a quiet and out-of-the-way small city, it was once, from the mid-eighteenth to the mid-nineteenth centuries, Taiwan's second largest city, and the main seaport through which all the trade between central Taiwan and the Chinese mainland was channeled. Both its rise and its precipitous decline in the first decade of the twentieth century were consequences of its location and its function as the node of a large-scale trading system linking central Taiwan with southern Fukien. In the last analysis Lukang's prosperity and indeed its very existence depended on a causally prior trading system that exchanged the rice, sugar, and fiber (hemp, ramie) of mid-Taiwan for the cloth, crockery, and other manufactured goods of southern Fukien.

From the earliest substantial Chinese settlement of the island under the Dutch East India Company (1624–1661) to the late nineteenth century, Taiwan can be considered an agricultural colony of Fukien. Fukien was importing rice by the end of the eleventh century, and by the seventeenth century it was a province with a chronic rice deficit.[1] Its people increasingly turned to the production of such high value commercial crops as sugar, oranges, and tea, to the manufacture of textiles and ships, and to fishing, foreign trade, and sojourning outside the province. The attraction of Taiwan, so close offshore, is obvious, and the surprising thing is that the island was not colonized earlier than it was. From its beginning under the Dutch, Chinese agriculture on the island was commercial and export oriented. Land on Taiwan was commonly opened up by development companies that brought in tenant farmers, and the capital for land development and the construction of irrigation systems came from the merchants of southern Fukien.

European travelers of the early nineteenth century noted the importance of the Taiwan trade for southern Fukien. Hugh Lindsay, an agent of the British East India Company who voyaged up the coast of China in 1832 to ascertain the prospects for trade, remarked of Amoy (Hsia-men, Xiamen) that: "The district in which this flourishing town is situated is one of the most barren in all China, and consequently yields nothing for export. It is dependent, even for the necessities of life, on the neighboring island of Formosa, which is most aptly described as the granary of the eastern coast of China."[2] The Rev. Charles Gutzlaff, a Prussian missionary who had learned some Fukien dialect in Thailand, accompanied Lindsay and says of Amoy that: "In proportion as the adjacent island, Formosa, has been colonized and yielded export produce, sugar, rice and camphor, Amoy has increased in wealth and importance. . . . Without Formosa the population hereabout would be starved, for the greater part of the supplies of rice come from that island."[3]

Although the trade between Taiwan and southern Fukien was essential for both areas, it operated in the face of many difficulties and obstacles. Although the Taiwan Straits are only about 200 kilometers (some 123 miles) wide and could be crossed by junks in a day or a day and a half, navigation was difficult and hazardous. The Straits are shallow, subject to gales in winter and typhoons in summer, and strong currents run through them. Until the nineteenth century they were haunted by pirates and the shoal coasts were lined with wreckers. There are no natural harbors along Taiwan's west coast between Tamsui in the extreme north and Kaohsiung in the south. The coast is low, flat, and bounded by tidal flats, sand bars, and ephemeral islands that extend several kilometers out into the Straits. The coastline moves out each year as heavy rain erodes Taiwan's steep young mountains, and at the mouth of the Cho Shui, the island's biggest river, in central Taiwan the coast moves out twenty meters a year. The mouths of most rivers are choked by sand bars, and the configuration of offshore mud flats and islands changes each year, as did the location of river mouths before the rivers were confined to their beds by massive dikes. Shipwrecks have been frequent, and Davidson's *The Island of Formosa* (1903) provides a long list of foreign vessels that met their end along this shore.[4]

A Western traveler in nineteenth-century China watching cargo being transshipped and hauled up the rapids of mountain streams remarked that Chinese commonly shipped goods on waters that no European would consider navigable, and one might

The seagoing bamboo raft, a vessel unique to Taiwan, moved cargo through the shoal waters of the west coast of that island for nearly three centuries.

add shipping along Taiwan's west coast as another example. Cargo was carried across the Straits on small ships of very shallow draft, whose fitness for their task was aided by the flat bottoms and retractable rudders common to all Chinese junks. The British merchant and consular official W. A. Pickering, who spent much of the 1860s sailing along the west coast of Taiwan in small craft, mentions tracking and poling small ships along a channel between the sandbanks, and the procedure appears to have been a routine response to adverse winds.[5] Davidson reports that during the French blockade of Taiwan in 1885 junks crossed the Straits at night and then sailed along the channels between the offshore sandbanks and islands where the French gunboats could not follow. In both the anchorages and the channels approaching them, junks frequently grounded at low tide, and extensive use was made of bamboo rafts for transporting both people and cargo along the coast. The seagoing bamboo raft is a vessel unique to Taiwan, and as late as the 1980s they were being outfitted with outboard motors and used for fishing.

Inland, transport was even more difficult. As in the rest of south China, roads and wheeled transport were poorly developed and the most common means of transport was the human carrier, supplemented in some area by ox carts. Taiwan differed from south China in that its rivers were nearly all unnavigable. The rivers that meander across the southwestern coastal plain are shallow and swift, with braided channels, wide stony beds, and a volume of water that fluctuates wildly with rainfall. Before they were confined by massive dikes they frequently flooded whole sections of the plain, making new channels and flowing into the sea miles from their former mouths. Furthermore, the many rivers that cross the relatively narrow coastal plain made movement of goods to the north or south very difficult. Banditry and subethnic strife made the roads dangerous as well as difficult to travel.

Under these circumstances, the best thing to do with goods was to get them to the coast as directly as possible. Then they could be moved by bamboo raft or small craft to some spot where it was possible for a junk to approach at high tide. The west coast was lined with port and market towns, located wherever a tidal lagoon or the mouth of a small river afforded relatively safe anchorage for some part of the year. With the exception of Chiayi, all the major cities of Taiwan before 1900 were along the coast. Each port had its own marketing territory stretching back to the hills and overlapping only to a limited degree with the territory of other ports. Rather than the overlapping and nested hexagons that G. W. Skinner employs as a model of the marketing and city trading systems of much of the premodern Chinese mainland, one might describe the west coast of Taiwan before 1900 with a segmentary, rather wormlike model. To some extent it resembles the pattern Skinner describes for the upper reaches of rivers, as in western Szechwan, where the cities were not located at the geographic center of their trading system but offset or even located at the edge.[6] In economic and social terms, though not in administrative ones, the Taiwan of that period might be thought of not as a single island but as an archipelago, an aggregation of similar regions, each of which had more contact with Amoy and Ch'uanchou across the Straits than with the other Taiwanese segments. The earliest settlers and officials commented not on how small the island was but on how vast it was, and they consistently overestimated its size. Settlers in one region looked back to the mainland and their native places rather than to other parts of Taiwan, and the general use of the term "island" for the place and "islander" or "Taiwanese" for the inhabitants dates only from the Japanese period (1895–1945).[7] One can question whether Taiwan had a central place in any but the administrative sense before the Japanese built a road network and the railroad. (The railroad running from Keelung to Kaohsiung was completed in 1908.)

Such was the context in which Lukang grew and prospered. As seaports go, it was never very good, and was used for two centuries only because there was no better way to move goods out of and into the Changhua Plain. It was built on the northern bank of one of the many small streams that cross the plain and the mouth of which afforded an anchorage. (The largest rivers carried so much sediment that their mouths were marked by extensive bars and shoals, which made them very dangerous to shipping and hence not suitable for ports.) The Changhua Plain, bounded by the Tatu River on the north and the Choshui River on the south, has some of the best soil on the island, a more reliable water supply than the plain further south and a longer growing season than northern Taiwan. In the mid-twentieth century it produced two rice crops a year, with an additional winter crop of wheat, flax, or vegetables. Since its settlement in the early eighteenth century it has been one of Taiwan's major rice producing areas.

Lukang lies in that narrow littoral strip that receives less rain than anywhere else on the island. The soil around the city is for the most part fertile enough, but low rainfall and high winds make agriculture and especially rice cultivation a difficult task. Rice cultivation along the entire coastal plain must rely on irrigation for dependable annual yields, but the problems are most acute along the dry and windblown coast. Rice can be grown with the least effort further inland, along the edge of the hills, where rainfall is higher and the wind, which damages standing crops and increases evaporation, is less strong. Even today the area along the coast, and especially to the south of Lukang, remains one of relatively sparse population and low living standards, where sweet potatoes are the staple and people eat rice only on special occasions. Lukang's immediate hinterland is thus a poor, thinly settled (by Taiwanese standards), and relatively unproductive region.

At the beginning of the eighteenth century Lukang was a minor river mouth port on the northern fringes of Chinese settlement. The Chinese colonization and population of Taiwan began in the south, around the present city of Tainan, and gradually moved north. The growth of Lukang's trade and population until it was the island's second city took place from 1730 to 1780. The fundamental reason was the settlement of the Changhua Plain and the production of an exportable surplus of rice and sugar. This began in the early 1700s and was greatly aided by the construction of the massive Pa-Pao irrigation system, which was completed in 1719. This took water from the Ch'o Shui River at the point where it emerged from the hills and used it to irrigate eight of the thirteen Pao (subcounty administrative units) of Changhua *hsien* and was built as a private venture by a Ch'uan-chou merchant.[8]

In the first years of the eighteenth century the channel through the offshore sandbanks leading to Lukang was narrow and shallow. But by 1740 all the other ports of central Taiwan were so badly blocked by silt as to be useless, while Lukang's harbor and channel became broad and deep. Consequently it became the major port for all of central Taiwan and maintained that position for 150 years, in spite of subsequent silting and blockage.[9]

The entrance to the channel that led to Lukang was fifteen or twenty kilometers south of the city, near the settlements of Fan Wa or Wang Kung. The course of the channel changed from year to year, as did its depth. From the early nineteenth century on, Lukang struggled with the silt that blocked the channel and the harbor. The Changhua County Gazetteer, compiled in 1831, says that Lukang harbor is blocked with sand but that the obstruction is not constant. "Sometimes it is deep, sometimes it is shallow. When it is deep, large ships enter; when it is shallow only small ships dare enter."[10] The channel could only be entered if ships had a favorable wind, and the port was closed from late October through March, when gales from the north sweep the Strait. During the 1860s the Ch'o Shui repeatedly flooded into the sea only seven kilometers south of Lukang. A small delta appeared in what had been called Lukang Bay, and silt choked all the channels leading to the city from the south. A new anchorage was developed in a creek mouth six kilometers north of the city, but it was shallow in the extreme and could only be reached at high tide. The China Sea Directory of 1884 describes the approach to Lukang.

> From Quang-wa (Fan Wa) to Lo-kiang (Lukang), a distance of ten miles, the coast continues low. This uninteresting seaboard becomes even more dreary at low water, when the mud and sand flats uncover for miles, outside of which again is shallow water with three, four and five fathoms. Ships should not approach this coast in less than ten fathoms, for the currents are very strong. . . . To the westward of the town of Lo-kiang and distant a little less than four miles is a small outlet marked by two bamboo beacons; in this creek a great number of junks find anchorage and shelter, but most of them ground at low water. They communicate with Lo-kiang, which is a large and straggling town, by boats and land.[11]

The trade across the Straits was also subject to official control and regulation, and Ch'ing administrative policy had a direct and significant effect on Lukang's commerce and general prosperity. In order to discourage piracy, limit overseas trade, and prevent illegal emigration, the imperial government in the eighteenth century attempted to limit the size of ships and the numbers constructed in Fukien. Each ship was to be licensed by the authorities and all crew members were to be registered. In the eighteenth century there were prohibitions on the shipment of certain articles between Taiwan and the mainland. Iron was not to be imported to Taiwan, lest the inhabitants use it to make weapons. Ships leaving Taiwan were forbidden to carry more than sixty *shih* of rice, so that the island's inhabitants could be assured of a sufficient supply. It is doubtful that the regulations were actually obeyed, but their existence and the threat of enforcement gave officials an excuse to extort bribes from merchants and ship owners as well as an incentive to keep track of ships.[12]

The officials attempted to control sea traffic not only by licensing ships and their crews but by permitting trade only at certain ports and voyages only between certain points. Ocean trade was to be reduced to fixed routes, like canal traffic. Thus in the early eighteenth century there was only one legal route between Taiwan and the mainland, that from Tainan (Anping) to Amoy. Military and civil officials at both ends inspected ships, passengers, and cargo, and placed their seals on the appropriate certificates and manifests.[13] So, to ship rice from Lukang to Ch'uan-chou City, for example, it was necessary to load the rice on a coasting vessel at Lukang and sail down to Tainan. There the rice would be inspected, certified, and perhaps be transshipped to a larger vessel. It would sail to Amoy, there go through customs, and then be shipped up the coast to Ch'uan-chou.

There was a temptation to avoid such fuss and expense and to sail directly to one's ultimate destination without going through official channels. Such voyages were "illegal crossings." As the Chinese frontier moved northward in Taiwan during the eighteenth century, illegal crossings became more and more frequent, and a series of apparently ineffective edicts commanded officials in Taiwan and Fukien to enforce the rules, and denounced the corruption that permitted the flourishing illegal trade.[14] One of the early eighteenth century editions of the *Taiwan Fu Chih* says:

> Various small craft set out from such northern ports as Penkang and Lukang and, taking advantage of the south wind, cross over to Amoy and Ch'uan-chou. Going from west to east they cross directly to the north of the Pescadores. This is called the passage to the west. It is most strictly

forbidden, but they flock to danger like ducks to the water.[15]

A thriving and technically illegal sea traffic between southern Fukien and the recently settled areas of central Taiwan grew up in the course of the eighteenth century. The restriction of sea traffic to the Tainan-Amoy route, a reasonable arrangement in the 1680s and 1690s when Chinese settlement was restricted to the area around Tainan, became increasingly irrational as the rest of the island was settled. The requirement that everything be shipped over this route not only inconvenienced merchants and caused higher prices for legal grain and goods in Fukien and Taiwan; it interfered with the army's grain supply. The policy could only be changed by the central administration in Peking, and it is likely that the officials on both sides of the Straits who were profiting from the squeeze on the direct trade opposed any change in the regulations.

As early as 1758 the governor of Fukien requested permission from Peking to open a legal route between Foochow and Tamsui. He cited the transport of the rice ration for the Fukien garrison, but his request was turned down.[16] In 1784 the commander in chief of the forces in Fukien suggested that Lukang be made a legal port for sea trade, linked with the port of Han-chiang on Ch'uan-chou Bay. He wanted to put the stamp of legality on existing practices, eliminate corruption, provide a new source of revenue, and reduce the cost of shipping rice. He argued:

> Fukien's Ch'uan-chou and Chang-chou are short of rice and depend on rice from Taiwan. Merchant ships go from Amoy to Tainan and back, being inspected by the subprefects in charge of ocean traffic. But, many make illegal crossings from other ports. Last year the Fukien commander in chief exerted himself to apprehend the criminals who make illegal crossings. Most of them came from Han-chiang in Ch'uan-chou, there being over twenty ships from there captured. The legal route is the southern one from Amoy to Tainan, but a northern route from Lukang directly over to Han-chiang also exists, and is much more convenient. So, many merchants are making great profits on illegal voyages over the northern route. I suggest that, taking the southern route from Amoy to Tainan as a model, a legal route be established between Lukang and Han-chiang and officials be posted to supervise it. This would benefit the common people; men would not be led into crime; and crafty people would no longer benefit from corrupt practices.[17]

His suggestion was accepted by the court and Lukang and Han-chiang were made legal ports for direct trade, as were Tamsui and Foochow in the north. A new yamen was built in Lukang to house the subprefect (*t'ung-chih*) who was posted to the city to oversee the trade. After this, Lukang which had been prospering on the illegal trade boomed on legal commerce. The sixty year period from 1790 to 1850 was its golden age and the peak of its prosperity. During that period it was the second city of the island and the economic center for all of mid-Taiwan.

In 1729 the *hsien* government established a granary in Lukang to store the tax grain that was remitted to Fukien. From that time until the late nineteenth century rice was Lukang's main export. The primary import was cloth, of cotton or ramie or a mixture of cotton and ramie. The cotton was probably grown in central China, but the ramie came from Taiwan itself, grown in the foothills of the central mountains. In a characteristically colonial pattern the raw material left Taiwan, was processed in Fukien, and the finished product was then reimported. The cloth was dyed (blue of course) at Lukang, dye-making and dying providing a rare example of an eighteenth- and nineteenth-century Taiwanese industry. Indigo grows well in central Taiwan, and individual farmers raised it as a cash crop to supplement their sales of rice. According to Davidson, the process used for extracting the dye from the plant was unsophisticated and the dye suffered in transit. It was possible to get more brilliant colors with less indigo if freshly made dye was used. He also notes that: "For some years it was customary to send manufactured grass cloth and other cloths to Formosa to be dyed and then returned to China."[18]

The *Changhua Hsien Chih*, compiled in 1831, says of Lukang:

At Lukang streets and lanes meet and cross like hairbands. The main street extends for three *li* (one *li* is about a third of a mile), and there are many businesses of the Ch'uan-chou and Amoy Guilds. It is a place where ships and carts come together, like spokes converging at the hub of a wheel, and all sorts of goods can be had in abundance. Except for Tainan, it is the most important market center of the island.[19]

The *Hsien Chih* says of Lukang's trade that:

Changhua and Ch'uan-chou are opposite each other. Lukang is a most important place for the commerce of the Ch'uan-chou and Amoy Guilds. The ships from Ch'uan-chou and Amoy come to carry rice, sugar, oil, and miscellaneous other goods to Han-chiang and Amoy. Lately small ships from Shen-hu and T'a-k'u (small ports on Ch'uan-chou Bay) have been coming to Lukang to buy rice, wheat, cattle bones, and such things. They carry them to Kwangtung, Macao, Che-lin, and other ports. They buy the mixed goods (eg. hardware, crockery) of Kwangtung along with salted and dried fish and bring them back to Lukang. They are called the South Ships.[20]

A later section of the *Hsien Chih* adds that ships came from the Pescadores with salt fish and seafood, and returned thence with rice, oil, and melons. Some ships carried sugar to Shanghai and Tientsin, but there were not as many of these "Sugar Ships" as there were sailing from Tainan. Sugar cultivation seems to have been concentrated in the relatively more arid southern end of Taiwan, while the well-watered Changhua Plain concentrated on rice. The section of the *Hsien Chih* on sea routes notes that Lukang had no North Guild and that few ships from Lukang went to central or northern China. In 1825 there was famine in north China and Lukang's subprefect asked the merchants of Lukang's Ch'uan-chou and Amoy Guilds to ship rice to Tientsin. They were rewarded by being allowed to carry cargo without paying any taxes on it. Such distant journeys remained rare, and the bulk of Lukang's trade remained the direct transport of rice and cloth to and from Ch'uan-chou, one day's sail across the Straits.

The ships that came to Lukang were fairly small junks carrying about one hundred tons of cargo. Fukien was famous for its great seagoing junks, which sailed to Thailand, Java, and the Philippines, but such craft were not suited to the shoal coasts of Taiwan and could not enter the shallow harbors of the island. (The distinctively Taiwanese craft is the seagoing bamboo raft, made from giant bamboos that grow in the central mountains and drawing only centimeters.) Ch'uan-chou Bay, where most of the junks trading with Lukang came from, is nowhere deeper than five fathoms and is dotted with shoals and tidal flats, a dangerous place for deep-draft vessels.[21] Amoy is a deepwater port, and the largest junks, called Sugar Ships or White Headed Ships, came from there, as did the smaller ones called Sea Crossing Ships. The junks from Han-chiang and the other ports of Ch'uan-chou Bay were smaller yet.

Most of the ships that came to Lukang were built in Fukien, where timber was cheaper and skilled labor more easily available.[22] They were usually owned by wealthy mainlanders.[23] One is left with the impression that few junks were based in Taiwanese ports or owned by Taiwanese merchants, an impression reinforced by the few Western references to the trade, which usually speak of "junks trading to (rather than from) Formosa," or of "small junks belonging to Amoy."[24] On the other hand, some Lukang families or business houses are referred to in historical documents and inscriptions as *ch'uan hu*, "ship households."[25] Today old men in Lukang assert that there used to be a ship guild, composed of ship owners. A Japanese-language account of the "Customs of Lukang" dated 1896 describes the "Ship Guild" as the largest of seven guilds, composed of businesses that shipped rice to Ch'uan-chou and imported various commodites from there. The brief account of the guild does not make it clear if the component enterprises actually owned ships or not, but describes the range of commodities they dealt in.[26] It does not contradict the impression that few if any ships were owned by Lukang houses.

According to G. W. Skinner's analysis of China's economic central places in 1843, Tainan ranked as a regional city (third from the top in an eight-step hierarchy), while Lukang and Meng-chia, the core of the present Taipei, both ranked as greater cities (fourth from the top of the eight-step hierarchy).[27] The closest port to the north was the minor anchorage of Wu-ch'e (the site of Taichung Port, developed in the 1970s) 25 kilometers away, while to the south it was 75 kilometers to the small port of Tung Shih Kang. Lukang's trading system covered most of central Taiwan south of the hills that rise just north of the Ta Chia River and north of the southernmost branch of the Ch'o Shui, known as the Huwei (Tiger Tail) River. It took in the present Changhua County, most of Taichung County, most of Nantou County, and the northern third of the present Yunlin County. The only detailed account of the trade within Lukang's marketing region is that contained in the Japanese *Report on Economic Affairs* of the Temporary Commission on the Investigation of Taiwanese Customary Practices, published by the Government-General of Taiwan in 1905. It describes the pattern of coastal and inland trade centered on Lukang at the beginning of the twentieth century, before the railroad was completed or the road network substantially improved. The most common method of overland transport was by human carrier. Oxcarts were used between Lukang and the settlements directly to the south, in the dry coastal belt. During the summer months it was possible to use bamboo rafts on the northernmost channel of the Ch'o-Shui, which ran from the market town of Peitou, and on the southernmost branch, the Huwei, the rafts then proceeding up the coast to Lukang. Small ships, able to carry 50 *shih* (6.3 tons), and bamboo rafts plied along the coast.[28]

During the nineteenth century, Lukang was a city of wholesalers and middlemen, with many large firms devoted to the trade in rice, cloth, sugar, timber, and pottery. Oxcarts and gangs of porters moved through its narrow streets, carrying the two annual rice harvests from further inland. Hundreds of workers loaded and unloaded the bamboo rafts and small boats that carried cargo to the larger junks aground several kilometers further along the channel. Thousands of men carried bales of unhusked rice across the Changhua Plain on shoulder poles, while some trekked down from the Puli basin carrying ramie fiber or camphor. How this army of porters and longshoremen earned their living during the winter when Lukang port shut down is anyone's guess. Lukang's merchants lived in solid, multistory houses, the very bricks and tiles of which had been imported from Fukien. The shoes they wore, the dishes they ate from, the paper they wrote their accounts on, and even the ancestor tablets they worshipped were all made by craftsmen in Fukien and shipped across the Straits. The immediate environs of Lukang contained much dry, uncultivated land and some small and relatively poor villages, their houses constructed of mud and thatch and their inhabitants occasionally walking into Lukang for shopping or entertainment. Lukang had official yamens, granaries, warehouses, temples, and academies, and was the site of magnificent annual festivals and conspicuous displays of wealth. But it produced practically nothing for itself, and depended on the trade that exchanged the rice and agricultural produce of central Taiwan for the cloth and manufactured articles of southern Fukien.

From the mid-eighteenth to the mid-nineteenth centuries Lukang was Taiwan's second city. It is to this period that the proverbial expression, still heard today, "*Yi Fu, Er Lu, San Meng-chia*" (first, Tainan-fu; second, Lukang; third, Meng-chia [Taipei]) refers. There are no reliable figures on the size of the city's population before the first Japanese count in 1896. There has been considerable outmigration from Lukang since the 1880s, and many of its people now believe that the past population was much larger. A figure of 100,000 is commonly quoted, and appears in many contemporary sources as well as some from the early Japanese period. I consider this an overestimate and doubt that the population was ever much over 20,000 people. Throughout most of the nineteenth century it was probably closer to 10,000 than to 20,000.

The Japanese *Report on Economic Conditions* gives figures on Lukang's population from 1896 through 1902, although it is not certain that the figures refer only to the built-up area. In 1896 the city had a population of 20,420. In 1897 it dropped to 17,334, but from then on it slowly increased until there were 19,165 people in Lukang in 1902.[29] If one accepts the figure of 100,000 people for the mid–1800s, then one must conclude that four-fifths of the city's inhabitants had left by 1896. Where they could have gone is a mystery, for in 1900 Taipei had only 70,000 people and Tainan, the second largest city, had 47,000. Furthermore, when they were in Lukang all those people would have occupied some space, and I could find no evidence that the city has ever occupied more ground than it does now with 28,000 people. All the major temples and the sites of such things as the guildhalls, the yamens, and the fort that housed the imperial garrison are well within the present built-up area. The city now is divided into named neighborhoods, which are named in local rhymes of the "Oranges and Lemons" sort, and listed in proverbs, genealogies, and the temple records. I found no vanished neighborhoods, nor did old men ever point to fields and claim that they used to be part of the city.

Nor does a population of 100,000 for Taiwan's second city fit with current estimates of urban population in nineteenth-century China. After exhaustive analysis and careful argument, Skinner concludes that in 1843 some 5.1 percent of the population of agrarian China, excluding Taiwan and Manchuria, was urban, while in 1893 some 6 percent were urban. When he breaks the figures down by region, he gets a figure for the Southeast Coast, the region that Taiwan belonged to, of 5.8 percent in 1843 and 6.4 percent in 1893.[30] Throughout the nineteenth century Taiwan's economy was overwhelmingly agrarian and there were no large-scale handicraft occupations like weaving. In 1898 the Japanese estimated the total population of Taiwan as 2.6 million. In the last quarter of the nineteenth century the population, especially in the north around Taipei, increased considerably. In 1850 there were probably no more than 2 million people. If one were to accept a figure of 100,000 for Lukang's population in 1850, then this would mean that 5 percent of Taiwan's total population lived in Lukang. Since it is generally accepted that Tainan's population was always larger than that of Lukang, this would mean that the two largest cities would have had 10 to 15 percent of the total population between them. A further 5 to 10 percent would have inhabited the other cities and market towns. It seems most unlikely that 20 to 25 percent of nineteenth-century Taiwan's population was urban, for that would have made Taiwan, an agrarian frontier province, one of the most highly urbanized parts of all China. In 1903 the Japanese authorities counted a total of 3,030,076 people on Taiwan, including 50,000 Japanese and 100,000 aborigines. In that year, 10.7 percent of the population (326,854) lived in the twenty-two cities with more than 5,000 people, and 16 percent (487,312) in all settlements with more than 1,000 people. Lukang, with 19,457, was Taiwan's fourth largest city, holding 0.6 percent of Taiwan's population.[31] All in all, an estimated population of perhaps 10,000 or between 10,000 and 20,000 seems right for the nineteenth century. This would also bring Lukang into line with Skinner's estimates of the mean populations of greater cities in regional peripheries in 1893, which is 17,200.[32]

By the second half of the nineteenth century Lukang's total share of Taiwan's trade and its relative importance in the island's economy had begun to decline. This was not so much the result of an absolute decline in the volume of trade at the city, although that may have been the case, as of the economic growth of the northern part of the island and of changes in Fukien's rice trade. The last quarter of the century saw the development of the tea industry in northern Taiwan. Foreign firms, primarily British, set up establishments in Taipei, and the Japanese began exporting such manufactured goods as textiles and matches to Taiwan. Taipei grew rapidly, and labor in the northern third of the island was so scarce that tea-pickers had to be brought in from Fukien each year.

Lukang's primary export had always been rice, but the rice trade appears to have fallen off by the end of the nineteenth century. Taiwan's population grew and more rice was consumed by the city dwellers, tea-pickers, and coal miners of the north. Fukien did not suffer, for it was able to import rice from Southeast Asia at a lower price. Coloquhoun and Stewart-Lockhart, writing in 1885, note that: "The export of rice from the island has dwindled down until it has almost ceased. . . . Rice can be brought cheaper from Indochina." They also report that: "The native junk trade has in some measure decreased, due to the introduction of the foreign steamer. The greater portion of the junk trade is with Chinchew (Ch'uan-chou), a port situated a short distance north of Amoy."[33] H. B. Morse, Commissioner of Customs at Tamsui, reported in 1892 that rice had actually been imported to Taiwan from 1882 to 1891. "Rice was in former years exported from Formosa in large quantities, mainly of course by junk. Even now the movement inward or outward of this bulky commodity is effected to a large degree in native craft."[34]

Since no steamship of even moderate size could get anywhere near Lukang or safely enter the shallow Ch'uan-chou Bay, the junks sailing in and out of Lukang were not directly threatened. But Lukang's trade with the mainland was threatened indirectly when large steamships were able to bring rice from Southeast Asia more cheaply than it could be shipped over from Taiwan in small junks. And any improvement of land transport, even in Fukien, directly threatened Lukang. The city functioned as a port, in spite of silt, tidal flats, the necessity of employing gangs of porters and longshoremen to load everything into small ships by hand, and the danger of storms and shoals in the Straits, only because there was no better way to move things into and out of the Changhua Plain.

The only available figures on Lukang's trade and population are those published by the Japanese colonial government, and it is not clear whether the city the Japanese found in 1895 had declined or changed in any major way since the middle of the nineteenth century. The only figure I have found is a statement quoted by Wang Shih-ch'ing, probably from an early Japanese source, that in the early years of the Hsien Feng period (1851–1862), just before the long decline began, over 3,500 ships came to Lukang each year.[35] In 1896 the Japanese customs authorities counted 1,051 ships coming to Lukang, although that number declined to 515 in 1897 and to 229 in 1900.[36] This looks like quite a drop in the last half of the century. But the Japanese totals probably do not include the coastal trade; the Japanese occupation of Taiwan in 1895 doubtless inhibited trade; and Japanese customs levies and the less corruptible Japanese civil service encouraged smuggling. According to residents of Lukang, the city used to be a major center for opium smuggling, and it is likely that many ships landed goods, especially opium, near Lukang without being counted.

By the end of the nineteenth century the trading system linking central Taiwan and Ch'uan-chou and Amoy was already declining as the rice trade dwindled and Japanese imports began to replace Fukienese cloth. Under the Japanese the commerce between Taiwan and Fukien dwindled yet further and the trade of Lukang, by then only a minor junk port, was practically extinguished. The Japanese built roads and the railroad, and so made it possible to move goods into and out of the Changhua Plain more cheaply than they could be shipped through Lukang's silt-choked harbor. The colonial government developed Keelung and Kaohsiung (then called Takao) as modern, deepwater ports, served by direct rail lines and equipped to load large steamships, while Lukang remained a haven for small junks. The Japanese pursued a policy of integrating Taiwan's economy with that of Japan, so that most of the island's trade was with Japan. Direct trade between Taiwan and southeastern China was discouraged by tariff barriers, preferential treatment for Japanese companies, and monopolies of essential consumer goods by the colonial government. Taiwanese farmers sent their rice and sugar to Osaka and Tokyo by Japanese steamships that sailed from Keelung and Kaohsiung, and bought cloth and hardware that came from the factories of Japan rather than the workshops of Fukien. The entire pattern of trade shifted, and Lukang was bypassed and left high and dry in a metaphorical as well as a literal sense.

The number of ships coming to Lukang fell off from 1,051 in 1896 to 229 in 1900, and dropped to 61 in 1910. In 1897, 5.4 percent of Taiwan's trade by value went through Lukang. In 1900, 2.5 percent went through Lukang, and in 1910 only 0.3 percent. In 1900, 2,413 junks came to Taiwan, 229 of them to Lukang. In 1910, 1,100 junks came, 61 of them to Lukang. In that year half the junk trade went though Tamsui, Anping, and Keelung, which took more than half the tonnage, indicating that the larger junks traded there. In the fourteen years from 1896 to 1910 Lukang's trade with Fukien dropped precipitously, thereafter remaining at the same low level until it dropped off once again in the 1930s and ceased entirely with the outbreak of war between China and Japan in 1937.[37]

In the first decade of the twentieth century the large-scale trading system that had linked central Taiwan with Ch'uan-chou and Amoy since the 1730s collapsed, the victim of improved transport technology. With it went the foundation of Lukang's prosperity. The railroad reached Changhua from the south in 1905, connecting the Changhua Plain with the southern port of Kaohsiung. In 1908 the last segment of the railroad, that tunneling through the hills north of the Ta Chia River, was completed, making it possible to go from Keelung to Kaohsiung by rail. By 1911, narrow gauge and pushcart railroads linked Lukang with Yuanlin and Changhua City, both on the main rail line. The Japanese authorities who had constructed the railroad in part with corvee labor also used corvee labor to improve roads. The surplus rice and sugar of the Changhua Plain then moved north to Taipei and Keelung along the railroad instead of west to Fukien through Lukang.

Lukang quickly slipped down the central-place hierarchy, and ended up serving as a market town for the farmers of the immediate surroundings. Before the Japanese period this aspect of the city's economy had been the least profitable and important. The area immediately around the city is an arid and windswept region, and the villages were populated by poor farmers who lived mostly on sweet potatoes. The villages along the coast were even poorer, the homes of fishermen and oyster cultivators who turned to wrecking whenever they got the chance. Lukang was left with a commercial population far too large to support itself by meeting the modest needs of the villagers. Some of its wealthy merchants had, in the usual Chinese fashion, diversified their interests and bought farm land. They favored the highly productive land around the town of Yuanlin, twenty kilometers to the southeast, which produces some of Taiwan's highest rice yields. Some simply became landlords and lived on their rents. But others, recognizing that they could not beat the modern transport technology that had doomed the city's commerce, chose to join it and took the train for Taipei or the booming port of Kaohsiung. The first decade of the twentieth century saw massive emigration from Lukang.

By the end of the nineteenth century some Lukang business-men had already established themselves in the thriving commercial quarter of Taipei, a city that was rising as Lukang sank. They were soon joined by crowds of their fellow townsmen, who sought opportunities in the growing cities along the rail line and in such recently opened frontiers as the Puli basin and Taiwan's east coast. Lukang, which had been settled by sojourners from southern Fukien, now produced its own sojourners. In the Taiwan of the early Japanese period, an overwhelmingly agricultural society undergoing rapid economic development and urban growth, the Lukang emigrants with their greater commercial expertise and literacy had an initial advantage over ordinary Taiwanese from the countryside. Furthermore, they did not go to Taipei, Kaohsiung, or Puli as isolated individuals. They went with introductions to other Lukang men who had already established themselves, and they joined the Lukang associations that existed in all Taiwan's major cities. (A Lukang Guild was founded in Taipei in the late 1800s, before the Japanese conquest, and was one of the five great guilds of Taipei.)[38]

The men who left Lukang were sojourners in the sense that they left their families at home in Lukang, sent money back, and returned to Lukang at New Year and at Ch'ing Ming, the holiday in early spring when people clean up the ancestral graves and report to the ancestors. Today people say that emigrants felt compelled to return at least for Ch'ing Ming, for if they did not, people in Lukang would say that they must have failed in business and their families would lose face. From the early 1900s to the present a considerable proportion of Lukang's population has lived on remittances sent back by sojourners. But the men who left Lukang differed from Skinner's model sojourners in that they followed no single, specific calling. They took any sort of job they could find, and Lukang folklore extols their ability to take advantage of any opportunity, to change occupations or businesses without hesitation, and their purported general intelligence and fitness.

Under the Japanese, and today as well, Lukang was a city that produced emigrants in considerable numbers. To some extent it came to resemble the emigrant districts of southeastern China, which sent sojourners to Southeast Asia and the New World, save that almost all its sojourners stayed within Taiwan. Today the local stereotype of the emigrants is that they are everywhere on the island, that they have an extraordinary talent for doing business, that they all stick together and help each other out, and that they have all done well for themselves, thus demonstrating that Lukang people are somehow a bit better or smarter than other Taiwanese. The poor but clever lad who goes to Taipei and strikes it rich through superior cunning and commercial acumen is celebrated in local folklore. Over time of course many sojourners became migrants. They either married local women in the places they were working (there is a Lukang proverb about going to Taipei to find work and finding Taipei women), or they prospered and moved their families out of Lukang to Taipei or Kaohsiung. They demonstrated their identification with their native place by contributing money to Lukang temples and charitable funds but seldom returned themselves.

Not everyone left Lukang of course, and some of those who remained were able to make a comfortable if not extremely profitable living. It seems that those most likely to leave were the very poor and propertyless on one hand, who had no choice, and the wealthy and well-connected on the other, who had many choices and moved into the wider economic and social system centered on Taipei. Like other rural towns, Lukang in the Japanese period had a number of mechanized rice mills, oil presses, brickworks, a wheat flour mill, and a soy sauce works. The 1903 statistical abstract, in a less than complete summary, lists twenty-four "factories" in Lukang, employing between them 99 workers. They consisted of eight dyeworks; six flour mills and noodle makers; three peanut oil presses; two lime works (using oyster shells as the raw material); two incense makers; two processors of tobacco leaves; and one workshop, employing twenty workers, that made wooden looms. The same sorts of establishments, devoted primarily to processing local crops, were found in all the towns of the region, such as Changhua City, Peitou, and Yuanlin. A survey compiled in 1929 lists 67 "factories" at Lukang, or rather in Rokkō Gai, the administrative unit corresponding to the present Lukang *chen* and Fu-hsing *hsiang*. There were 43 rice mills, many certainly located in the countryside or in crossroads hamlets rather than in Lukang proper. There were also six flour and noodle factories; four furniture makers; three dyeworks; three peanut oil presses; two brickworks; two canneries; one incense maker; one soy sauce factory; one printer; and one goldsmith.[39] Changhua City, on the main railroad line, although its population was only slightly larger than Lukang's in the 1920s, had many more factories and many more sorts of them.

The sorts of enterprises found in Lukang and the other market towns not on the main rail line processed local agricultural produce and were limited by the variety and amount of produce available. Some enterprises that depended on local agricultural production actually declined, as did Lukang's dyeworks. The Japanese introduced more effective ways of making dye from indigo, made dye that could be stored and so did not have to be made from fresh plants, and imported textiles from Japan that came in colors other than blue. The local dyemaking and dyeing trade thus faded away, one more victim of technical progress. During the Japanese period the bulk of Lukang's income consisted of remittances sent back by sojourners, and of money extracted in one form or another from the farmers of the Changhua Plain, who paid rent and interest to Lukang landowners and moneylenders, sold them their surplus and commercial crops, and bought necessities such as cloth from their shops. Lukang families could own land quite a distance from Lukang, but their marketing and commercial functions were restricted to a small area around the city. The most profitable enterprise in Lukang before the Second World War was a combination of landholding, ricemilling, and moneylending.

Some wealthy men were able to send their sons to the university, where a few places were available for Taiwanese. If possible they studied medicine, a career that had a number of attractions. It was one of the few professions open to non-Japanese; it required extensive formal education and was therefore worthy of respect in a traditional Chinese way; and it was lucrative to boot. But ultimately all the ways the people of Lukang earned their living, from landholding to rice milling and even medicine, depended on the surplus produced by the agricultural sector of the economy, and the portion of this surplus available to them was quite limited. Under the Japanese, Taiwan's agriculture went through a "Green Revolution" in the 1920s and 1930s and production increased quite considerably. But the profits from this expansion were not available to the landlords and small-scale merchants of Lukang and other country towns, for they were concentrated in the hands of the colonial government, a few large Japanese corporations, and a few very wealthy Taiwanese. The profits were not shared out to the farmers, whose living standards and incomes appear to have risen only marginally during the Japanese period.[40] Since the farmers' incomes were low, the merchants of such towns as Lukang could expect only a limited volume of business. They were better off than the farmers and the colonial authorities supported them in their role of landlords, but their possibilities were limited.

Some of the men of Lukang attempted to respond to the collapse of the city's trade with Fukien by using political influence to bolster Lukang's economy. In the long run they were not successful, but their attempts had antecedents that went back at least to the mid-nineteenth century. A complete understanding of Lukang's history and economic history, and of the forces that shaped its social structure demands that some attention be paid to the city's relations with central and regional administrative structures, that is to administration and politics. The topic deserves a chapter of its own.

Notes

1. See Mark Elvin, *The Pattern of the Chinese Past* (Stanford: Stanford University Press, 1973), pp. 207ff; Evelyn Sakakida Rawski, *Agricultural Change and the Peasant Economy of South China* (Cambridge: Harvard University Press, 1972).

2. Hugh Lindsay, *A Voyage to the Northern Ports of China in the Ship Lord Amherst* (London: B. Fellowes, 1834), p. 13.

3. Ibid, p. 272.

4. James W. Davidson, *The Island of Formosa* (New York: Macmillan, 1903) (Reprint, Taipei: Ch'eng-wen, nd.).

5. W. A. Pickering, *Pioneering in Formosa* (London: Hurst & Blackett, 1898).

6. Skinner, 1977, p. 293.

7. See Harry J. Lamley, *The Taiwan Literati and Early Japanese Rule*. Unpublished Ph.D. dissertation in History, University of Washington, 1964, pp. 28–29.

8. See Wang Sung-hsing, "Pa Pao Chun Yu Taiwan Chung-pu te Kai-fa" [The Pa Pao Canal and the Development of Central Taiwan], in *Taiwan Wen Hsien* 26, 4 and 27, 1 (1975), pp. 42–49.

9. Wang Shih-ch'ing (Chang Ping-nan, psued.), "Lukang Kai Kang Shih [History of the Opening of Lukang as a (Legal) Port], *Taiwan Wen Hsien* 19, 1 (1968).

10. *Changhua Hsien Chih* (compiled 1831). Taipei: Bank of Taiwan, 1964.

11. Lords Commissioners of the Admiralty, *China Sea Directory* (London: Admiralty, 1884), vol. 3, pp. 287–288.

12. See Chou Hsien-wen, *Ch'ing Tai Taiwan Ching-chi Shih* [An Economic History of Taiwan in the Ch'ing Period] (Taipei: Bank of Taiwan, 1956), p. 58.

13. See Chou (1956); and Laurence G. Thompson, "The Junk Passage Across the Taiwan Straits: Two Early Chinese Accounts," *Harvard Journal of Asiatic Studies* 28 (1968).

14. Chou, 1956.

15. Quoted in Wang Shih-ch'ing, 1968.

16. Chou, 1956, p. 60.

17. *Changhua Hsien Chih*, vol. 3, p. 415.

18. Davidson, 1903, p. 515.

19. *Chuanghua Hsien Chih*, vol.1, pp. 40–41.

20. *Changhua Hsien Chih*, vol. 1, pp. 21–25; vol. 3, p. 290.

21. On navigation on Ch'uan-chou Bay, see the 1884 edition of the *China Sea Directory*, vol. 3, p. 215. "Chin-Chu (i.e., Ch'uan-chou) bay has shoals eleven feet, and when the swell rolls in it is dangerous to vessels of over ten feet draft. The channels to Chin-chu are shoal and intricate, and the large junks have to wait in the neighborhood of Aisai for the tide before they can cross the flats, which are covered with artificial oyster beds."

22. On the organization of southern Fukien's maritime trade, see Ng Chin-keong, *Trade and Society: The Amoy Network on the*

China Coast, 1683–1735 (Singapore, Singapore University Press, 1983).

23. Wang Shih-ch'ing (1968). He quotes the Amoy gazetteer on this point. See also Clark (1896), p. 10: "Owing to the scarcity of wood and the high price of labor here (Anping), the vessels are built on the mainland, where the owners dwell."

24. See, for example, Charles Gutzlaff, "Journal of a Residence in Siam and of a Voyage along the Coast of China to Mantchou Tartary," *The Chinese Repository* (Canton) 1, 3 (1832), p. 7: "Formosa has several deep and spacious harbors, but the entrances are extremely shallow. The trade is carried on in small junks belonging to Amoy; they go to all the western ports of the island, and return loaded with sugar or go up to the north of China with sugar." See also A. R. Colquhoun and J. E. Steward-Lockhart, "A Sketch of Formosa," *The China Review* 13, 3 (1885), p. 193. Pickering, on his trips up and down the west coast of Taiwan in the 1860s usually employed a small yawl. He makes passing reference to a fleet of big junks from the mainland coming to Takao (Kaohsiung) to load sugar for the northern ports (p. 177). He once, with great difficulty, was able to hire a small boat of about ten tons at the port of Ta Chia to attempt a brief journey to the port of Wu Ch'e (pp. 81 ff.)

25. See, for example, *Taiwan Chung-pu Pi Wen Chi Cheng* [A Collection of Stone Inscriptions from Central Taiwan] (Taipei: Bank of Taiwan, 1962). The list of donors for the reconstruction of Lukang's Ch'eng Huang Temple in the 1850s lists some contributors as *ch'uan-hu*, either as *ch'uan* "ship" or as *hao* "business name," pp. 144–145.

26. The source is a hand-written, Japanese-language document with no author listed that is in the library of the Department of Anthropology at National Taiwan University. A Chinese translation is included as a supplement to a book on Taiwan's Traditional Chinese Society, published in 1987. "Ch'ing-wei te Lukang" [Lukang in the Last Years of the Ch'ing Dynasty], in Ch'en Ch'i-nan, *Taiwan te Ch'uan-t'ung Chung-kuo She-hui.* [Taiwan's Traditional Chinese Society] (Taipei: Yun Ch'en Wen Hua [Asian Culture Co.], 1987), pp. 181–258.

27. Skinner, 1977, pp. 285–286, 525.

28. Taiwan Sotokufu (Government-General of Taiwan, 1895–1945), Rinji Taiwan kyukan chosaki, Dai Niibu, ed., *Dai Niibu*

chosa keizai shiryo hokoku [Report (of the Second Section) on Economic Conditions], vol. 2 (1905), p. 169.

29. *Report on Economic Conditions*, vol. 1 (1905), p. 581.

30. Skinner, 1977, p. 229.

31. My calculations, from the figures in Taiwan Sotokufu [Government-General of Taiwan], *Chosaka Tokeishu* [Annual Statistical Summary] (1903), pp. 273–277.

32. Skinner, 1977, p. 287.

33. Colquhoun and Stewart-Lockhart, 1885, pp. 189, 193.

34. Clark, 1896, pp. 52–53.

35. Wang Shih-ch'ing, 1968, p. 12 (no source cited).

36. *Report on Economic Conditions*, vol. 2 (1905), p. 332.

37. Taiwan Sotokofu, *Annual Statistical Summary*, 1903, 1905, 1911. Also, *Taiwan Boeki Nempyo* (Annual Returns of the Trade of Taiwan), 1922, 1925.

38. Wang Yi-kai, "Taipei San Chiao yu Taiwan-te Chiao Hang," [The Three Guilds of Taipei and Taiwan's Guilds and Wholesale Firms], *Taipei Wen Hsien* [Taipei Historical Journal] 6, 1 (1957), p. 19.

39. *Annual Statistical Summary*, 1903, 1911; *Taiwan Kojo*, [Taiwan's Factories] (Taipei: 1929).

40. The literature on Taiwan's economic development under the Japanese is large and growing. See George Barclay, *Colonial Development and Population in Taiwan* (Princeton: Princeton University Press, 1954), especially chapter 2, "Economic Development in Taiwan."

Chapter 5

Politics at Lukang

An old Chinese proverb says that "Heaven is high and the Emperor is far away." In premodern China the imperial government rested relatively lightly on local communities and regional power structures, and the few mandarins in the emperor's administrative service ruled with the cooperation of local elites, the characteristic Chinese gentry. In the past the emperor was certainly far away from Lukang, and my initial assumption, when my efforts to understand Lukang as it was in 1967 and 1968 inevitably led me to its past, was that the imperial bureaucracy was not directly relevant and could safely be ignored. This assumption turned out to be wrong, and I was forced to learn more than I wanted to about Ch'ing administration and the governance of eighteenth- and nineteenth-century Taiwan. Although to some extent this reflects the administrative bias of most of the easily available historical sources, it also stems from the city's commercial and regional role. In much the same way that soil conditions and water supplies shape the growth of farming villages, the administrative and taxation policies and regimes of the central and provincial governments are part of the environment of a regional trading city. Not only was Lukang, as a thriving seaport with a lucrative trade, the natural target of mandarins out to line their own pockets, but official policies and practices had a marked effect on the city's development and its internal structure. They could no more be ignored than its location or economic foundation. One of the major themes in the 275-year history of Lukang has been the shift in the balance of power between local and national forces.

In thinking about politics at Lukang I have found it useful to employ a fairly simple model of different political actors or groups contending for a share of the surplus produced by the local community. In the Ch'ing period the parties to the contest are, in brief, the emperor, the bureaucracy reaching from Peking down to the local magistrate, the nonofficial staff of the local yamen (government office) such as clerks and runners, and the local elite, who are liable to be divided into many potential groups by regional, occupational, and factional loyalties. Each party needs the others, and they engage in negotiations and trade-offs that make up local-level politics.[1]

Taiwan's Population and Its Segments

The official side of the political system operating in any county or city is fairly easy to picture, but the other, local, side is not, in part because one would expect its composition to vary from place to place. For understanding local-level politics in Taiwan in the eighteenth and most of the nineteenth centuries, it seems necessary to begin with migration from the mainland and the resulting regional and speech or subethnic groups that loomed so large in Taiwanese politics and local administration.

Although Taiwan lies only a hundred miles or so off the coast of southeastern China it was not settled by Chinese in any appreciable numbers until the seventeenth century, and only in the eighteenth century did they occupy the entire west coastal plain. From 1624 to 1661 Taiwan was ruled by the Dutch East India Company, which encouraged Chinese settlers to come to Taiwan to grow sugar and rice, which the Company used in its trade with Japan. From 1661 to 1683 the island was the base of Cheng Ch'eng-kung, known to Westerners as Koxinga, who drove out the Dutch. The head of a large trading/pirate fleet, he was a seagoing warlord who had been fighting the newly established Manchu Ch'ing dynasty (1644–1911) in the name of the deposed Ming dynasty (1368–1644). After Ch'ing forces drove him from his base in southern Fukien, he expelled the Dutch from Taiwan, built up an independent kingdom there with its capital at Tainan, and encouraged immigration from war-ravaged Fukien. After his death an imperial fleet, led by a former subordinate of Cheng's, Admiral Shih Lang, who was a native of Ch'uan-chou prefecture in southern Fukien, conquered Taiwan in 1683.

Once it had Taiwan, the Ch'ing Court was not eager to develop its new possession. It held the island mostly because it did not want it used by a hostile power, rebels, or the Japanese and Ryukyuan pirates who were then harrying the coasts of south and central

China. The imperial government attempted to restrict migration to Taiwan and considered the island to fall into the same category as the "South Seas," the term applied to Southeast Asia. An ineffectual series of edicts attempted to halt migration to Taiwan and southeast Asia, and the imperial government attempted to limit and control trade with both places. Although the central government was not wholly successful, it was powerful enough to exert a strong influence on the economic fortunes of the Southeast Coast region and on the settlement of Taiwan. Because Taiwan in the eighteenth century was regarded as a frontier, a malarial region inhabited by fierce and uncivilized savages, only the more adventurous or desperate Chinese were willing to risk the crossing and take their chances on the frontier.[2]

The somewhat haphazard nature of migration to Taiwan, usually carried out by solitary individuals or small groups of acquaintances who crossed on small ships or were recruited as laborers from the cities of the mainland, meant that entire social units such as villages or lineages were not transplanted to the island. Many of those who went to Taiwan doubtless considered themselves sojourners, short-term workers who would return to their native places and families, rather than emigrants or pioneers. Once safely ashore in Taiwan, they formed communities and effective groups by using such criteria as common place of origin and common speech, as did Chinese sojourners in Southeast Asia and in China itself. The criterion of common place of origin (*t'ung hsiang*), which could be applied to units as small as villages or as large as provinces, when combined with language, which usually varied with provenance, permitted the use of a set of nested binary distinctions to define the major categories of the population.

The primary distinction was between Chinese and aborigines. All Chinese would unite to fight the aborigines. The aborigines were divided into the assimilated or sinicized, known as the *"shu fan"* the "cultivated" or "cooked," and the unassimilated aborigines, called *"sheng fan,"* the "wild" or "raw." The Chinese were divided, in the first instance, into the Hokkien and the Hakka. Hokkien and Hakka are mutually unintelligible southern Chinese languages, and their speakers represent distinct "subcultural" or "subethnic" segments of the Han Chinese population. The Hokkien come from the coastal regions of southern Fukien Province, while the Hakka come from the hilly interior of southern Fukien and northeastern Kwangtung Provinces. The Hokkien were the dominant group among the settlers. They were internally divided by reference to their places of origin, the primary distinction being between Ch'uan-chou and

Chang-chou, adjacent prefectures in southern Fukien with minor dialectical differences.

On Taiwan the native place and speech groups formed large-scale, endogamous segments of the population. They clustered together, and during the eighteenth and nineteenth centuries tended to fight with each other, sometimes burning villages and driving the losers off their land or out of their quarter of a city. Much of the turbulent history of Taiwan can be summed up as conflicts between speech groups. Rebellions against imperial authority were frequent, and the usual strategy employed by the authorities was to quell the rising with the aid of militia enlisted from an opposing segment of the Taiwanese population. Hakka helped imperial troops defeat rebellious Hokkien, and Ch'uan-chou men attacked Chang-chou villages in the name of the ruling emperor or a local would-be emperor, as the case might be.

Imperial control over the Taiwanese seems to have been rather weaker than it was over the inhabitants of most areas of the empire inhabited by Han Chinese. When rebellions did break out (prover-bially, every seven years) they were usually put down by enlisting local militia and bringing troops in from the mainland. Local mil-itary forces, commanded by local men and locally financed, which came to play a significant part in mainland Chinese politics after the great rebellions of the mid-nineteenth century, were important elements of the power structure in Taiwan throughout the Ch'ing period, and imperial officials were forced to come to terms with them.[3]

Enter Lukang

Lukang first appears in the historical records as the site of a small garrison of coast guards. The *Chu Lo Hsien Chih*, compiled in 1718, records that a military guard post was established at Lukang as early as 1685.[4] The troops were coast guards, their duties being to deny pirate ships the use of the harbor, and to keep watch for pirates and for commercial vessels making unauthorized crossings or bringing in illegal migrants. In 1723 Changhua *Hsien* (county or district, the smallest administrative unit of the Chinese state) was formally established, taking in the northern portion of the previ-ous *hsien* of Chu Lo. This may be seen as an administrative response to the growing population of the area, as settlers brought the plain under cultivation. The *hsien* seat (always known by the same name as the *hsien*, here rendered as Changhua City) was established at the site of a small military post along the edge of the hills inland, where the road to the north passed. Twelve kilometers inland from Lukang, this has been the seat of the *hsien* government ever since, in spite of several attempts to transfer it to Lukang. In 1731 the authorities of Fukien Province (Taiwan was a prefecture of Fukien until it was elevated to provincial status in 1886.) declared Lukang to be a port legally open for trade along the coast of Taiwan, and stationed a minor official there to supervise the trade. He was a *hsun-chien*, usually translated as sub-district magistrate, who held the lowest of the eighteen ranks of the civil service (Civil Rank 9b). He and a staff of twenty underlings were responsible for keeping track of shipping along the ninety kilometer stretch of coast from the mouth of the Ta Chia River in the north to the mouth of the Hu Wei in the south, that is, along the entire coast of Changhua *hsien*.

When Lukang was made a port legally open for trade across the Taiwan Straits in 1785, an official was posted to supervise that trade. An official with the rank of subprefect (*t'ung-chih*, Civil Rank 5a) had since 1768 been stationed in Changhua City with the title of Northern Route Barbarian Managing Subprefect. The incumbent was responsible for all relations between Chinese settlers and aborigines in the entire northern two-thirds of Taiwan. When Lukang was made a legal port for trade with Fukien this official was given the concurrent title of Sea Defense Subprefect and instructed to supervise the trade between Lukang and Han-chiang, enforcing all the regulations on trade and migration. After the first holder of the position died with the rest of the officials in Changhua City during a major rebellion in 1787, his successor was posted directly to Lukang, where a new yamen was built in 1789, and supervision of trade came to occupy more of his time than relations between Chinese and aborigines, which eventually came to be handled by other officials.[5]

Alignment of Commercial and Administrative Systems

In 1789 Lukang was the largest city and the commercial center of mid-Taiwan. But it was not an administrative seat. This is a bit odd, since the imperial government usually (though not always) chose the largest and most commercially active city in a region to be the administrative seat. Like banks, that's where the money was. As

Skinner puts it: "Since the extraction of economic surplus is every-where a critical enabling mechanism of politics, it was efficient for political institutions to focus on commercial centers in their efforts to control and regulate the means of exchange and (indirectly) pro-duction, and to tap the wealth of any given local system." He also notes that: "a regular feature of the periodic adjustments and reor-ganizations of the imperial field administration was the incorpo-ration as capitals of newly prominent trading centers."[6] On general grounds one would also expect the commercial center of a region to be the cultural and religious center, as well as the center of the informal, locally based political system whose members were con-cerned to tap the wealth of their own local system. In as much as a good deal of the work of imperial officials consisted of dealing with local leaders, it was to everyone's advantage to be in the same place. In Skinner's terms, Lukang looks like a "misaligned" city, where the commercial hierarchy and the administrative hierarchy did not mesh in the most efficient way.

But even though Lukang was not the district capital, it was hardly bereft of officials or in danger of being overlooked by the imperial government. With the posting of the subprefect in 1789 it had two resident officials, and the district magistrate in Changhua City was only 12 kilometers away. And the officials were certainly well aware of the wealth of Lukang. In his paper on the construction of walled cities in northern Taiwan, Lamley cites the case of the holder of a high military post who successfully resisted the attempt of the governor-general to shift the post from Changhua to Hsinchu. The official wished to remain in the more flourishing Changhua area.[7] The subprefect who was posted at Lukang from 1789 to 1875 was a direct subordinate of the prefect at Tainan. The prefect, the island's highest official directly concerned with administration, was located in the island's largest and most flourishing commercial center, Tainan City. His direct subordinate was, logically, located in the island's second largest city and commercial center, Lukang. This arrangement bypassed the Changhua district magistrate, but made sense in both administrative and bureaucratic political terms. Lukang's subprefect, who held Civil Rank 5a, outranked the Chan-ghua district magistrate who held only Rank 7b. The *Changhua Hsien Chih* explains that the subprefect was appointed to Lukang because the district magistrate couldn't be expected to administer his district and to supervise trade as well. It says:

> After Lukang was formally opened as a port (1785) mer-chant ships flocked there. There were problems with evil-

doers trading, and it was necessary to supervise trade to prevent unauthorized voyages and trade in contraband. To do all this and look after the official grain transport Lukang had only a subdistrict magistrate, and it was too difficult for him to manage it all. The district magistrate had the local responsibility but he could not take concurrent responsibility (for both administering his district and supervising trade at Lukang). There was the Tamsui Marine Affairs Subprefect (stationed at Hsinchu) but even a long whip would not reach (i.e he was too far away). There was only the Barbarian Managing Subprefect at Changhua City, only twenty li from the port. He could come and go to investigate cases, and could supervise the Lukang subdistrict magistrate. So he was made concurrent Marine Affairs Subprefect.[8]

The burdens of office, especially on district magistrates, were indeed heavy in Ch'ing China, but here one cannot help suspecting the higher level officials of pushing the district magistrate out of the way so that they themselves could get first crack at extracting that economic surplus. And if that meant denying the Lukang elite the benefit of making their city an administrative seat, the prefect could live with their discontent.

Official Power

Some idea of the activities and powers of the subprefects and their fellow officials is provided by an account of a case of an "unauthorized voyage" in 1843. Upon receiving word that a suspicious ship had entered the small harbor of Hsia-hu Kang, south of Lukang, the Lukang subprefect dispatched the Lieutenant (*Ch'ieh-tsung,* Military Rank 6a) of the coast guard force with a patrol craft to investigate. They found the ship, which had just come from Amoy. Neither the ship, the crew, the passengers, nor the cargo had any of the necessary documents or licenses for trading with Taiwan. It was clearly a case of an unauthorized voyage, and the thirteen men aboard were put in the custody of the assistant magistrate (Civil Rank 8a, assistant to the magistrate of Chiayi district) at Pei-kang. They were then sent to the jail at Chiayi City, where the Chiayi district magistrate began the investigation. The master of the vessel had rented it at Amoy and, being illiterate, had not realized that the official license for trade with Taiwan that he had bought was in fact the previous year's and no longer valid. He had never been to Taiwan before, but there was famine in Fukien that year and business was very bad. None of the six crew members, who had made previous voyages to Taiwan, had the required personal documents. They were suspected of being in league with pirates. Along with the cargo of pottery and dried fish, the ship was carrying fifty-one iron cooking pots. Since the import of iron to Taiwan without a permit was illegal, the master and the merchant who owned the pots were also charged with carrying contraband. The five passengers were all poor men who had hoped to join their kinsmen in Taiwan. A complete report was made to the prefect in Tainan, and the authorities in Chiayi and Lukang continued their investigation into three suspicious letters the ship was carrying. The thirteen men were transferred to the jail in Tainan, where the prefect would try their case.

The three mysterious letters turned out to be innocuous business letters being sent to the Amoy and Ch'uan-chou Guilds of Lukang, and the charges of collusion with pirates were dropped. While awaiting trial at Tainan, the master of the vessel fell ill, "afflicted with fever and chills," and died. The other prisoners were sentenced to flogging, the number of strokes depending on the severity of their offence and their status. The merchant who had tried to import the cooking pots got an extra ninety strokes and had to wear the cangue for a month. The ship and its cargo were confiscated by the officials.[9]

This case demonstrates the power the officials could exercise over trade, and the sanctions they could apply to traders who had neither the proper documents nor an established working relation with the officials. One may suspect that had the master of the ship been able to make a suitable payment to the investigating military officer, or had he been affiliated with the group of merchants who usually carried on the trade across the Straits, such as the guild merchants of Tainan or Lukang, the case would not have turned out as it did. Knowing that this sort of thing did sometimes happen would perhaps make a Lukang rice exporter or cloth importer a bit more willing to contribute to a fund for the celebration of the prefect's mother's birthday, or to pay his guild dues.

Official Vulnerability

In 1787 a great rebellion broke out in Changhua county. It was led by Lin Shun-wen, the head of a secret society or religious sect called the Heaven and Earth Society. He captured Changhua City, burned the yamen, and killed the district magistrate and all the resident officials. Gathering support, he proclaimed himself emperor in Changhua City and then marched south, capturing cities and scattering officials before him. The rebellion was finally put down when Fu K'ang-an, a high-ranking Manchu general and personal favorite of the Ch'ien-lung emperor with successful campaigns in Mongolia, Tibet and Nepal to his credit, landed at Lukang with a large army in the autumn of 1787.[10]

The inhabitants of Lukang, which had not been occupied by the rebels, who were busy besieging the island's last Ch'ing officials at the city of Chiayi, welcomed General Fu, sending small craft out to meet his fleet and help ferry troops ashore. One reason they did this was that Lin Shun-wen was a Chang-chou man, as were most of his supporters, while by the 1780s Lukang and the coastal area to the north was a stronghold of the Ch'uan-chou people. The Chang-chou settlers lived further inland, and Lin Shun-wen himself had only arrived from Chang-chou in 1784. Armed bands of Ch'uan-chou men therefore offered their support to the imperial army as "loyal militia."

After the rebellion was put down, the governor-general of Fukien suggested to the imperial court that the seat of Changhua county be moved to Lukang. He pointed out that the population of central Taiwan had increased considerably since Changhua county had been established in 1723, and that the prefectural capital was at Tainan, far to the south.

In the past the only seaport was Lu-Er-Men (Tainan), which is 800 or 900 *li* from Amoy. Today there is a lot of traffic with Changhua's Lukang, whose location is more in the middle of the island. From Ch'uan-chou's Han-chiang it is but 400 *li* by sea, and with a favorable wind it can be reached in but half a day. Lukang is therefore a most important "gate" to Taiwan, and can be more easily depended on in times of adversity than Lu-Er-Men. Fortunately, Lin Shun-wen and his fellows were all mountain brigands who, though they knew enough to attack walled cities, were not intelligent enough to seize the seaports. Therefore our officials were able to set sail and land on Taiwan. Since it is not possible for very large ships to land troops at Lukang, it is necessary for smaller ships to put out some twenty *li* from Lukang to ferry troops ashore. Now, were the brigands to have only a little forethought, they would first attack Lukang.

Lukang has no wall to defend it and is easily captured. Once captured it can be held and small ships kept in. Should our officials approach in ships they would be unable to land troops. So, to get troops into Taiwan one would have to depend on Lu-Er-Men as the only "gate." From there, troops could enter the prefectural seat and then slowly advance to the north, along a roundabout and disadvantageous route. They would certainly not be able to attack the rebels as promptly or move as rapidly as they could by way of Lukang.

The present seat of Changhua county is twenty *li* distant from Lukang. It does not border the mountains; there are no water communications to it; it is really not at all the sort of place to establish a *hsien* capital. If the district capital were moved to Lukang and high civil and military officials posted there, then in time of peace they could command the areas to the north and south and information could easily be gathered. In times of disturbance the port could be guarded and held to ensure access to the interior. Lukang and Lu-Er-Men would thus act as pivots to the door, that is, as the key points for the control of Taiwan, and there would always be two routes by which to enter Taiwan. Thus calamities could be averted.[11]

The suggestion was turned down by the court (the *Changhua Hsien Chih*, which includes the proposal does not include the response to it), and the district magistrate's yamen was rebuilt in Changhua City. But the court did respond to the military and strategic argument, for in 1789 it stationed a battalion (*ying*) of the An Ping Marine Force at Lukang. The battalion, with an authorized strength of 708 men, was commanded by a Major (*Yu-chi*, Military Rank 3b) and occupied a mud-walled fort overlooking the harbor at the north end of the city.[12]

The importance of the local system's own resources and armed strength was demonstrated in 1795. The price of rice was unusually high that year and a man called Ch'en Chou-ch'uan, a former member of Lin Shun-wen's Heaven and Earth Society, began organizing groups of bandits in the countryside and seizing stores of rice. At the beginning of the third month the band, numbering some 400, swore to kill all officials. One night they suddenly attacked and captured Lukang. While a few small vessels made a diversion in the harbor, Ch'en's forces attacked the fort from the landward side and most of the garrison fled. The band then attacked the subprefect's yamen, killing the subprefect, whom the official history eulogizes for having gone down with his sword in his hand. They then went on to loot the official granary. The bandits marched on Changhua City, taking it after the garrison there managed to accidentally blow up the powder magazine along with most of their officers. Within five days however, Ch'en's band was scattered by the local militia, who were financed by local landholders and the Lukang merchants. The remaining bandits fled to the hills and order was restored. A new subprefect and major arrived in Lukang and the fort was rebuilt on a different site at the south end of the city where the road to Changhua City begins.[13]

The case of the unauthorized crossing demonstrates the power the officials could exercise over individual merchants and traders, and suggests the need of the Lukang merchants to establish close relations, both official and unofficial, with the civil and military officials. But the rebellions of 1787 and 1795, which killed two sub-prefects in an eight-year period, demonstrate the officials' need to rely on local armed forces to maintain their own position and, in some cases, to keep their heads. This point was illustrated yet again in 1862 when a Chang-chou man called Tai Wan-sheng, a landowner from south of Changhua City, organized yet another Heaven and Earth society, rose up, and captured Changhua City. The subprefect of the Tamsui T'ing (whose yamen was in Hsinchu City) had come south to urge the Changhua district magistrate to take a hard line and suppress the Heaven and Earth Society. Tai Wan-sheng hung the head of the subprefect from the city gate. The Changhua district magistrate had been more conciliatory with Tai, and he only had his queue cut off before being allowed to flee to Lukang with a placard around his neck reading "Ch'ing Officials Go Home!" The Ch'uan-chou men who lived in Changhua City were escorted to the south gate and permitted to flee to Lukang.

All the officials from Changhua City fled to Lukang, where the commander of the garrison laid gunpowder mines to defend his fort and called on the "gentry and merchants" of Lukang to raise the militia. Tai Wan-sheng and his co-leader declared themselves kings and sent expeditions against Yunlin, Chiayi, and Lukang. The Ch'uan-chou Militia beat off that attack, aided by the goddess Matsu who appeared in the sky with a white banner and a celestial army. (The Ch'uan-chou Militia were also known as the White Banner Militia.) After several months of skirmishing an imperial officer finally landed at Lukang with 400 troops from the island of Chinmen. They set out with 1,000 men of the Ch'uan-chou Militia and defeated the rebels at a great battle halfway between Lukang and Changhua City.[14]

Walls and Symbolic Urbanity

The resident officials and the local merchants and gentry who made up Lukang's elite collaborated in more than military affairs. By 1825 Lukang had such ornaments of a proper Chinese city as a yamen (the sub-prefect's), a charitable foundation, several large temples, and an academy (*shu-yuan*) where local men could prepare for the civil service examinations. One of the temples, founded by the Eight Guilds and the sub-prefect in 1814, was a Wen Wu Miao, a temple dedicated to Confucius and to Kuan-ti, the god of war and of loyalty. Such a temple was not part of the official state cult, for those temples were found only in administrative capitals, but it was the next best thing. The city's temples included a Ch'eng Huang Miao. This seems a bit irregular, for Ch'eng Huang is the God of Walls and Moats, often called the City God, who is thought of as the supernatural counterpart or colleague of the district magistrate, or prefect, or governor. But, although Lukang had a Ch'eng Huang, it didn't have a wall or a magistrate.[15] The usual Chinese word for "city," *ch'eng*, actually means "wall," and in the past most Chinese cities were walled. Just as a proper Chinese house, one with pretentions to being more than a shelter, had a wall, so, it seems, did a proper city have a wall and gates. Lukang's elite apparently wanted a wall and were willing to pay for one. Their persistent efforts to get official permission to build a wall and to have their city made an administrative capital failed, but they seem to have had the support of the local officials.

The collection of documents in the *Changhua Hsien Chih* contains a proposal for the construction of a wall at Lukang. Although the authors of most of the documents contained in the *hsien chih* are carefully listed, this one is anonymous. It was composed sometime between 1827 and 1831, when the *hsien chih* was compiled, for it refers to the construction of walls at Fengshan (1825–1826) and Hsinchu (1827–1829). Official sanction was necessary before a city wall, which was a substantial military installation, could be constructed, and that sanction had to come from fairly high up the administrative ladder, from the provincial governor and perhaps from Peking as well. In the eighteenth century the imperial court had prohibited the construction of substantial stone and brick walls around Taiwanese cities, on the grounds that if such strong places were lost to rebels, it would require long and costly campaigns to recover them. The policy was summed up in the slogan, "easily lost, easily regained." The island's administrative centers, like Chang-hua City, had official yamens and temples of the state cult, but they were protected by earthworks (which were eroded in a few years by Taiwan's heavy rains) and hedges of thorny bamboo. The cost of wall building also deterred the circumvallation of Taiwanese cities, for most of the cost was met by the local residents.

Official policy changed after the last Ch'ing officials on the island were able in 1787 to hold out against the superior numbers of Lin Shun-wen's rebels behind the palisades of Chiayi City. This impressed the Ch'ien-lung emperor, who recommended that stone and brick be used to wall cities on Taiwan. By the first decades of the nineteenth century the Taiwanese economy had developed to the point that it was possible to raise the funds for wall-building. One of the first such projects was in Changhua, where a group of prominent gentry and nondegree holding local leaders from all the county's subethnic communities (Ch'uan-chou, Chang-chou and Hakka) submitted a petition to the Fukien-Chekiang governor-general when he arrived on a tour of inspection in 1809. Between 1811 and 1815 a brick and stone wall was built around Changhua City. This effort, at its time the most costly wall construction project yet carried out in Taiwan, cost 190,000 silver dollars (Taiwan was on a Mexican silver dollar standard), with almost all the funds being raised locally.[16]

The proposal for a wall at Lukang notes the construction of walls at Chiayi, Changhua, Hsinchu and Fengshan (all of them, unlike Lukang, district capitals), and points to the utility of walls for protecting administrative offices, treasuries, granaries, and ordinary citizens. It describes Lukang as a center of the rice and sugar trade, and the site of the official granary and the subprefect's yamen. It also notes the strategic importance of Lukang's location for control over the area. The proposal suggests that the wall be built over a period of years, beginning with an earth rampart.[17]

If we assume that the proposal was either made by an official or that it had official approval, which seems likely, we can also assume that whoever wrote the proposal must have assured himself that local support for the undertaking would be forthcoming. By 1830 the local elite at Lukang were willing to provide the considerable sums necessary. A wall, if built, would serve the utilitarian purpose of protecting them from bandits, rebels, or hostile Chang-chou men. It would also serve as a concrete symbol of the city's wealth, importance, and elevated status.

While it was reasonable for Lukang's leaders to want a wall, there were precedents for their situation. Many quite substantial cities in China, such as Foshan in Kwangtung and Ching-te-chen in Kiangsi, had no walls and were not administrative capitals. (It is possible that the suggestion I made earlier about higher levels of administration reaching down to directly tap the wealth of the trade at Lukang, to the detriment of the district magistrate, may have applied to these mainland cities as well.) Once the massive investment in walling Changhua City had been made (with, no doubt, substantial contributions from Lukang merchants), there was clearly less chance of moving the district capital to Lukang, where the whole expensive process would have to be repeated. There may also have been other political reasons for the refusal of higher authorities to move the district capital to Lukang or permit construction of a wall there.

Skinner points out that not only must the alignment of administrative systems with commercial systems be imperfect, because administrative territories are discrete while commercial ones always overlap, but that administrators sometimes deliberately minimized the convergence of the two systems. The state did not want to strengthen local gentry and merchants to the point where they threatened bureaucratic power, and one way to limit the power of local elites was to divide them by focusing different subtypes on different centers and systems. Merchants were oriented to the places they bought from and sold to, while the interests of the gentry were more channeled by the hierarchy of districts, prefectures, and provinces.[18] The Lukang merchants were concerned with central Taiwan, conditions in which would affect the price of rice in the markets of Ch'uan-chou and Amoy, and they were very concerned with people and events across the Straits. They were less concerned with events in northern Taiwan or with those around the prefectural capital of Tainan in the south. Local politics, in which they could not help being involved, centered on the district magistrate's yamen in Changhua City, where the interests of Chang-chou landowners, Hakka settlers, and even of sinicized aborigines, were taken into account along with those of Ch'uan-chou merchants.

Administrative or Commercial Cities

The subethnic division of the local population and its role in local-level politics may also been a significant factor in the decision to refuse permission to build a wall at Lukang. Lukang, it must be kept in mind, was from the end of the eighteenth century a solidly Ch'uan-chou city in an ethnically mixed county. There was nothing unusual about this, and Lamley points out that in Taiwan it was common for port towns and market towns to be enclaves of one subethnic group or another. Administrative cities, on the other hand, though they often had smaller populations, served and were inhabited by representatives of all the subethnic groups. Building walls around administrative centers was one of the few occasions in which the usually opposed if not downright hostile subethnic groups cooperated, but the neutrality of the administrative center was an obvious condition for the cooperation. When in the late nineteenth century the capital of the newly established province of Taiwan was sited at the flourishing commercial center of Taipei (where the money was), an entirely new settlement was constructed, walls and all, on the rice paddies adjoining the old commercial city.

The commercial cities along the Tamsui River (which were the core of Taipei City), Meng-chia and Ta-tao-ch'eng were, as the result of bitter subethnic fighting in the 1850s, each ethnic enclaves. The new walled city of Tai-pei-fu, which was constructed between 1879 and 1884 as the seat of the newly established Taipei prefecture, was not only above the rivalry between T'ung An and An-ch'i people and merchants; it had a distinctly more cosmopolitan population as well. After it became the capital of the new Taiwan province in 1886 it came to house many sojourners from Fukien and the lower Yangtze region as well as mainland scholars and officials.[19] In the mid-eighteenth century Lukang seems to have had an ethnically mixed population, but by 1800 it had become a solid Ch'uan-chou base. By successfully driving out or assimilating the Hakka and Chang-chou people Lukang's Ch'uan-chou merchants won a victory, but that victory may well have doomed their sons' attempts to make the city an administrative capital. It appears that in eighteenth- and nineteenth-century Taiwan you could either have ethnic purity, which in that context meant control of trade, or you could have a yamen and walls, but not both. Had the seat of Changhua *hsien* been moved to Lukang before the investment in walls and public buildings at Changhua City, a new walled enclosure would most likely have been built beside commercial Lukang, and the walled settlement at least would have housed representatives of all subethnic groups. If the officials had permitted the construction of a wall around Lukang without making it a district capital, they would have been granting a major concession to the Ch'uan-chou community, and would have come under pressure to permit the Chang-chou people and perhaps the Hakka as well to wall their principal towns. It was not in the interest of any official to encourage a subethnic arms race, nor, considering that in the next rebellion the rebels were quite likely to be Ch'uan-chou men, was it in the government's interest to permit them to fortify Lukang.

Subethnicity and Segmentation

The spirit of militant parochialism exhibited in the incessant strife between subethnic communities in Taiwan was an expression of that same sentiment of native place solidarity that underlay successful sojourning and the establishment of commercial relations of mutual trust within *t'ung-hsiang* communities. Local solidarity, in a pan-Han context, was an expression of partiality and favoritism, in other words of *ch'ing*, and it is important for our comprehension of the political role of subethnic communities and loyalties to realize that loyalty to one's subethnic community was never total nor an end in itself. Opposition and competition between subethnic and regional communities took place within a context of bureaucratic administration. Not only were the units of native place loyalty always identified in administrative terms as counties, prefectures, or provinces rather than as city trading systems, but I believe that bureaucratic administration represented, even in eighteenth- and nineteenth-century Taiwan, values which lent it legitimacy and so limited subethnic loyalty. In ideal terms the yamen and the official represented both the largest cultural and political community—that of Chinese civilization—and the values of rationality, equity, and evenhandedness, that is, of *li*.

In some respects such Chinese subgroups as Hakka or Teochiu or San Yi Ch'uan-chou are just as much ethnic groups as any discussed in recent anthropological literature.[20] But it is necessary to keep in mind that although Ch'uan-chou men, say, considered themselves better than Chang-chou men or Hakka and were perfectly willing to compete with or to fight them, they did not do so in the name of an independent Ch'uan-chou. In this way they differ considerably from Basques or Catalans or Serbs. An independent, sovereign Ch'uan-chou just doesn't make sense in a Chinese context. The goal was to maximize Ch'uan-chou's share of money, honor, scholars, and anything else that could be competed for, within the taken for granted arena of the Chinese empire. Here one may note that in Chinese political culture the only regime whose legitimacy is accepted is one that controls or purports to control the entire country, and that there is no way to establish a legitimate administration based on a province or a larger region. This helps to explain the recurrent habit of minor bandit chieftains proclaiming themselves emperor, since they could claim no lower status and be recognized as the proper rulers of even a village. In places like Taiwan one thing the mandarins did, inadequately and ineffectually perhaps, was to serve as neutral third parties. In the same way that a guarantor represents the larger, public interest or a mediator represents principles of abstract equity and rationality, so did the bureaucrats serve as third parties, above the strife between the subethnic communities. The problem is thus not strictly one of choosing between local and national loyalties; it is one of deciding where the balance point lies, as is the analogous problem of deciding when to follow the value of *li*, rationality, and when to follow the equally valued principle of *ch'ing*, affect. Just as one man's human feeling is another man's corruption, so commendable loyalty to one's fellows may also be interpreted as subversive and anarchic clannishness. The line is hard to draw, and the common Taiwanese strife between subethnic communities, which appalled the officials, can be interpreted as the result of just leaning a bit too far to one side, of carrying a normally good and honorable principle just a bit too far.

All this is significant not only because it helps to bring local politics and subethnic strife into the same frame of reference as personal relations, commerce, and associations, but because it helps to make sense of some of the more puzzling features of subethnic strife. On the one hand, the fighting was real enough. Men died; villages were burned; people were driven out of their homes and made refugees. But, on the other hand, total extermination of the opposing group does not seem to have been the goal, and the fighting never seems to have approached the ferocity and general slaughter that marked the great rebellions in China proper. Usually the fighting ceased after a year or so, and the opposing communities settled down to live next to each other for another decade, exchanging mutual insults no doubt, but also cooperating, if only grudgingly, in local politics and economic relations. Rent, for instance, seems to have been regularly paid to landholders, even if they belonged to opposing subgroups, and commodities somehow got in and out.[21] Much of the rice that was exported from Lukang was grown by Chang-chou men further inland, and that's where a lot of the cloth and manufactured goods from Fukien went after passing through Lukang. Rent strikes and economic blockades don't seem to have been part of the normal tactics of the sub-ethnic conflicts. The overall picture one gets is of a serious but limited opposition, within a larger political context whose legitimacy everyone accepts. A similar picture, although with more commonalities and less open conflict, will emerge when we look at political relations within nineteenth-century Lukang.

Last Try for Administrative Status

Lukang's elite made a last effort to win administrative recognition of their city's importance in 1887. When Taiwan became a province in its own right in 1886, the new governor, Liu Ming-ch'uan, decided to build a provincial capital in the center of the island. In 1887 he received a petition urging him to establish the new capital at Lukang. The petition was signed by twenty-two members of the Lukang gentry, that is, those who held imperial degrees. One of them, Tsai Te-fang held the coveted *chin-shih*, (the highest degree, won in national examinations in Peking) and had served as a district magistrate in Kwangtung. The petition pointed out that all Taiwan's administrative centers, save Chiayi, were located on or near the coast, as was the former prefectural seat of Tainan. It stressed the military importance of Lukang, noting that most rebellions broke out in the interior and were put down by mainland troops who landed along the coast. The disadvantages of the city of Changhua were listed, and its easy capture by Tai Wan-sheng's rebels in 1862 was noted. Lukang, on the other hand, occupied an advantageously central position both for military affairs and for civil government.[22] Governor Liu was not impressed by the petition and rejected it, replying that Lukang's altitude (or perhaps, relief) was too low and its harbor too shallow. The petitioners, he said, were acting with the selfish commercial interests of Lukang in mind rather than the best interests of the government of Taiwan. Finally, as a geomantic site, Lukang was clearly not suitable for a provincial capital.[23] He decided to build his new capital on open ground on the site of the present city of Taichung, but lack of funds prevented this and the seat of government remained at Taipei.

The Mandarins Depart

Lukang's trade declined in the 1870s, as a result both of further deterioration of the harbor and of changes in the sources of Fukien's rice supply. As Lukang's trade fell off and as the junk trade across the Straits became less important as a source of official and nonofficial revenue, the officials who had been posted to the city to supervise and tax its commerce were withdrawn. The subdistrict magistrate, who had been assigned to Lukang in 1732, was transferred up the coast to Ta Chia in 1810. In 1875 the Lukang subprefect was transferred to the Puli basin on the edge of the central mountains and resumed the title of Northern Route Barbarian Managing Subprefect, which had been the title of the office before the move to Lukang in 1787. He was replaced by a much lower ranking subdistrict magistrate, a *hsun-chien.* In 1885 the subdistrict magistrate was transferred over the hills to Nantou and for the first time since 1732 Lukang had no civil officials at all. In 1888 the subdistrict magistrate was returned to Lukang.[24]

In 1888, when the city's prosperity had already begun to fall off and Lukang men had begun to migrate north to Taipei, Lukang's local elite, which had enjoyed a relation of mutual accommodation with the representatives of the central government during the period of prosperity, turned against the central government in a misguided assertion of local solidarity. Liu Ming-ch'uan, the first governor of the province of Taiwan, was an unusually able administrator. He set about "developing" Taiwan with plans for everything from pacifying the aborigines to building a railroad. But all his modernizing and self-strengthening projects took money, and his attempt to raise additional revenue earned him the fierce opposition of Taiwan's landowners and merchants, especially those in the southern part of the island who got little in return for their taxes. In 1861 branches of the Fukien likin office (likin was an internal transit tax levied on goods, originally to help raise revenue to put down the Taiping rebels) were established in the ports of Taiwan, and the merchant guilds contracted to collect the duties on opium imports as well as on various export commodities. In 1886 Liu Ming-ch'uan put a likin tax of 5 percent on sugar exported from Taiwan. The merchants of the south refused to move the sugar to the ports, and threatened to burn the sugar fields and plant rice instead. Liu refused to back down (he may have known there wasn't enough water to grow rice in place of sugar anyway) and the merchants ended up paying the tax.[25]

Governor Liu also planned a cadastral survey, as the records on which the land tax was based had not been revised since the mid-eighteenth century. A great deal of land had been brought under cultivation since then, but no taxes were paid on it. Registering all the land would vastly increase the provincial revenue and would be a relatively equitable way of distributing the tax burden. The scheme aroused the predictable opposition of the landowners and a great deal of unrest ensued. In Changhua, the magistrate put down disorders and locked up troublemakers.

Tax Protesters in Arms

In the autumn of 1888 a mob destroyed the office of the Salt Monopoly in Lukang. Similar incidents had been occurring all over Changhua county for the past several months. The mob was led by a man whose brother had been imprisoned for his part in earlier disorders, and by Shih Chiu-tuan, a landowner and onetime Lukang rice dealer. The group then marched on Changhua City and surrounded it. Others joined them, and soon the walled county seat was encircled by several thousand insurgents, while further disorders broke out in the countryside. The district magistrate was isolated in his city, but managed to send a message ordering the head of Lukang's Chuan-chou militia to call out the volunteers and come to the rescue. The magistrate also used the just completed telegraph line to inform the governor in Taipei of his plight.

The Lukang militia did not stir, but Governor Liu, using the telegraph and chartered steamships, reacted far more quickly than the imperial government had in the past, when it normally took several months for imperial troops to arrive to put down a Taiwanese uprising. Within a week, picked troops from the Pescadores (Peng-hu) and Chinmen were landing at Lukang, while others marched up from the south. Although the district magistrate had called for 200 militia from each *pao* (a sub-district administrative unit roughly corresponding to the present *hsiang* and *chen* in size), none arrived. The insurgents continued to besiege Changhua City, and an account of the affair written by a member of the local gentry rather weakly accounts for the failure of the militia to come to the aid of the district magistrate by saying: "The summons was so sudden that no response was possible. The roads were all blocked (with pits and sharpened bamboo stakes) and the men of each *pao* were suspicious, so no one came. In the Lukang garrison there were only a few tens of soldiers to defend the fort, and the scholars and merchants of the city were hard-pressed to arrange for its defense, so they could not send help to Changhua City."[26]

After Changhua City had been surrounded for a week, word came that imperial troops were on their way and a group of 800 militia finally arrived from T'ien-chung, 25 kilometers south.

They attacked and scattered the insurgents and Shih Chiu-tuan escaped to the mountains. The district magistrate was furious that Lukang's Chuan-chou militia had not come to his aid. He talked of attacking them, so they blocked the roads and barricaded the villages of their districts. The magistrate accused the Lukang guild merchants of collaboration with the insurgents, and the leader of the Ch'uan-chou militia with having abetted the escape of Shih Chiu-tuan. He therefore ordered the commander of the Peng-hu battalion to attack Lukang. On the evening of the sixteenth day of the ninth lunar month the troops from Peng-hu surrounded Lukang, many of whose people fled the city. In Changhua City a group of influential local gentry presented petitions and asked the magistrate and military commanders to call off the attack on Lukang, but they would not. According to the account later written by one of these local gentry, they finally managed to send a telegram to Governor Liu Ming-ch'uan asking if he approved of the attack on Lukang and pointing out that if this were done, the Ch'uan-chou militia of the 24 villages of Pai-sha (immediately south of Changhua City) and the 53 villages of Hsien-hsi (the coastal district north of Lukang) would go over to the rebels. They asked how this would aid in pacifying the region. Liu telegraphed back an order to halt the attack, and Lukang was spared.

When order was finally restored after a fair amount of bloodshed and the death of one of Governor Liu's subordinate generals, Liu summoned everyone involved to Taipei for an investigation. Somehow in the course of the troubles the official land register of Changhua County had disappeared and the matter had to be explained to Peking. The district magistrate repeated his charges that the Lukang guild merchants had been involved in a conspiracy with Shih Chiu-tuan. It was pointed out that Shih was not the usual local bandit type. He was over sixty, a wealthy landowner, and had been a prosperous rice merchant in Lukang for many years. It was claimed that when the likin tax had been imposed on the movement of ordinary goods (as distinct from opium and tea) the previous year, all the merchants of the island had complied, while only Lukang had resisted it, albeit feebly, for the past year. It was further charged that only Lukang *pao* had gone so far as to oppose the cadastral survey. The major commanding the Lukang garrison, the head of the Ch'uan-chou militia, and a number of important merchants and degree holders of Lukang were accused of conspiring with Shih Chiu-tuan, their old acquaintance, and aiding his escape.[27] They in turn protested their innocence, and claimed that the disorders were the fault of the harsh magistrate and the arbitrary and corrupt way he and his minions had carried out the land survey.

The governor responded by punishing everyone involved. He reprimanded the district magistrate for losing the hearts of the people, and dismissed the major commanding the Lukang garrison from office. The heads of the Ch'uan-chou militia were dismissed from their posts, and the city as a whole had a fine of 30,000 taels imposed on it. (A tael is a unit of account corresponding roughly to an ounce of silver.) The work on the land survey went ahead, and in January 1890 Liu reported to Peking that it was completed for the whole island. He postponed collection of the land tax in Changhua for one year because of the insurrection and consequent damages, but thereafter the Lukang landlords, like everyone else, had to pay the tax.[28]

Decline and Adaptation

The rising of Shih Chiu-tuan was a bloody failure, and the Lukang merchants and landowners, whether they supported it or not, or whether they supported it fervently or halfheartedly, suffered severe losses. If, as seems likely, they did in some fashion support it, that support can be seen as a mistaken and anachronistic attempt to stop or turn aside those forces that threatened to put an end to Lukang's prosperity and parochial preeminence. Lukang, which had been a booming city at the end of the eighteenth century, found itself at the end of the nineteenth up against the forces of progress and modernity, and sure to suffer for it. Economically, Lukang with its armies of porters and carrying poles and fleets of small junks and rafts was up against steamships, railroads, telegraphs, the international market for rice and sugar, and, by Taiwanese standards, a rational and effective bureaucracy that was bent on bringing "progress" to the island and the empire as a whole. Whoever planned the rising seriously underestimated the speed and strength of the military response that Governor Liu (himself a military hero who had risen through the ranks while supressing the Taiping and Nien rebels) could make. Instead of several months, the imperial troops took only a week to land.

As Lukang's economy declined and the trading systems of which it was the node lost their relative importance, land rents became an increasingly significant element in the income of the local elite. That elite resisted the attempts of the central government to extract more revenue through the land tax, which was normal enough, but they failed to realize how far the balance of power had shifted toward the central government and away from the local system. An endeavor that might have succeeded in 1788 or 1838 had no hope of success in 1888. In 1895 Taiwan was ceded to Japan, and the Japanese colonial government quickly incorporated Lukang into a far more effective and centralized administrative structure than that of the late Ch'ing dynasty.

The Japanese army arrived in Lukang on the afternoon of August 28, 1895. They were preceded by Ku Hsien-jung, one of the Lukang men who had left to seek his fortune in Taipei. Reputed later to have left Lukang with nothing but the clothes on his back, he had prospered in Taipei and became a well-to-do businessman. A good eye for the main chance is said today to be one of the requisites for mercantile success, and Ku demonstrated his when he and a few other merchants went out in 1895 to invite the Japanese army to come into Taipei and restore order after the Chinese troops had fled and looting broke out. That incident was the beginning of a new and profitable career as a mediator between the Japanese and the Taiwanese populace. To the extent that he could be persuaded to use his position and powers for Lukang, the city might benefit more than it otherwise would under the new dispensation. He and several degree-holders welcomed the Japanese forces to Lukang, led them to the recently abandoned barracks of the Chinese soldiery, collected provisions, and enrolled men to serve as porters.[29] Ku and a few other local notables formed a pro-Japanese militia group, to guard the city and themselves against armed men who could be described either as "bandits" or as "loyal anti-Japanese resistance fighters." During the period of disorder after Chinese civil authority collapsed but before the Japanese arrived and took control, the area around Lukang was plagued by bandits and partisan groups, who were often difficult to tell apart. Rich families hired private guards or raised their own armed bands, but found the guards almost as much trouble as the bandits.[30]

Some of Lukang's wealthy and influential men cast their lot with the Japanese and prospered. Others, the scholars in particular, were unhappy under the new regime. Many crossed over to Fukien where traditional Chinese scholarship still brought respect and they could continue to compete in the imperial civil service examinations. Most of them eventually returned to Lukang. Many scholars withdrew from an active role in a society that did not value their learning, with some living in retirement on their land rents and others supporting themselves by teaching or seal carving. Lukang, after a thriving career as a philistine commercial city had just reached the point when it could begin producing cultivated, genteel scholars when not only did the commercial foundation collapse, but the painfully acquired scholarship was suddenly devalued as well. Looked at in the most favorable light, the disgruntled scholars preserved the heritage of traditional Chinese culture, teaching the classics and preserving a sense of Chinese identity under alien rule. But they were cut off from the centers of modern Chinese thought and devoted to a cultural tradition that soon became anachronistic, not to say sterile. The more they tried to preserve the high culture of the past, the more provincial they became. They cultivated their calligraphy, formed societies devoted to poetry and wine, and on the whole lived in a peculiarly shabby-genteel world, insulated both from the lives of the common people and from the intellectual currents of early-twentieth-century China, or Japan, or the West. The tangible remains of their activity consist of some calligraphy on the walls of Lukang's temples, some privately printed collections of verse, and the conviction of the city's present inhabitants that Lukang was once a center of scholarship and learning.

Ironically, the greatest blow to Han learning in Lukang came not from the Japanese but from Taiwanese resistance groups. In August 1896 a band of partisans came down from the hills and attempted to "liberate" Lukang. They were driven off by the small Japanese garrison and the thousand-man militia that Ku Hsien-jung had helped to organize. The Japanese were not driven out nor were their Taiwanese collaborators harmed, but several old houses were destroyed, and the library of the academy (the *Wen Kai Shu-yuan*), reputed to be one of the largest libraries of the island, was burned and totally destroyed.[31]

In Lukang the Japanese set up a customs house and police force, and stationed a small force of Japanese military police. In 1896 they established a school, housed in a temple, to teach the Japanese language, and from this nucleus grew the public school system, which expanded in Lukang at much the same rate that it did in the other towns of central Taiwan. There never were a lot of Japanese in Lukang and the colonial government rather ignored the city, concentrating its attention on Taipei, Kaohsiung, and the other major ports and commercial centers of the island. The Japanese authorities of course exercised much closer control over Lukang than had their Ch'ing predecessors, working through the Japanese mayors of Lukang (Rokkō) and the ubiquitous *hokō* system of mutual supervision and responsibility by small groups of neighbors, but in this respect Lukang was no different from any other Taiwanese community.[32] In the main, the city was affected more by indirect results of government policy and subsequent economic and demographic changes than by direct actions or policies of the central power.

Salt in the Pork Barrel

During the Japanese period Ku Hsien-jung was Lukang's wealthiest man and most prominent citizen. He was one of the very few Taiwanese who had a substantial share in the islandwide, centralized economic structure that collected the profits from Taiwan's economic growth. By the end of his career he owned a sugar company, an import-export firm, several cement factories in Kaohsiung, a land development corporation, and had become a member of the Japanese House of Peers. He built an immense and imposing mansion in Lukang, a three-story, Nippo-rococo structure in red brick, which is today claimed to be the largest private dwelling on the island. However, he actually spent very little time in Lukang, and was usually to be found in his Taipei mansion or in Tokyo or Shanghai. He contributed funds to the rebuilding of some of Lukang's major temples, and housed the offices of his land development corporation in one of the spare wings of the Lukang mansion. He employed some of the sons of the old degree-holding Lukang gentry in this enterprise, which bought farm land, built irrigation works for the land, and then rented it out to tenants. At the time of the Land Reform in 1953–54 this corporation owned over 4,000 *chia* (one *chia* equals 2.39 acres, or 1.03 hectare) of land scattered all over Taiwan, and was the island's largest landholder. In 1899 he had urged the Japanese authorities to set up a salt monopoly, and when they did so in the next year he became its head. He rewarded those members of the Taiwanese elite who collaborated with the Japanese with posts in the salt monopoly.[33]

His position with the salt administration led to a scheme to help reverse Lukang's declining prosperity by establishing a salt field there. Sometime in the early twentieth century, (accounts of the date vary from 1899 to 1907,) Ku and another wealthy Lukang man formed the Lukang Salt Production Corporation and set up salt fields at the shore to produce salt by evaporating sea water. Sometime between 1905 and 1911 a sugar company built a narrow gauge rail line linking Lukang with Changhua City and the main rail line. This was then extended down to the salt fields, which began producing as much salt as possible. The owners of the salt field may have made money, and the installation most probably would not have been built at Lukang if an emigrant had not been the head of the Salt Monopoly, but the salt fields were a dubious asset to Lukang. At the most they employed a few hundred of the area's poorest people, who worked very hard for very low wages. The salt workers came to be recognized locally as an exceptionally deprived and miserable group. For various technical reasons the Lukang salt fields were never as productive as those elsewhere in Taiwan, and had the decision of whether to build them or not been made on technical rather than political grounds, they would not have been built. The Cho Shui River lowered the salinity of the seawater off Lukang, and though it does not rain very much along the shore, it is overcast fairly often. Furthermore, most of Lukang's rain comes in the summer, which is the salt-making season. The rest of the island's salt fields were further south, around Tainan and Kaohsiung, where the summers are drier and sunnier. As the coast at Lukang continued to move out by a meter or two a year the salt fields came to be further and further from the water and it became more and more expensive to produce salt there.

By 1955 the cost of production at the Lukang salt fields was 3.7 times that of the other salt fields and the yield was very low, with only 12,490 of Taiwan's total salt production of 658,585 metric tons being produced at Lukang.[34] The salt fields became an issue in local politics, with some local leaders trying to persuade the provincial government (which took over the assets of the colonial Taiwan Salt Corporation) to help the salt workers and the city's economy by expanding the salt fields while the provincial government tried to close down the uneconomical Lukang fields. They were finally closed down in the early 1960s, and the local leaders were mollified by being appointed to the committee that would oversee the conversion of the salt fields to rice fields, an expensive and protracted process of leaching the salt from the soil that would be managed by the committee on behalf of the salt workers, who would eventually gain title to the new rice lands.

Dig a Harbor and the Cargo Will Come

After the restoration of Taiwan to Chinese rule in 1945, Lukang's elite made a commendable if quixotic attempt to bring back the good old days by reopening the harbor. Today old men, some of whom were influential twenty years before, claim that the decline of Lukang's sea trade was due to the deliberate policy of the Japanese colonial government, that, they claim, disliked Lukang because it was a center of traditional Chinese culture and opposition to Japanese rule. They also say that the Japanese decided not to run the main railroad line through Lukang for the same reason. While this is a characteristic example of local opinion on Lukang's place in the scheme of things (more fully discussed in later chapters), it is hardly convincing. It is hard to imagine the Japanese colonial administrators in Taipei worrying a great deal about Lukang, and a glance at a map will explain why the railroad was built where it was. But if the local leadership really believed these things, it would help to explain their doomed attempt in the decade after restoration of Taiwan to Chinese authority to bring back the golden age before the 1860s by recreating the harbor as it had been. It was decided to begin by dredging the mouth of the creek north of Lukang that had served as an anchorage in the early 1900s. A breakwater would then be built, and eventually the channel leading to Lukang itself, most of which had been filled in the 1930s, would be cleared out and ships would be able to sail into the basin next to the customs house again. This would all require some money, and an application was made to the provincial government, while funds were raised locally to get the work started. After intense lobbying by Lukang's leadership, the vague assent of the provincial government was obtained along with a token grant, most of which seems to have gone to set up a Lukang office of the Keelung Harbor Bureau. There was no machinery for dredging or earth moving, so gangs of men were hired to do the work by hand. Most of the funds were raised locally or from well-off emigrants.

It was estimated that the work would take several years, and not very much had been accomplished when the communist armies occupied Fukien and all traffic across the Taiwan Straits ceased. This rather undercut the argument for reopening Lukang's harbor. But the city's leaders were committed to the project, and a more modest plan for developing the creekmouth as a fishing harbor was announced. This was then made part of a master plan for developing the whole poverty-stricken coast of Changhua with roads, land reclamation, and a greatly enlarged fishing industry. This plan had the support of the Changhua county government and Lukang was able to get some money from the county administration for work on the harbor, but much more was necessary. The provincial government chose to spend its limited funds on restoring the railroad and the ports of Keelung and Kaohsiung, all of which had been heavily damaged by U.S. air attacks in 1945. It regarded those tasks as of more importance to Taiwan as a whole than the re-creation of Lukang's vanished harbor.

As the gangs of men with shovels, baskets, and carrying poles toiled away, it became more obvious that the project would require a great deal of money. A new obstacle arose in the form of the Nationalist army, which declared the entire coast a military zone, prohibited it to all but the villagers who actually lived there, and discouraged the development of the fishing industry on the west coast.[35] Nevertheless, the local leadership attempted to carry on with the project. A journalist who visited Lukang in 1953 reported the county government's plan for developing the coast and said of Lukang that; "The harbor reconstruction work is now going on with vigor and will be completed next year. It is said that the Japanese government planned to build up Taichung and its port (Wu-ch'e) to replace Lukang because of Lukang's strong spirit of Chinese nationalism. The people here all hope that Lukang will be able to recover the prosperity of those years before the Japanese. There is a fine sugar refinery nearby (in the town of Chihu) and Lukang is one of the closest points to Fukien. If only the fishing harbor is completed, then Lukang's future is unlimited. . . . We went out to look at the first stage of the harbor reconstruction, but unfortunately the coast defense troops would not allow us to approach the shore, so the only thing we could do was to go to the top of a nearby sand hill and look toward the north. There were a lot of fishing boats and fishermen to be seen."[36] Assertions of communal solidarity notwithstanding, the next year (1954) the project was abandoned with nothing to show for the money and the six or seven years of work. It ended in a cloud of rumors, scandals, and accusations of corruption leveled against the men who had been in charge of the project.

Lukang's prosperity had since the 1780s been associated with the state and with official categories, statuses, projects, and concessions. Its local elite took an omnicompetent if distant state for granted, and seem to have assumed that the way to collective or community (rather than private) prosperity was through state-granted categories and concessions and the decisions of officials. Although the view of politics as the shifting balance of power between local and central forces that is presented in this chapter reflects the historical sources (largely compilations of official documents) used to construct it, it also reflects the realities of community life in a centralized bureaucratic state, even one so imperfectly centralized and bureaucratized as Ch'ing China. Although when seen from a great distance Lukang's 1946–1954 harbor reconstruction project has overtones of a cargo cult, or of one of the failed mainland projects of the Great Leap Forward, it is evidence of the local leadership's awareness of the need for both local initiative and central government action.

In the harbor project the local leadership had raised funds and used its political influence with higher levels of administration in an attempt to revive a past that most of them could remember only dimly if at all. It failed utterly. On the one hand it demonstrated an impressive ability to rally support and raise funds, and showed that fifty years of Japanese occupation had not destroyed the spirit of local initiative. The harbor project was the sort of thing that the Chinese gentry had been doing for centuries. On the other hand, the spectacle of gangs of people trying to use shovels and muscle power to reverse the geological processes of sedimentation in a Canute-like fashion has an almost proverbial quality. One can argue that one reason for the failure was precisely because the project was so local, parochial, and so narrowly focused on trying to revive the glorious past in a literal (and littoral) manner. The men who made the decisions probably didn't include any civil engineers or economic geographers, and their attempt to resuscitate Lukang's port ignored the economic changes that had taken place since 1895. Those changes were the product of forces that had been evident as far back as the time of Liu Ming-ch'uan in the 1880s. By the 1950s the prospects of reviving the cross-straits junk trade were subminimal, and to actually construct a harbor at Lukang that could be used by modern seagoing ships would have required far more money than could have been raised in Lukang itself. The decision to do so would have been one involving the economy of the entire island of Taiwan.

In 1940 the Japanese authorities had announced plans to develop Wu-ch'e, 27 kilometers north of Lukang and convenient both to the main rail line and the city of Taichung, as a major deepwater port, but because of the war nothing came of this. In the late 1960s the provincial government finally provided money to construct a fishing harbor, but, on the advice of professional planners and engineers, it was built at Wang Kung, 15 kilometers south of Lukang. In 1969 the central government decided to open a new international port to handle anticipated foreign trade and relieve the congestion at Keelung and Kaohsiung. It retained a team of harbor development specialists from Japan, and finally decided to develop the port at Wu-ch'e. (It was called Taichung Kang—Taichung Harbor) The funds for construction would come from the World Bank and the port development would be coordinated with improvements to the road and rail systems and with establishment of an export processing zone. Lukang's leaders dominated their own town, had influence with the Changhua county government, and some connections to individuals in the provincial administration, but they were in no position to influence the central government's cabinet or to deal with the World Bank, which is the sort of thing that would have had to be done to establish a seaport at Lukang.

School Building

When the men of the 1940s and 1950s looked back at Lukang's past, they saw the city as a center of learning as well as a seaport, and attempts to improve education through local initiative and effort were rather more successful than the harbor project. By the 1920s the Japanese had established primary schools throughout the countryside, but in Lukang more children, and especially more girls, attended school, and literacy rates were higher than in the countryside, although no higher than those of Changhua City and the other towns of the region. After the end of the Second World War, local leaders decided that Lukang should have a middle school of its own so that its children who graduated from the city's three primary (six year) schools would be better prepared for success in the world. The idea proved popular and the middle school committee won general support. As there was no money for a middle school to be had from the county government, funds were raised locally. Representatives of the committee were sent to Taipei and Kaohsiung to solicit money from emigrant Lukang men, one of whom, the owner of a canning factory, went so far as to endow a scholarship fund to help graduates of the new middle school to attend college. The school received 5 *chia* of rice land belonging to the large Lung Shan temple, 1 *chia* from the Ch'eng Huang temple, and the proceeds of the sale of 15.6 *chia* belonging to the government of Lukang *chen* (township). The school opened in 1946 with three classrooms and expanded over the next few years as some money became available from the county and provincial governments. By 1950 it had 500 pupils, two-thirds of them male, and two of the twelve classes were senior middle school students. By the mid–1950s it had become a county-funded, six-year middle school. During that decade it was chosen as one of a group of "model community middle schools" and received a considerable amount of United States aid money, which went for vocational and agricultural training, an up-to-date home economics program for girls, and an American-style extension program aimed at improving rural life. By 1968 the middle school had about 2,000 students, fine airy buildings, and an impressive collection of equipment and "teaching aids" ranging from power tools to sewing machines to life-sized plaster torsos to teach human anatomy.

Unfortunately, Lukang middle school never became quite what its founders had in mind, for, as mentioned in chapter 3, with only 3 percent of its graduates passing the all-important college entrance examination and going on to higher education, it is very much a second or third choice school. All primary and secondary school students wear uniforms with badges that proclaim their school and year, and there are stories in Lukang of boys from Changhua County Middle School, the best in the county, who never wear anything but their school uniform, while those attending Lukang Middle School try to change out of their school uniform as soon as they get home, for they are ashamed to be seen wearing a uniform that brands them as failures. Once again the attempt to revive the imagined past failed, and the forces of local initiative had to give way to those of the islandwide political and economic system.

The Landlords Depart

The Japanese colonial authorities generally supported the position of Taiwan's rural landlords, upholding their property rights as long as they cooperated with the government. The Nationalist government however, which owed nothing to the Taiwanese local elite and may even have feared it as a source of anti-Kuomintang leadership, put through a land reform scheme that abolished the landlord class. During the 1950s Lukang's landlords, as a class, disappeared, to be replaced by a new dominant class of petty industrialists. In 1950, 6 percent of the households in Lukang *chen*, which includes a large (perhaps 50 percent in 1950) rural population, were classified as landlords, and 4.9 percent as semi-landlords. The average for all Changhua county was 2.89 percent landlord households, and the entirely rural township (*hsiang*) of Fu Hsing just south of Lukang, whose villages seem much like those to the north of Lukang, had only .58 percent of its households classified as landlords and .48 percent as semi-landlords.[37]

In the city of Lukang proper then, probably at least 10 percent and perhaps 15 percent of the households were those of landlords.

When the central government carried out its land reform in 1953–54 the landlords lost title to all but a small amount of their lands, being recompensed with shares in government enterprises and with long-term bonds, payable in rice or sweet potatoes as a hedge against inflation. While the land reform did not in fact operate as smoothly or equitably as the government today claims, it did very effectively eliminate the landlord class and did contribute to the prosperity of the farmers. The landlord class fragmented, with some former landlords opening shops or small factories, others going into teaching or public administration that offered relatively high prestige and low pay, and others slipping down into what can loosely be called the lower middle class. Some of those who went into commerce or small-scale industry failed; others became rich. Lukang's parochial landholding elite was the successor to a mercantile elite that had held land primarily for security and as diversification of their estates. With the land reform program that elite was finally defeated and destroyed by the centralized, rational bureaucracy it had coexisted with and resisted for so many years.

With their land gone, many of Lukang's old elite families moved away to Taipei, leaving the city to those of their fellows who had decided to stay on in administrative posts or to join the rising class of potty industrialists. In the 1960s Lukang's elite became more and more like those of other Taiwanese towns and small cities, and political activities in Lukang changed from romantic attempts to revive an idealized past to more pragmatic efforts to win concessions from the bureaucratic organizations that were reluctantly acknowledged to have the final say about what happened to Lukang. Office holders took credit for using their personal influence with the county government to get roads paved, or win a larger grant for the middle school, or persuade the provincial government to locate the experimental eel-culture station on part of the old salt fields. Local political figures also acted as helpers and facilitators in local citizen's increasingly common contacts with the state. In this way politics at Lukang came more and more to resemble local politics in most of rural and small town Taiwan.

By the 1960s the city was far more prosperous than it had been in the early 1950s, but this owed nothing to local political action. It was the result of the general growth of Taiwan's economy. That growth reflected such factors as the central government's macroeconomic policies, the expansion of world trade, and the entrepreneurial strain in Chinese economic culture. In Lukang economic growth took the form of a substantial increase in the number of small-scale factories or handicraft enterprises that sold to island-wide or international markets. Although no longer the economic hub of the region, Lukang in the late 1960s was by no means a depressed or exceptionally poor settlement. Nobody was about to get rich there, but a large number of people were making comfortable livings.

The Imagined Past

Looking back, much of the political activity of Lukang's elite in the 1945–1955 period can be seen as misguided, overambitious, and ultimately wasteful. The program to restore the legendary past couldn't possibly have succeeded since in the last analysis it represented nothing less than an attempt to abolish the past sixty or seventy years' history. At this remove it is impossible to tell if the men responsible for it actually believed it possible to bring back the glorious past, did not believe it but considered it a useful device for mobilizing support and serving the community, or did not believe it but were cynically using it for their own benefit. It may also indicate that the leaders of the time, who were those men who had chosen not to depart for Taipei or Kaohsiung, were simply not well educated enough, either in economic history or civil engineering, to realize that their project could not possibly succeed. What they were skilled at, if they were anything like their current successors, was mobilizing support, persuading people, and managing a fairly large project, all of which were traditional skills of Chinese local elites. The technical feasibility of the scheme was not their department, but in the Lukang of the immediate postwar years it wasn't anyone else's department either and it does not appear to have occurred to them to consult anyone more expert than they.

In any case, their success at raising funds from a shrewd and financially sophisticated Chinese business and landlord class, in the midst of a confused period of inflation, political turmoil and postwar economic prostration, testifies to the strength of attachment to Lukang and of the picture of a golden age that might be recovered. To me, this indicates something of the significance of ideas and of local culture and demonstrates some of the limits of the external, historical, and economic perspective that looks at

Lukang as an object and as a component of larger regional systems, and which, up to this point, I have used to look at the city.

What I see when I look at Lukang over the past 275 years is the overwhelming priority and causal weight of large-scale economic and political systems and of long-term historical movements. Lukang would never have prospered or even existed were it not for the combination of a whole host of factors, ranging from southern Fukien's demand for rice to the cost of land transport in Taiwan, which I have tried to outline in the past two chapters. The other side of Lukang's prosperity and glory was a vulnerability and a dependence on a kaleidoscopic array of factors, systems, and random events. The trading network that, in an ultimate sense, created Lukang was inherently much more mutable and capable of transformation than the rice and sweet potato fields that support a single village. In a very real sense the houses of the great Lukang merchants were built on the sands.

As a detached, neutral, outside observer, I look at Lukang and see contingency, mutability, and complex concatenations of causality. Except for Taoist philosophers though, this is not a very common or comfortable way for people to see their communities and their lives, and it is not the way the people of Lukang prefer to see it. The anthropological literature is full of accounts of villages in change; Lukang presents itself as a city in stasis. It is not really in stasis any more than those villages are changed utterly, but to understand its present social organization and the way its people talk about their community it is necessary to have some idea of the internal structure of the city in the past. Since we have very few accounts of the social structure of a traditional Chinese city the topic is also worth attention for its own sake.

Notes

1. See John R. Watt, *The District Magistrate in Late Imperial China* (New York: Columbia University Press, 1972); also, Watt, "The Yamen and Urban Administration," in G. W. Skinner, 1977, pp. 353–390.

2. On Ch'ing policy on trade and emigration, see Chen Ta, *Chinese Migrations* (Washington: Bulletin of the U.S. Bureau of Labor Statistics, no. 340, Miscellaneous Series, 1923); and G. W. Skinner, *Chinese Society in Thailand: An Analytical History* (Ithaca: Cornell University Press, 1957). On early migration to Tai-

wan, see James W. Davidson (1903), *The Island of Formosa* (Reprint, Taipei: World Book Co., 1964); and Harry J. Lamley, *The Taiwan Literati and Early Japanese Rule*. Unpublished Ph.D. dissertation, University of Washington, 1965.

3. The best sources in English on the early history of Taiwan are Davidson, 1903; Lamley, 1965; and J. R. Shepherd's magisterial *Statecraft and Political Economy on the Taiwan Frontier, 1600–1800* (Stanford: Stanford University Press, 1993).

4. *Cho Lo Hsien Chih* (1718) (Reprint, Taipei: Bank of Taiwan, 1962), chapter 7, p. 122.

5. *Changhua Hsien Chih* (hereafter CHHC), vol. 1, pp. 67–68; *Taiwan T'ung Chih* (1893) (Reprint, Taipei: Bank of Taiwan, 1962), vol. 3, p. 580.

6. Skinner, 1977, p. 276.

7. Lamley, "The Formation of Cities: Initiative and Motivation in Building Three Walled Cities in Taiwan, " in G. W. Skinner, 1977, p. 172.

8. CHHC, vol. 1, pp. 67–68.

9. Wu Shu, "Tao-kuang Nien Chien-t'ou Tu Yi P'an Li" [A Case of an Illegal Crossing in the Tao-kuang Period], *Taiwan Feng Wu* [The Taiwan Folkways] 18, 1 (1968).

10. The best English-language accounts of the rebellion of Lin Shun-wen are to be found in Davidson (1903); and in the biographies of Ch'ai Ta-chi and Fu K'ang-an in Arthur Hummel, *Eminent Chinese of the Ch'ing Dynasty* (Washington: Library of Congress, 1943), pp. 23, 253.

11. CHHC, vol. 3, p. 406.

12. On the Lukang garrison, see CHHC, vol. 1, pp. 67–68, and *Taiwan T'ung Chih*, vol. 3, p. 580.

13. See Davidson, 1903, pp. 81–82; CHHC, vol. 3, pp. 377–378; *Taiwan T'ung Chih*, vol. 3, p. 580.

14. Davidson, 1903, pp. 97–98; Wu Te-kung, *Tai Shih Liang An Chi Lueh* [A Record of the Two Cases (of Rebellion) of Tai (Wan-sheng) and Shih (Chiu-tuan)] (Taipei: Bank of Taiwan, nd., Taiwan Provincial Historical Commission Research Report No. 47).

15. There is also a Ch'eng Huang Miao in Ta-tao-ch'eng, the commercial settlement along the Tamsui River that is now the Yenping District of Taipei, which never had a wall or a resident magistrate either, so that Lukang was not unique.

16. Lamley, 1977.

17. CHHC, vol. 3, p. 418.

18. Skinner, 1977, pp. 341–344.

19. Lamley, 1977, p. 201.

20. Skinner, 1977, p. 544.

21. This point was made by Myron Cohen in his oral comments at a conference on the anthropology of Taiwan, sponsored by the subcommittee on Research on Chinese Society of the Joint Committee on Contemporary China of the American Council of Learned Societies and the Social Science Research Council and held at Wentworth, N.H., in August 1976.

22. The petition is included in *Taiwan T'ung Shih*, vol. 1, p. 107.

23. Ibid. vol. 1, pp. 146–148.

24. *Taiwan Tung-Chih*, vol. 1, pp. 146–148.

25. Speidel, 1967, pp. 231–236.

26. Wu Te-kung, nd., p. 107; Speidel, 1967, pp. 232–233.

27. *Taiwan T'ung Chih*, vol. 4, pp. 885–886.

28. Wu Te-kung. nd, p. 107; Speidel. 1967, pp. 232–233.

29. Lamley, 1965, p. 251.

30. Lamley, 1965, pp. 188–189. See also Davidson, 1903, chapter 21, "The Japanese Occupation of Mid-Formosa," pp. 314–344.

31. See Lin Heng-tao and Feng Tso-min, *Taiwan Li-shih Pai Chiang* [One Hundred Lectures on Taiwan's History] (Taipei: Ching-wen, 1966), chapter 14, "The Recovery of Yunlin and Lukang", p. 189.

32. Chen Cheng-chih, "The Police and Hoko System in Taiwan under Japanese Administration," in *Papers on Japan*, vol. 4 (Cambridge: Harvard University Press, 1967), pp. 147–176.

33. Lamley, 1964, p. 342.

34. Chen Cheng-hsiang, *Taiwan: An Economic and Social Geography* (Taipei: Fu-Min Institute of Economic Development, Publication No. 96, 1963), p. 456.

35. For brief accounts of west coast fishing communities and the army in the 1950s, see Norma Diamond, *K'un-Shen: A Taiwanese Fishing Village* (New York: Holt, Rhinehart and Winston, 1969); and Vern Sneider, *A Pail of Oysters* (New York: G. P. Putnam's and Sons, 1953).

36. Teng Hsueh-ping, *Taiwan Neng Tsun Fang-wen.* [A Visit to Taiwan's Agricultural Villages] (Taipei, 1954), pp. 32–33.

37. Changhua Hsien Cheng-fu [Changhua County Government], *Changhua Hsien T'ung-chi Nien-chien* [Changhua County Statistical Abstract] (Changhua City, 1951).

Chapter 6

Social Structure in Old Lukang

By combining the Ch'ing local gazetteers and histories, contemporary memoirs and notes on folklore, old men's tales of the past, and the projections of some contemporary patterns into the past, it is possible to get some idea of Lukang's social structure in the now legendary days before the Japanese. With a past made simple by the loss of detail, an account of corporate groups and formal rituals can be put together, but there is no information available on families, kinship, business relations, personal networks, factions, or other social institutions or practices. Social structure here refers to the major, enduring corporate groups and to the relations between them. My account will necessarily be rather spare and skeletal, and will probably make nineteenth-century Lukang appear rather more orderly and neatly patterned than it in fact was, but there is no way to avoid this.

Subethnic or Speech Groups

The date of the earliest settlement at Lukang is unknown. It is quite possible that the first Chinese to use the harbor were fishermen or pirates who stayed for a season or so, but there is no record. The aboriginal inhabitants of the area left no trace save some place names, disguised by Chinese characters, and doubtless some genes. The first Chinese settlers, mostly Hokkien from Ch'uan-chou, arrived on the coast of the Changhua Plain during Koxinga's reign (1661–1683), but the plain was not really settled until the first quarter of the eighteenth century. Local accounts claim that the first settlers at Lukang were from the prefecture of Hsing Hua, which is on the coast of Fukien just north of Ch'uan-chou. I don't know what evidence supports this claim, and I've not seen any reference to Hsing Hua settlers in the gazetteers and histories that I've looked at. Lukang does have a temple called the Hsing Hua Matsu Temple, which oral tradition claims was founded by Hsing Hua people as early as the 1690s. If this is true, then it is the city's oldest temple. Other settlers came from Chang-chou and from Ch'ao-chou prefecture in extreme northeastern Kwangtung Province (the Swatow region). The Ch'ao-chou settlers were probably Hakka, for their temple, which still exists, is dedicated to San Shan Kuo Wang, a deity peculiar to Ch'ao-chou Hakka. The temple contains a stone tablet, dated 1791, bearing a semi-legible inscription of an edict concerning Kwangtung people resident in Taiwan. It assures them that they may return to their native places in Kwangtung without penalty, and says that they may obtain the necessary documents, at a set fee, from the Lukang subprefect.[1] In 1783 the merchants from Chang-chou constructed a temple dedicated to Kuan-Ti and called it the Nan Ching Kuan Ti Temple (Nan Ching is the name of a *hsien* in Chang-chou). The settlers from Ch'uan-chou built a temple dedicated to the goddess Matsu at some unrecorded date in the early eighteenth century. Today it is claimed that the image in this temple was presented to the Ch'uan-chou settlers by Admiral Shih Lang, the Ch'uan-chou native who conquered Taiwan for the Ch'ing dynasty in 1683. That is highly unlikely.

The original settlers came from different areas of the mainland and, like all migrants to Taiwan, organized themselves into groups defined by common place of origin. Each group had a patron deity and founded temples to that deity, organizing itself as a group united by (and defined by) common worship. By the beginning of the nineteenth century Lukang was a solidly Ch'uan-chou city, and the Chang-chou, Hsing Hua, and Hakka people had either left or been assimilated. The armed clashes between subethnic groups would have provided pressure for both flight and assimilation.

One such clash began in Lukang. In the early spring of 1807 the subprefect at Lukang got word that the notorious pirate Tsai Ch'ien, who had attacked Tainan and destroyed the city of Fengshan the previous autumn, was going to attack Lukang in conjunction with local bandits. The subprefect prudently called for the Changhua Militia, who had defeated many bandit groups, to come and help guard the city. These militiamen came from the inland and foothill areas of the district and were Chang-chou men. As they marched into Lukang the citizens greeted them with insults, and the militia finally opened fire with their matchlock "fowling guns," killing several inhabitants of the city. A full scale riot ensued, with the subprefect and the commander of the militia trapped in the yamen while fighting raged in the streets. The outnumbered militiamen finally withdrew, being ambushed by Ch'uan-chou villagers as they went. The incident started a bitter struggle that continued until the end of the summer. By that time Lukang was crowded with refugee Ch'uan-chou people whose villages had been burned, and the public granaries had to be opened to feed them.[2]

The temples of the non-Ch'uan-chou people still exist, but today they function as neighborhood temples and the people who live around them are either ignorant of or quite uninterested in the original ethnicity of their neighborhood gods.[*] In the nineteenth century, groups defined by common place of origin played no part in Lukang's social structure. Just about everyone claimed to be a Ch'uan-chou Hokkien from the three coastal counties of the prefecture, the *San Yi*, and spoke with the same distinctive accent. Everyone was *t'ung-hsiang*. But within the boundaries of common place of origin and common residence in Lukang, the population was divided into many sorts of groups that both opposed and overlapped with each other. There were surname groups, neighborhood groups, and occupational groups. Within the city the groups cut across each other, and each individual belonged to several groups, each defined in a different way. Both the limited opposition of groups and the ultimate solidarity of the city itself were expressed in periodic public rituals.

Surname Groups

The settlers of Lukang came from an area of China well known for its large corporate lineages, and descent groups were one significant element of the city's social structure. As was often the case in Taiwan, the descent groups were not replicas of nor segments of the lineages of Fukien. The groups in Lukang held no common property, had no ancestral halls, lacked comprehensive written genealogies, and were less corporate—however that term be defined—than the classic southeastern Chinese lineages. Today

---

[*]Dr. Hsu Chia-ming, a Taiwanese anthropologist with the Academia Sinica in the late 1970s who has done field work with the assimilated Hakka of Changhua, informs me that several families living around Lukang's San Shan Kuo Wang Temple are indeed Hakka, although they speak Hokkien with the characteristic Lukang accent and keep rather quiet about their Hakka origins.

they are usually referred to simply as *hsing* "surnames" and they are probably best labelled as clans or surname groups. The three major surnames -Shih, Huang and Hsu- account for up to half the city's present population. Other names, such as Lin, Ch'en, Wu, Li and Ts'ai are quite common. In speaking of the past, it is only the three big surnames to which some degree of solidarity and corporate character is ascribed. In the past they fought with each other, and this is the activity for which they are best remembered. A proverb current in Lukang says: "Shihs, Huangs, Hsus; their women all are shrews." (In Hokkien, *Se, Ng, Kho; chia: ca-bo*) This is explained as meaning that women from the three big surnames made bad, quarrelsome wives, for they were proud and unwilling to accept the authority of their husband's families. The internal organization of each surname group differed, and it is best to briefly describe each.

The largest surname group, the Shih, most nearly resemble the classic southeastern Chinese lineage. All Shihs claim to be descended from a common ancestor thirty-nine generations back. The founding ancestor, one Shih Lin-pu, was an official during the reign of the T'ang dynasty's Chao Tsung emperor (A.D. 889–905), and lived in Nan Kuang Chou in the province of Honan. Around the end of the T'ang dynasty (A.D. 618–907) and the beginning of the Sung (A.D. 960–1280), some of the Shihs left Honan and settled in Ch'uan-chou in Fukien. Today, Shihs in Lukang know which generation they belong to, and the generation is written along with the surname on the lantern that stands before the domestic altar table in Taiwanese homes, as well as on the special lanterns carried in funeral processions. No complete genealogy of the Lukang Shihs exists, although a few families possess handwritten genealogies listing only their immediate ancestors.

The Shihs are divided into two main segments, each of which has a name. They are the Ch'ien-chiang and the Hsin Hai, also known as the Ch'ien Kang and the Hou Kang, front and rear harbors. In Lukang today these two segments are said to stem from two brothers who lived "three hundred years ago in Fukien." The two main segments in turn are divided into branches (*fang*), known as the senior, second, and third branches. These are in turn divided into lower level segments called, in Hokkien, *thiau*. This word, written with a character whose Mandarin reading is *chu*, has the primary meaning of pillar or post, forming part of the architectural metaphor for kinship groups, with lineages being halls or houses (*t'ang*), segments being rooms (*fang*), and smaller segments being posts (which defined the modular units that made up most traditional Chinese construction.) In central Taiwan at least, the term often used for "lineage" *tsu* (in Hokkien, *cok*) is assumed to refer to large groups of many hundred members, while *thiau* is the usual term for the sorts of small, shallow descent groups that can be found in villages. Neither term implies very great solidarity or any degree of corporate structure. The Lukang Shihs are divided into many (between twenty and thirty) named *thiau*. The names of the *thiau* are those of streets and neighborhoods, and all members of the same *thiau* are said to live in the same area. Thus one speaks of the Ch'ien-chiang Shihs of the Axe Street Thiau, or the Hsin Hai Shihs of the "Behind the Temple" Thiau.

In 1968 members of a *thiau* could not trace descent from a common ancestor nor did members of the same *thiau* employ generation names. A few people, once I had raised the question, said that it should be possible for all members to trace descent from a common ancestor; others were not sure. What is probably most significant is that in 1967 and 1968 no one but me seemed at all interested. Residence and locality seemed far more important than descent, and people generally agreed that were a Shih from another part of Lukang to move into their neighborhood he could, once he had been there a while and gotten to know people, be considered a member of the *thiau*. A *thiau* then is a named group, residing in a given part of Lukang, all of whose members share the same surname. The primary criterion for membership is residence, little stress being put on descent. A *thiau* is more of a locality-focused than an ancestor-focused group, though an individual is thought to belong to only one, which in almost every case is the same one that his father belonged to. A *thiau* has no formal internal structure and all adult males are equals. It has no head or leader. It was claimed that *thiau* had never held any common property, any estate, and that neither the branches, the two major segments, or the Shihs as a whole had ever held any common property either. Membership in a *thiau* conferred no particular rights or duties on individuals, although it was said that members of the *thiau* all knew each other and would therefore "help" and "support" each other.

The Lukang Shihs had no ancestor halls, but the Ch'ien-chiang segment had a temple, dedicated to the popular Taiwanese deity Shang Ti Kung (or, to use his proper title, *Ch'uan-chou Hsuan T'ien Shang Ti*, the Ch'uan-chou God of Profound Heaven), who served as patron god for the segment. The temple has existed at least since 1851, the date of the wooden eulogy board hung over the altar, and was refurbished in 1964. The temple looks and functions like any other small temple in Lukang, save that it serves only the Ch'ien-chiang Shih. In the not-so-distant past the management of the temple's annual festival rotated each year among the *thiau* of the Ch'ien-chiang segment. Other *thiau* participated in the procession, providing a dragon team or a drill squad. The Hsin Hai segment had in the past no temple, but did have a ritual connection to the great Matsu temple of Lukang's Ch'uan-chou people. Admiral Shih Lang, who conquered Taiwan for the Ch'ing dynasty in 1683, was a Hsin Hai Shih from Ch'uan-chou (of the sixteenth generation). It is said today that when the emperor asked him how many troops he would need, he replied: "I have 7,000 Hsin Hai and 3,000 Ch'ien-chiang, and that's all [I need]." Not every lineage can claim to have conquered Taiwan.[3] The image of Matsu in the temple is said to have been brought directly from Fukien's Mei-chou Island, the original, root, temple of the cult, by Admiral Shih Lang, who left it off with his lineage-mates at Lukang before he returned to Peking to report to the emperor on his conquest. His easy crossing of the Straits and subsequent conquest are also attributed to Matsu's supernatural intervention. Not every patron god can claim to have conquered Taiwan. (These claims, it should be clear, have no historical foundation, and it is not at all clear that a settlement even existed at Lukang in 1683.) Some people claimed that the land the Lukang Matsu Temple stands on was donated by Shih Lang's eldest brother's son. As a matter of fact, the land was donated by a Shih, but he was a son of the wealthy Ch'uan-chou investor who built the great Pa-Pao irrigation system in 1709–1719, and, as far as I know, was not a member of the Shih lineage represented in Lukang.[4]

In the past, the Lukang Shihs appear to have had no common organization and the relation between the two segments was one of rivalry and some degree of hostility. Each claims to be the senior segment. In 1968 a building called the "Lukang Shih Surname Association" was constructed in the Hsin Hai neighborhood of *Kieng Au*, "Behind the (Matsu) Temple." A small booklet printed up for the occasion described the association as the Lin Pu Hall Changhua County Shih Surname Association, and declared the purpose of the association to be honoring the ancestors and strengthening the sentiments of common kinship. The association made no reference to internal segmentation, and proposed to worship or revere the ancestors as an undifferentiated body. The building, a one room structure of reinforced concrete, is arranged like a temple, with an altar table holding a glass case containing three small statues. These are said to represent Lin Pu, the founder of the lineage, and the founders of the Hsin Hai and Ch'ien-chiang segments. In 1968 the association was moribund and the hall always deserted. According to an elderly man who was associated with the management of the Ch'ien-chiang temple, the surname association began as an attempt by some men in the Hsin Hai segment to form an association and build a hall that would serve the Hsin Hai segment in the same way as the Shang Ti Kung Temple served the Ch'ien-chiang segment. But the Hsin Hai people were unable to raise enough money and so decided to form an association embracing all the Shihs, and appealed for contributions from the Ch'ien-chiang segment. Since it was "to honor the ancestors" the latter contributed, but when the Hsin Hai men insisted on running the association themselves and allowed the Ch'ien-chiang group no say, they refused to participate. The surname association was really just a front for the Hsin Hai group. I have no idea how far this story corresponds to what happened, and I am sure the Hsin Hai people would explain it differently, but it demonstrates something of the quality of the relationship between the segments.

In fact, the distinction between Ch'ien-chiang and Hsin Hai and their mutual rivalry goes back to Ch'uan-chou and was brought to Lukang by the early settlers. In Lukang, Shihs said there were other branches of the lineage in Tainan and in the Philippines. I heard of a man who possessed a great genealogy of the Shihs and finally arranged an introduction to him. His genealogy turned out to have been printed in Manila and to be devoted to the activities and glories of the Shihs in the Philippines. He had obtained it from a group of visiting Philippine-Chinese businessmen, some of whom were Shihs. It happens, happily, that the Shihs of Ch'uan-chou are discussed in Amyot's study of the Chinese community of Manila.

He says that Chinchiang was another name for the city of Ch'uan-chou, and that Yak'ou *hsiang* (a subcounty administrative unit) in Chinchiang *hsien* was known as a Shih *hsiang*. It had 40,000 people and over 30 villages. The Shih lineage of Yak'ou was divided into two branches along a small river that crosses the *hsiang*. The larger of the two branches, with 30,000 members, had its ancestral hall in the village of Houchiang, and was distributed along the upper reaches of the river. Downstream the other branch, with 10,000 members, had its ancestral hall in Ch'ien-kang. As was common, the two major segments of the lineage were on bad terms, and brought their mutual hostility with them to the Philippines, where each maintained a distinct organization in Manila [5] An attempt to unify the two Shih associations only led to

the creation of a third association, the claims of which (to represent all the Yak'ou Shihs) were rejected by most of its putative
members. Amyot's list of Chinese clan associations in Manila in
1959 includes the three Shih groups, which are the Lin Pu, the
Hsin-chiang or Yak'ou, and the Ch'ien-chiang. He notes that the
last two were registered with the Chinese embassy as same-place
associations rather than as clan associations.

The distinction between Lukang's Ch'ien-chiang and Hsin Hai
segments thus is based on a split in a truly immense lineage in
Ch'uan-chou. Ch'ien-chiang and Hsin Hai turn out to be the names
of the villages (or market towns) that are the centers of these
groups. Groups of this size are as much territorial or local groups
as descent groups. The distinction between the two groups, or perhaps two standard marketing systems, was preserved in Lukang,
but interpreted in forthrightly genealogical terms as representing
a split between younger and older sons in a rather simpler lineage
"three hundred years ago." It is also possible to understand why
there is no complete genealogy of the Lukang Shihs or of the two
main segments, since the settlers at Lukang represented only individuals or small groups of men from so large a lineage that they
might well have to go back thirty-nine generations to find a common ancestor. In early Lukang the distinction between the Ch'ien-
chiang and Hsin Hai Shihs served as an exact equivalent to the
usual distinctions among migrants to Taiwan based on place of
origin, and indeed it was a distinction of place of origin.

The lower level groups, the *thiau*, were organized within the
common framework, but the identification of *thiau* with sub-
branches (*fang*) was, in 1968 at least, quite problematic, and the
thiau were defined by place of residence in Lukang. In the past in
Lukang the *thiau* seem to have been relatively solidary groups and
to have been units of the social structure to a far greater extent than
the two big segments or the sub-branches. The *thiau* were residential groups, and participated as groups in ritual. They also appear
to have been the basic units in the fighting between surname
groups that characterized Lukang in the past. That is, the most
common sort of fighting did not involve all the Shihs against all
the Huangs, but rather one specific Shih *thiau* against an equivalent group of Huangs. The topic of fighting between surname
groups leads to a discussion of what they fought for, which in turn
gives one some idea of the sorts of rights and property that *thiau*
as corporate groups could hold or have rights to, but this topic is
best deferred until after a brief discussion of the other two big surnames, the Huangs and the Hsus.

The second most common surname is Huang. The Huangs recognize no common ancestor. They are divided into five groups, each of which is said to have come from a different place in Fukien. Each occupies its own neighborhood in Lukang, and is usually known by the name of that neighborhood, so that one speaks of the Ch'uan-chou Street Huangs or the Huangs of the Market Garden neighborhood. Such groups can be called *thiau*, but their members cannot trace descent from a common ancestor. It is assumed that most of the members are in fact the descendants of the original settlers, but it is recognized that anyone who stemmed from the same place in Fukien could be accepted as a member of the group. One elderly man of the Market Garden Huangs said that once a young man called Huang came to Lukang from Chiayi. He had no kinsmen in Chiayi and knew only that his old father, who had died a few years before, had been a Pi Su man, though he didn't really know what that meant. Someone told him there were a lot of Huangs in Lukang so he came to look for kinsmen or to find out who his ancestors were. The Market Garden Huangs come from a place called Lun Feng in Ch'uan-chou while another group comes from Pi Su. The young man said his father was a Pi Su man but was not believed until he mentioned his father's personal name, which was recognized as a generation name used by a or the Huang lineage of Pi Su, and the young man was then recognized as a kinsman by the Lukang Pi Su Huangs. He did not settle in Lukang, but presumably derived some satisfaction from learning about his ancestry and being recognized as a kinsman.

Although they came from different places and claimed no common ancestor, the Lukang Huangs did, on occasion, act as a unit. In 1968 the Huangs were still collaborating in a ritual cycle. Every thirteen years, one of the five Huang groups unites to celebrate the Festival of Hungry Ghosts, the fifteenth of the seventh lunar month. The schedule follows the twelve-year cycle of animal names for years, so that in the Year of the Monkey the Huangs of Market Garden put on a festival, while in the Year of the Snake it is the Huangs of Ch'uan-chou Street. The ritual cycle is restricted to the Huangs, and since there are only five Huang groups, in seven out every twelve years there is no celebration.

The third most common surname is Hsu, and the Hsus are most easily described, since they are said to have no formal organization whatsoever. They came from different places on the mainland, and none save descendants of the same grandfather consider themselves members of a *thiau*. Most of the Hsus live in one neighborhood of Lukang, a place called, in Hokkien, *Gu-thau*.

(Ox Market) While the various subgroups of Huangs and Shihs live scattered throughout the city, most of the Hsus are said to be concentrated in *Gu-thau*, which is, roughly, the northeastern section of the city. It must be understood that the association between surnames and neighborhood is not absolute, and that in a neighborhood identified with a given surname often no more than half the residents will bear that surname. There are Chens, Lins, Wus, Ts'ais, and Wangs living all over Lukang, sometimes in small clusters of their own. It is quite likely that a family's next-door neighbor will bear a different surname. Only the three big surnames are associated with specific named neighborhoods, where they constitute from 40 percent to perhaps 80 percent of the inhabitants.

Relations Between Surname Groups

In the past in Lukang, as elsewhere in China, surnames were, of course, exogamous, even when common descent was not assumed. The Lukang surname groups therefore took brides from other surname groups and married their daughters out to other surnames. But there is no evidence that Lukang's surname groups ever exchanged women in any systematic fashion, as groups. Marriage and the matrilateral and affinal ties it created was an affair of families, not of surname groups.

The most common thing exchanged between surname groups seems to have been blows. The big surname groups were famous for battling in the streets, and fighting is the attribute of surname groups that is most often recalled today. In 1891 Tang Tsan-kun wrote of Lukang in his book *Tai Yang Chien Wen Lu* [A Record of Things Seen and Heard on Taiwan] that: "There are three big surnames, with some 40,000 to 50,000 adult males in all. Each, because of its great strength, goes so far as to start fights."[6] The fighting between Lukang's major surname groups seems to have resembled that between the lineages of Ch'uan-chou, which is described by Amyot as being about "everything and about nothing . . . The use of a water passage or harbor, field boundaries, or personal insults."[7] In Lukang today the usual explanation for fighting or brawling between surname groups is that they didn't like each other, so they fought, and the more they fought the less they liked each other. Members of the big surname groups are said to have been very touchy and to have gone around with a chip on their shoulder, elbowing members of minor surnames out of their way and looking for confrontations with those of other major groups. A chance insult could lead to a pitched battle, fought with sticks or rocks. Today old men say that if men of the big surnames jostled in the market, it could easily lead to insults, which would in turn lead to an agreement to meet that afternoon or the next morning at a certain place to fight. "Each would go off and round up the men of his surname, and they would meet to fight." Such groups might range in number from twenty up to a hundred or so, and usually the fight resulted in nothing worse than bruises, lost teeth or an occasional broken bone. There were apparently standard insults for each group, and an elderly man called Huang recalled that "in the old days" one could insult a Hsu in the market by pointing to or referring to a cow's head, since the name of the Hsu neighborhood, *gu-thau*, an abbreviated version of the term for a periodic cattle market, sounds much like the word for cow's head, which in turn sounds like the term for "stupid head."

Some of the flavor of the battles between surname groups can be obtained from a story I heard from an elderly man called Shih. His grandfather was a wealthy merchant who lived in a large house cum warehouse on Axe Street. He was a big man, very strong, and famous for his prowess as a master of the arts of Chinese boxing and fencing. When he married, his bride of course had bound feet. He told her to remove the bindings. When she questioned this most unusual command, he explained: "We're going to fight the Huangs next month, and how can you fight with bound feet?" He taught her to fight, and she turned out to be rather fierce.

In those days the harbor was right behind Axe Street, and everyone who lived there had a small boat that they used for local transportation, like people use bicycles today. One afternoon as Mr. Shih returned, he noticed some strange boats tied up at the quay, boats that did not belong to any family on Axe Street. As he walked to his house he noticed some strange men hanging around the end of the street. Suspecting trouble, he hurried home, stopping only to advise his great-uncle who lived across the street to close up his shop. It was early, about 5 p.m., and the shops were usually open until about 10 p.m., but his great uncle immediately began to close up his shop. When he put the great wooden shutters across the open front of his shop, the owners of the neighboring shops saw this, and they too hurried to close up their shops. It was quiet, and the only sound was that of shutters being put up all the way down Axe Street, one after another.

Mr. Shih went to his own house, where no one was at home but one of his daughters-in-law and some young man of the neighborhood. The daughter-in-law had just brought water for him to wash when there was a tremendous noise at the door. The Hsus were attacking. Mr. Shih had put the horizontal bar across the double doors at the front of the house, but had not bothered with the vertical bolts that secured each door to the lintel and the threshold. The Hsus were hacking at the wooden door with halberds and swords and using a small log as a battering ram. With each blow of the log the doors bulged inward and the horizontal bar was about to break. Mr. Shih, who was very strong, held the doors shut and sent his daughter-in-law off to fetch the cowardly young man, who was about to flee out the back door. She brought him back and together they managed to get the vertical bolts in, but while holding the doors shut both of Mr. Shih's thumbs were crushed. For the rest of his life he was known by the nickname "flat thumbs." People on Axe Street claimed that one could still see the holes in the door made by the Hsus' halberds, but in fact the door was replaced long ago.

The house is still standing, and like most of the old merchant houses on Axe Street it is a substantial two-story house, made of the best Ch'uan-chou brick. There are no windows on the ground floor, and the houses on both sides of the street, which is some three meters wide, form an unbroken line of masonry. Many have a small window on the second floor above the door, which could be used to throw bricks or other objects down on men in the street or at the door. Many people attribute the distinctive architecture of Lukang town houses to the demands of defense, for the city had no wall and each house or street could serve as a fortress. With the front doors closed, it would be difficult for bandits from the countryside or men from another Lukang surname to break into the houses of the merchants.

Battling surname groups seem to have been common in many Taiwanese cities, for in 1867 Pickering found himself in the midst of a fight between the Chens and the Ts'ais in the port of Wu-ch'e, 27 kilometers north of Lukang. He had engaged what he describes as "the head of the clan Ch'oa (in Mandarin, Ts'ai)" as an agent to collect camphor. At that time the Intendant, the highest Ch'ing official on Taiwan, claimed a monopoly on camphor, and Pickering was involved in a dispute over his right to deal in the substance. He says of Wu-ch'e that it:

> was practically populated by the two clans, Tan and Ch'oa (Ch'en and Ts'ai), each of which, according to North Formosan fashion, possessed a strong, loopholed mud tower, into which the warriors could retreat during a clan fight. . . . On arriving we found our warehouse beseiged by

the clan Tan; but, with the help of our seven-shooter rifle and two boat guns, we and our agents, the clan Ch'oa, succeeded in routing the enemy for the moment. . . . When I had been up there a week, the Taotai's troops, composed of militia under the district magistrate of Lok-kang (he means the Lukang subprefect) came in sight. The clan Tan's evaporating courage returned to them, whilst our clan, on the contrary, promptly removed their women and children and furniture in carts, and ran away.[8]

Pickering, his servants, and the agent were beseiged for a week in the Ts'ais' tower by the Ch'ens and by what he describes as the "rabble militia" from Lukang. He eventually sallied out to confront the Lukang subprefect, who was staying at a house in the Ch'en quarter. "We found a guard of some twenty men, armed with spears fifteen feet long, whilst behind them gathered the whole of the clan Tan." Pickering claims to have persuaded the subprefect of his right, under the treaties, to deal in camphor, and the official returned to Lukang with the militia. During the hostilities most of the Ts'ais appear to have been going about their daily business in their quarter of the town, for Pickering reports that they cheered him as he went off to meet the subprefect. He continued to stay in the tower while trying to find a boat to take the camphor to Tainan, but:

> Meantime the retirement of the Lok-kang mandarin impressed the clan Tan with some slight respect for my power. They ceased open hostilities, contenting themselves with pot-shots from the roofs of their houses when we chanced to exhibit our heads above the parapet of the tower and with annoying our leper whenever he visited the market to buy provisions.
>
> They however gradually wearied of this one-sided enmity, until at last we ceased hostilities to the extent of joining in a model yacht or junk race upon a big pond outside our fort, competitors on both sides being armed in case of misunderstandings arising.[9]

From this account one learns that Wu-ch'e, like Lukang, was the home of large surname groups, each living in its own neighborhood, and given to mutual strife. The fighting does not seem to have been so fierce as to seriously disturb the life of the town, nor to have engaged very many of the inhabitants at any single time. Not only did the market remain open and patronized by both Ch'ens and Ts'ais, but Pickering could send his leper servant out to buy food.

In Lukang the battles between the surname groups seem to have resulted in few deaths, and the conflict was limited in many ways. The relations between the major surname groups appear to have been marked by pervasive but low-keyed hostility, and the antagonism was marked by gossip, rude stories, and by occasional brawls. But there never seems to have been any concerted effort to decisively defeat another surname group or to drive it out of town, as the Ch'uan-chou men from San Yi (the three counties on the coast) drove the T'ungan and the Anchi (the two counties of the interior) people from Bangka in the core of the Taipei settlements in the 1860s. Conflict between Lukang's surname groups was circumscribed within what were at least tacitly recognized limits. The parties to any single brawl or fight were the neighborhood surname groups, the *thiau*, rather than the entire body of people named Huang or Hsu. One hears of the Shihs of the neighborhood around the market place fighting with the Huangs from the area around the New Matsu Temple, or the Hsus of *gu-thau* battling with the Huangs of Market Garden, but not of such groups being joined by others of the same surname.

The Annual Rock Fight

On occasion the entire body of Shihs and Huangs did come together to fight, but they did so only once a year, in a very well-defined and bounded situation. This was the famous Lukang rock fight, which is cited today as one of the city's peculiar local customs. Each year in the spring, on a day sometime between the lunar New Year, which usually falls in late January or in February, and the Ch'ing Ming festival, which comes 105 days after the winter solstice, on April 5th, members of all Lukang's surname groups would gather at a field on the northwestern side of the city to fight. According to elderly men who took part in their youth, the surname groups would form up around the edge of the field, facing inward and toward each other. The Shihs, Huangs, and Hsus provided the bulk of the combatants, but members of such smaller surname groups as the Ch'ens, Lins, Wus, and Ts'ais took part as well. The minor surnames could either form a side or team of their own, or they could choose to help one of the larger groups such as the Huangs. There was no fixed order and where a particular group stood does not seem to have made much difference. Some men described the annual fight as a contest between the Shihs and everyone else, others spoke of it as a four-sided match, while others said it began as a circle. The participants began by throwing rocks at each other, and then eventually moved inward and fought with sticks and fists. Most of the participants were young, but anyone who wanted to could take part, for: "If you were too old to throw rocks you could always pick them up and hand them to younger men." Some older men are said to have used sticks like lacrosse rackets to hurl their stones further. I was assured that no one was ever killed in this melee, and that injuries could be healed by using water from ponds in front of certain temples. "Besides, people were tougher then than they are now. If someone got hurt or lost some teeth, he would drop out and wash his injury off, apply a plaster made of tobacco leaves and cow dung, and then go back and fight some more."

The purpose of the fight seems to have been the fighting itself. No one won and there were no losers. The day of the rock fight is described as a festive holiday, very exciting. "It was very *lau-ziat.*" Thousands of people turned out to watch, the spectators standing along the sidelines, often near the fighters of the same surname. Hawkers sold snacks and toys, and a good time seems to have been had by all. The Japanese police tried to stop the annual battles, but the site was simply moved further out into the country, to the other side of the huge cemetery to the north of Lukang.[10] It was still happening, on a reduced scale, in the 1930s, but has not been indulged in since the Second World War.

The most common reply to questions asking why the surnames fought in so formal a fashion once a year is that it was "an old Lukang custom." A few people go beyond this apparently definitive and satisfactory explanation and cite the prevailing hostility between the surname groups, and a few old men explained that: "People in those days were very superstitious (*mi-hsin*) and believed that if blood was not shed during the spring, then there would be bad luck during the rest of the year. The harvest would be bad, business would be depressed, there might be an earthquake or a typhoon, or something of that sort would happen." Such "customs" with their Frazerian explanation were not unique to Lukang, but were known and observed in southern Fukien. A nineteenth-century missionary account of life in T'ung An *hsien*, which included the city of Amoy, reports that:

> Some villages in this *hsien* have a curious custom of going out to the fields on or about the fifteenth of the first moon and then pelting each other with stones, lumps of earth, sticks or whatever comes to hand. One clan, Yeh, residing

at Ling-Hsia Yeh, regularly set out thus to maul each other at the close of a feast in the ancestral hall. The idea seems to be that a certain amount of suffering is fated to fall on the clan or village during the year, and they prefer to take it in the form of broken heads, lest otherwise it may come in the form of fever, cholera or famine. The same custom prevails at Shih Ma, in Changchou.[11]

A Chinese account of the local customs of Hsing Hua Prefecture, published in 1842, includes a note on annual rock fights.

On New Year's Day, villages fight each other with stones, as a custom. The youth come into action, and later also all fathers and elder brothers. At first there are only a dozen people, then several hundreds. Some are wounded and start bleeding, and leave the field. Then they may return with a larger force. The women stand giggling and there is laughter everywhere. One says: this entire year there will be no disasters and diseases.[12]

Annual rock fights, then, seem to have been a southern Fukienese custom, involving either villages or subgroups of a single lineage (which could also be distinct villages). In Lukang, a multi-surname city, the parties to the fight were surname groups who acted out a ritual, though not a mock, battle. The rock fight is, I think, best interpreted as a ritual, because it had no victors, was an annual event, and the combat was restricted by time, place, and intent to do serious or lethal harm to the other participants. Like much ritual, it represented action for its own sake, with no other overt purpose. As a ritual, it may be interpreted as a statement about Lukang's social structure. The vernal brawl brought together all the natives of the city, and no outsiders played any part. It defined the limits of the community, and defined one of the sets of internal segments into which the city was seen to be divided. The surname groups of Lukang, whose members could not trace descent from a common ancestor or claim rights to a common estate, were defined primarily by their opposition to each other, and their internal solidarity and mutual opposition were made clear at the annual battle. Their only common activity was gathering together one day of the year and throwing rocks at each other.

Georg Simmel pointed out a long time ago (1908) that conflict is a form of sociation, and Simmel is quite relevant to an analysis of Lukang's social structure.[13] One could also interpret Lukang's rock fight in the spirit of Durkheim and Mauss as expressing a model of mechanical solidarity. Equivalent groups or segments of a total society are united by exchange of the same commodity. Perhaps because we tend to identify Mauss's term "prestation" with the English "gift," it is difficult to think of a rock flying at someone's head as a prestation. The usual anthropological examples are yams, cattle, or women. It is, however, a sociological truism that exchange is the foundation of social life, and blows and insults may, under some circumstances, be exchanged and create as much social solidarity as yams, as long as their exchange is limited and a balanced payback is maintained. In fact, if the groups involved are not internally undifferentiated and their members interchangeable, as the ideal model of mechanical solidarity assumes, then blows and insults may be more appropriate than prestations that would call attention to such matters as disparities in wealth and so invalidate the assumption of equivalence. Competitive sports, especially those in which a high degree of specialized skill is not necessary, come to mind, and one thinks of the annual battles between classes that seem to have been common in American colleges in the early twentieth-century. For a more baroque instance of a community whose solidarity is expressed through a fairly rough ritual contest, there is the magnificent example of the *Palio* at Siena, which is, to oversimplify, a horse race between jockeys representing highly corporate neighborhoods of an Italian city.[14]

The inhabitants of Lukang were thus participants in an almost sportsmanlike contest, an agon performed in the rather bloody ritual idiom of southern Fukien. Such relations of limited mutual opposition, which may be called agonistic rather than antagonistic, existed between all the recognized sub-groups into which Lukang's population was divided. That between the surname groups was perhaps the most overtly hostile and most crudely expressed. This, I would argue, was a consequence of the very dubious and weak internal solidarity of the surname groups, which had no common property, were residentially dispersed, and were composed of people of different occupation and class. Mechanical solidarity presupposes equivalent groups, but Lukang's surname groups were not like Nuer or Tallensi lineages where every man earns his living in the same way. They were, rather, arbitrary samples of the population of a commercial city with a high degree of division of labor. Their principle of recruitment, patrilineal descent, cut across the occupational and class groupings. Under the circumstances, it is not surprising that the groups so formed had little internal solidarity or that they reinforced that solidarity by exchanging blows with other groups recruited in the same way. It is hard to think of anything else that Lukang's surname groups could have exchanged that would not immediately have brought factors of differential wealth and social status into the picture and made balanced reciprocity impossible.

That the balanced opposition of the surname groups was expressed by tossing stones at each other was an accident of cultural history. The settlers at Lukang brought with them a cultural repertoire that included annual rock fights that were associated in some dimly discerned way with blood and with good and bad luck in the coming year. Settlers in Taiwan did not mechanically reproduce all aspects of the culture and society of southern Fukien. Although perfectly familiar with large internally segmented patrilineages, the settlers do not seem to have attempted to reproduce them in Taiwan. And if they chose to retain such practices as the annual rock fight it was not because of blind adherence to tradition, but because it was an appropriate vehicle for something they wanted to express or found useful to practice. If we focus on the issues of the definition and internal structure of the surname groups and on the social field in which they interacted, on the patterning of their relations, then they could as well have been playing cricket.

Possible Economic Rationality of Clan Fights

Organized fighting between surname groups is, I should reiterate, not part of the current scene at Lukang, and is therefore more difficult to reconstruct and understand than behavior such as ritual exchange and rivalry that offers contemporary examples. From the perspective of the present, it appears that on some occasions groups recruited by common surname may have contended, not for contention's sake, but for rational economic goals. But in these cases the units involved were not the entire surname groups, but either the small *thiau* or groups with a common occupational or class interest which recruited members from within a social field restricted to those of the same surname. I was told that once a *thiau* of Shihs fought with the Huangs of Ch'uan-chou Street over fishing rights and rights to oyster fields along the shore. They first clashed and began brawling at the shore, but then returned to Lukang to round up their fellows and fought again. The Shihs won, but the Huangs retaliated by refusing to let the Shihs use the shortest path to the shore, which passed through Ch'uan-chou Street. Said the Huangs; "If we can't use the sea, then they can't use the land." (The tidal flats offshore seem to have been or to be a no-man's-land with no secure title to any area. On at least two occasions in the winter of 1967–68 the people of two villages, one north of Lukang and one south of the city, engaged in pitched battles on the tidal flats over rights to establish oyster fields.)

I was also told that in the more recent past many of the poorer Shihs worked as fishermen and porters, carrying things through Lukang's narrow lanes on shoulder poles. All the cargo that was shipped through Lukang had to be carried at least a short way by gangs of porters. Many of the poor people who worked in the salt fields were also Shihs from the north end of Lukang. It is claimed today that the porters and salt workers had some sort of organization restricted to Shihs, though it is not clear if there was only one organization or many small ones, or if only Shihs worked at those trades. Nor is it clear in what way the organization corresponded to any genealogically or residentially defined unit. In the salt fields, at least, groups of people, however they were defined or organized, worked as a unit with a recognized head. The group was composed of both strong young men and of women and older men who could not do as much work. The young men did the bulk of the work, with the others doing what they could, it perhaps requiring two of them to carry a load that one man in his prime could lift. The wages were paid to the head of the group, who gave everyone an equal share, no matter how much work was done. "People stuck together and shared like that because of the sentiments of common surname."

Work as a porter or in the salt fields was unskilled labor and could be done by anyone with a strong back, or perhaps by any two less robust people. On the basis of what we know about other Chinese cities, it seems that unskilled labor was often regulated by some sort of organization, either a secret society or perhaps a formal guild, like the Peking Street Porters' Guild. Unskilled labor at Lukang, at least around the turn of the century, seems to have been organized by groups defined on the grounds of common surname. One can argue that such groups would probably not have corresponded neatly with groups of agnates defined in either genealogical or residential terms. It seems likely that any group of agnates in urban Lukang would contain people with different occupations and amounts of wealth. At present the neighborhoods of the city are not segregated by class, and rich and poor live next to each other. There is no reason to assume that things were different one hundred or seventy-five years ago. Organized groups of laborers probably drew their members from several *thiau*, if not from different major segments. To the list of groupings defined by common surname, one would have to add groups of proletarians, membership in which was restricted to those of one surname, and perhaps to those of a certain segment or quarter of the city as well.

By the turn of the century Lukang's economy was declining and many residents were emigrating. For the unskilled though, there may have been some advantages, such as family support, for doing unskilled labor in Lukang rather than Taipei or Taichung. One can assume some level of competition for unskilled jobs in Lukang, even if the pay was low. It would then be to the advantage of a group of workers if they could organize and keep others from competing for their jobs. On the basis of sheer numbers, it would be likely that there would be more workers called Shih, the most common surname, than any other. Given the consciousness of common surname and the tradition of fighting with those of other surnames, it would not be unusual for workers to organize themselves into work gangs limited to those of the same surname. They could win support from those of the same surname if they described their efforts to monopolize jobs as porters or salt workers as yet another clash between surname groups. As long as their opponents were other unskilled laborers, their organization posed no threat to the upper classes, some of whom might support them because of the claim to solidarity of those with a common surname. Were the workers to act as a trade union and try to win higher wages, their employers, no matter what their surnames, would act in terms of their membership in a class rather in a descent group. This is all speculation of course, but it suggests that what is remembered and described as fighting between surname groups may in fact have been another sort of conflict altogether, but one that was presented as a dispute between surname groups in order to win support from the powerful and to strengthen the solidarity of groups of workers.

Surnames, Descent, and Alliance

The internal structure of the great surname groups varied from the elaborate internal differentiation of the Shihs, who claimed to be a real lineage descended from a distant common ancestor, to the amorphous Hsus, who seem to have acted as a solidary group only because they had to defend themselves against the Shihs and the Huangs. In the context of Lukang the surname groups were defined primarily by their opposition to each other, and this mutual opposition was of more significance than their internal organization. Such attributes as the numbered generations of the Shihs can be regarded as historical accidents, survivals, interesting enough in a folkloric sense but of no consequence in Lukang. The existence of a fairly solidary body of Hsus was not the result of several generations of natural increase and the principle of the solidarity of the (male) sibling group; rather it was a response to the exigencies of a particular situation and the possibility in Chinese culture of using common surname as a foundation for an enduring group. The Hsus, with nothing but their surname in common, were the social and functional equals of the Shihs with their numbered generations, internal segmentation, and links to a localized, real and huge lineage back in Ch'uan-chou.

This being so, then the profound lack of interest I found in 1968 in such matters as genealogical reckoning, segmentation and the ways *thiau* fit into *fang* becomes more understandable. Those matters would have been quite significant back in Ch'uan-chou, as they are today in the lineage villages of Hong Kong's New Territories, but in Lukang all that mattered about surname groups was their association with certain neighborhoods and their opposition to each other in certain specific and restricted ways. In anthropological terms, alliance theory, which focuses on groups as parts of systems and on the exchanges that define the system, seems more relevant than descent theory, which focuses on the internal structure and continuity over generations of groups like lineages.

The theme of limited opposition between equivalent groups within the city, which was most crudely expressed in the ritual annual battle between surname groups, characterized the relations between neighborhoods and guilds as well. Neighborhoods expressed their competition primarily in rituals and festivals, while guilds were involved in more straightforward commercial and political rivalry.

Neighborhoods

In the past, as now, Lukang was divided into many named neighborhoods. Today a man identifies himself to a stranger first as a Lukang man, then by his surname, then by his neighborhood. "Yes, I'm a Lukang man, surnamed Ts'ai, and I live in Anping

Street." The other will respond with a question about someone he knows who lives in Anping Street, and the first will reply, "Oh yes, I know him, he's a good friend of mine." He may then remark that his younger brother's wife comes from the same neighborhood as the other man. Thus links are established and almost all natives of Lukang can find some common acquaintance. The key to this is one's neighborhood.

Although some neighborhoods were associated with certain surnames, the identification was never complete. Even the most solidly Shih neighborhood always had a sizeable number of families of other surnames, and some neighborhoods, such as that around the Lung Shan Temple or the "End of the Street" were not identified with any single surname. Neighborhoods have names, and one speaks of "a man from Channel Bank" or "people from Cart Field." Neighborhoods are recognized as having special characteristics— one is where the oystermen live, in another there are a lot of woodworkers. There are local proverbs like "The End of the Street for opera; Market Garden for pigs," that indicate that in ritual observances the people of one are especially fond of opera while those of another will slaughter a lot of large pigs. A wealthy man of the first neighborhood would demonstrate his standing by paying for an operatic performance, while his peer in the second would contribute an especially large pig. One neighborhood, the North End, is seen primarily as the home of poor fishermen and oystermen, and the most consistently lower class and distinctive of Lukang's neighborhoods. It has its own accent, which might be described as an exaggerated Lukang accent, and its people are said to stick together more than the inhabitants of some other neighborhoods.

Each neighborhood has a temple, supported by all the local residents. Everyone in the neighborhood contributed to the cost of the annual festivals and to the periodic refurbishing or reconstruction of the temple. At least once a year the deity of the temple could be carried on a tour of his district, expelling evil influences and being greeted by each householder with incense. The day of the annual festival was also an occasion on which to invite the gods of other temples as "guests," and festivals not only marked off the neighborhood as a ritual unit united by common worship, but also involved them in complex patterns of exchange and emulation with other neighborhoods and their temples. A temple festival was also marked by domestic feasting, to which guests from other neighborhoods were invited by every household, the invitation being reciprocated later when the guest's neighborhood temple celebrated its festival.

Neighborhoods might also be said to have exchanged people in marriage. In the past most inhabitants of Lukang married other Lukang people. The wealthy were more likely to take brides from or to marry their daughters off to equally wealthy families of other towns of the region, such as Changhua City, Peitou, or Yuanlin, and marriages with people from the villages around Lukang were not unknown. But on the whole most marriages were within the city but between people of different neighborhoods. One can speak of a tendency toward endogamy for Lukang and exogamy for neighborhoods. It must be understood that there was no rule on the matter and that neighborhoods were not jurally exogamous in the way that surname groups were. Neighborhoods were thus linked by exchange of women, and any person's network of matrilateral and affinal ties was likely to be confined to Lukang but to extend to several other neighborhoods.[15]

Neighborhoods were ritual units, each celebrating the annual festival of its temple and participating in exchanges with the temples of other neighborhoods. Apart from this activity, two distinct sets of rituals or festivals linked all the neighborhoods together in ritual exchange, competition and emulation. Each demonstrated the solidarity of neighborhoods and their ritual interdependence, and underlined the limitation of that interdependence to the city itself.

The Seventh Month Cycle

The first of these was the great festival of the hungry ghosts in the seventh lunar month. In Taiwan in the past this was the year's largest and most important festival, more so than New Year's, and a considerable sum was spent on it. In Lukang the celebration lasted the entire month. On the first, seventh, fifteenth, and thirtieth days of the month, all of Lukang, every household, feted the hungry ghosts. On the other days, one neighborhood put on a festival each day, in strict rotation. A Lukang song lists the days of the seventh month and the neighborhood responsible for each day's festival. It begins, "First day—put out the floating lanterns; second day, Pu Wang Kung; third day—Rice Market Street;" and goes on day by day and neighborhood by neighborhood. Every day in the seventh month one of Lukang's neighborhoods was the scene of opera performances, rituals by Taoist priests, and of elaborate banquets. Every day in the month the people of one neighborhood were inviting those of other neighborhoods to come and share special foods. For the rest of the month they would be guests and others hosts. The rotating festival, an orgy of hospitality and of exchange of food between neighborhood residents and their fellow townsmen and between the living and the dead, was confined to Lukang and its natives, the inhabitants of the surrounding villages playing no part in it.

On the first day of the seventh month the front doors of the temple to Ti Tseng Wang, the bodhisattva who releases souls from the Buddhist hell and is popularly described as the king of hell, were opened. This was said to release multitudes of hungry ghosts, who would be at large until the doors were shut again at the end of the month. Each family took a sacrifice to the temple and then returned with it for a festive meal. On the same day professional opera troupes and entertainers performed, competing to put on the best show. The seventh month was when they made most of their money, being hired to perform at festivals each day, and the contest provided a form of advertising. This contest, with the elements of competition and display that seem to have characterized much public ritual in the Lukang of the past, is described in the reminiscences of a Lukang man who became a professional journalist in Taipei.

> What was most fascinating on the first of the seventh month was the contest between the two theatrical troupes. Lukang had two permanent theatrical stages, and there the drama companies put on especially elaborate performances on the first of the seventh. This was called the "Drama Contest." Each troupe tried to demonstrate its superiority. When the first played a scene from the "Three Kingdoms," the other put on something from the "Journey To the West." They competed in the costumes and the acting, and eventually the audience could make up its mind which troupe was better. At that point, the inferior troupe, to save its reputation, might take a chance and display acrobatic fighting. Not only would one actor turn a somersault, but he would "throw the wheels" as well. The opposing group couldn't sit still and watch this, so the battle began. . . .
>
> My home was on Pine Street, and that neighborhood celebrated on the nineteenth day. We children really enjoyed that day. My father didn't have much money, but we had to spend a lot on the festival. In the morning when it was barely light the servants were sent to Yuanlin to buy fruit, and others went to kill pigs and goats at the slaughter house. When we got back with the meat it was about eight

The sedan chair bearing the image of a visiting diety approaches a pan-Lukang temple in a cloud of incense smoke.

in the morning, and the streets had become temporary markets, filled with pork stalls and vegetable stalls, and with great bundles of food and fish. The cackle of cocks, the quacking of ducks and the bargaining over prices all made a great noise. Children ran about here and there. My mother sat at the door and ordered this and that from the sellers. Gradually food piled up in the hall. About noon the food stalls and peddlers disappeared from the streets like the ebbing tide, leaving the street littered with leaves and garbage. After lunch every family decorated their front parlor (*k'e-t'ing*), cleaned the house and brought out the best paintings, pottery and objects d'art. The fruit the servants brought back was packed away in big barrels that stood with the other offerings on trestles on each side of the parlor. On each barrel were flags with such expressions as "Happy Pu Tu" or "Sincerity." Pasted to the tops of the flags was gold paper made in the shape of weapons, like knives, axes, tridents or halberds. These were the toys the children liked best. After the seventh month when the adults did not notice, the children took the toy weapons and played with them, pretending they were the heroes of antiquity.

The festival officially began in the afternoon, when the theatrical performances began. The stages were erected in the busiest streets and there were people everywhere. Where the crush was worst people actually erected temporary bridges across the streets. While the opera was going on, the young Taoist priests came around to go from house to house to perform their ritual. All they did was stand in front of the domestic altar table and mumble for a few minutes. Then they took their red envelope (containing their fee) and left. The more famous Taoists did not come around to perform this ritual, because they were concerned with their reputation. They just sent their apprentices to pick up a little extra money. The young Taoists didn't know much, just a few spells, and the children always mocked them. They were embarrassed and tried to hurry along, stopping only at the houses of the rich families. There, while one Taoist was going through his performance, another would be standing by waiting his turn.

At dusk the feast was held in the parlor, which gleamed with the light of the extra candles and lanterns. Then the drums began to beat again and the evening theatrical performance began. It went on till midnight. Many friends and relatives dropped in on their way to watch the drama. They would admire the paintings and art objects and chat a bit. At this time we children usually fell asleep. When we got up the next morning my mother was busy sending the servants to take some of the food to our relatives. . . . Afterwards all the old dishes appeared at every meal, because the family had to eat not only its own leftovers, but all the food sent by the relatives. People got to the point where they could hardly stand it. Everybody suffered from stomach trouble and the doctors were extremely busy during the seventh month.[16]

The seventh and the fifteenth days of the month were marked by elaborate celebrations at Lukang's major temples. On the fifteenth, Lukang's eight guilds sponsored a huge ceremony at the Lung Shan Temple, a Buddhist temple founded by the Ch'uan-chou Guild in 1785. On the thirtieth of the month every household feted the hungry ghosts for one last time and then the doors of the Ti Tseng Wang Temple were closed, confining the ghosts to the underworld for another year. The first day of the eighth month was the beggar's festival. The beggars had done very well during the seventh month, especially as it was their habit to take the food set out for the hungry ghosts, who in some ways could be considered the supernatural analogues for the beggars.[17] On the first they had their own celebration, a riotous occasion of license and clowning, eagerly watched by the respectable people of Lukang. The monthlong rituals and feasting alternately stressed the common solidarity of Lukang and its internal differentiation into interdependent neighborhoods. The seventh month was a period of concentrated exchange and interaction, one of the few times of the year when many families invited guests or were themselves guests, and the one event for which migrants tried to return to the city. All the exchanges were confined to Lukang itself, and for the hungry ghost festival Lukang formed a closed, self-sufficient community whose constituent neighborhoods and households exchanged food and hospitality.

Flutes, Floats, and Moieties

The internal differentiation of Lukang and the solidarity of its neighborhoods and larger territorial units was demonstrated periodically in an event known as the *biou hui* (Hokkien) or "temple association." Essentially, this consisted of competitive street processions with elaborate floats and tableaux, marching bands and acrobatic cum military drill teams. For the purposes of this event, the city was divided into two halves, called the upper quarter and the lower quarter, *tieng-kak* and *e-kak* (Hokkien). The north-south line bisected the city and did not correspond with any other form of distinction, such as surname, neighborhood, or occupation. On any major ritual occasion, such as the rebuilding of, or the installation of a new image in any of the several temples common to all Lukang, the residents of each half, subdivided into neighborhood groups, would arrange float parades each night for up to a month. This happened at irregular intervals, "about every seven years, but that wasn't certain."

The first night the Uptown people would provide three floats, representing scenes from the "Three Kingdoms" or the "Journey to the West" or any other story or episode from the rich body of Taiwanese folklore. If the Downtown people had only two floats while the Uptown ones had three, they would consider themselves bested, and perhaps prepare five for the next night. In this way the contest quickly escalated until there were as many as sixty or seventy floats moving through the narrow lanes, lit by torches and elaborate paper lanterns and accompanied by the din of gongs, pipes, drums, and flute-playing troupes of children (another Lukang specialty). The topics of the floats played off against each other in subtle counterpoint and folkloristic one-upmanship, and the occasion was used to make fun of the other half of town. A rich man and leader of the Uptown people had a reputation as an uncultured boor, and the Downtown people built a float poking fun at him.

The cost of this exercise in local emulation and competition is said to have been borne primarily by the wealthy merchants. The nightly processions stopped only when one side could no longer raise money for the procession. Since the reputation and face of each half of town and of its wealthy men was at stake, no one wanted to give up before the other side did. The exact role of individual neighborhoods is not clear. Obviously at some point in the process, especially if it went on every night for a month, neighborhoods cooperated and divided up the labor of constructing floats and providing bands and mummers. From the accounts of old men, who took part in their youth, it seems that toward the end of the contest every street and small neighborhood was actively involved, constructing new and overwhelmingly impressive floats, and it is claimed that everyone in town was caught up in the frenetic preparations for the evening's procession. If one could assume that there were a number of discrete neighborhoods and that each neighborhood contributed a float, band, or drill team, the matter would be simple. But, as the contest escalated the number of floats went up from three or four to a hundred, and the organization of the early stages is not clear. The first few floats might have been provided by only a few men from quite large districts, such as the entire main street, and subsequent floats by progressively smaller units, with more and more of the population becoming involved. Or, each float could have been provided by the cooperative efforts of several contiguous neighborhoods, each of which would supply its own in the later stages of the contest. Or, the floats could have been supplied by single neighborhoods acting in turn, with the periodicity of the cycle growing shorter until each neighborhood was providing one every night instead of every ten or five nights. The question cannot be answered with any degree of satisfaction, but is significant in the context of the problem of the nature of neighborhood units and the extent to which they formed discrete and bounded entities.

The tales of the old men are, unfortunately, none too specific on such matters, and, as is often the case, their significance was not apparent at the time I heard them. What is quite clear, though, is the strength of the rivalry and passions that were involved in the potlatch-like display of wealth. As with the tales of the surname groups, the accounts one hears today devote more attention to the

rivalry between the two halves of the city than to the internal organization of the competing groups. "One side would do something
and the other would immediately respond, like a shout and an
echo." As with other demonstrations of group solidarity in
Lukang, the excitement generated in the nightly display often
spilled over into brawls, and the affair often ended with a pitched
battle. I was assured that the wounds incurred in such melees, like
those sustained in the annual rock fight, were never lethal, injured
people leaping into pools in front of the major temples in their
quarters and so being healed. This tells us more about the ideology
of community solidarity than about the level of violence.

Street Gates

In the past, Lukang was divided into discrete territorial segments
by small gates, called (in Hokkien) *ai-mng*, that blocked the streets
at intervals and also closed off the entrances to the built-up area
from the countryside. What is not clear is whether the territories
demarcated by the *ai-mng* corresponded to any recognized social
grouping. The gates were said to have been closed at night and
guarded by a watchman, who could open a small door in the main
gate through which people could stoop. The gates are said to have
provided protection against bandits, pirates, and bad elements in
general, since Lukang had no wall.

Lukang's main street, which runs the length of the city like a
backbone and is about two kilometers long, had, before the Japanese period, five street gates. Two marked the ends of the city and
the other three were spaced at roughly equal intervals. They
divided the main street into four segments, and the street was
called "Five Fortune Street," (*Wu Fu Lu*) the number five referring
to the gates. All the households on the street worshipped at the
temple of San Shan Kuo Wang, the former Hakka temple that
stands halfway along the street. Each year one of the four segments
defined by the gates was responsible for the annual festival of the
temple, the others taking responsibility in turn and forming a ritual cycle that repeated every four years.

Villages in the City?

Save for this example, the relations between the segments defined
by gates and sociological neighborhoods is obscure. The real

question, of course, is the nature of the units that I have been referring to simply as neighborhoods. It is possible that neighborhoods were discrete cellular units, the urban analogues of the villages that surrounded the city. Chinese villages of course were not self-sufficient social or economic isolates, and there is ample evidence of the existence of "intervillage systems" and "primary marketing communities." One might then consider Lukang as a collection of villages with no open space between them, a collapsed primary marketing community rather like a neutron star. It is clear that for some purposes at least, Lukang's neighborhoods, however defined, formed solidary units, acting together for rituals, festivals, and sets of exchanges with equivalent neighborhoods. However, there are reasons for doubting that the analogy between urban neighborhoods and villages is really a very good one.

Villages tend to be physically distinct and compact and, in central Taiwan at least, are often surrounded by a bamboo hedge, sometimes of a special sort of thorny bamboo, that makes for a sharp boundary. Lukang, on the other hand, is a compact huddle of houses, and before the Japanese widened some streets in the 1930s it was even more compact. The alleys and street gates gave it a certain segmentary structure, but there were, and are, none of the "urban ecological" features like large highways, railroad tracks, streams, or industrial zones that divide many Western cities into "natural" regions or neighborhoods. In 1968 I found the exact boundaries of neighborhoods very difficult to determine. It was also very difficult to determine the total number of named neighborhoods. There are many names for sections of the city, but it proved impossible to line up the names with any limited set of territorial units. This was because of the fractal quality of the system of names. Some names like "the North End" (*pak-thau*) or "*Gu-thau*" are applied to large sections of the city. The people who live there make much finer distinctions, but those distinctions are not usually known to people who live on the other side of the city, and the situation is reciprocal. The closer one gets to home, the finer the distinctions one can make. Furthermore, even in one family the grandparents might know names the younger generation would not. This relativistic effect means that there is probably no person who knows the names of all the parts of the city. The physical form of the city's buildings and the pathways between them is determinate and could be mapped, but the set of names people apply to that physical structure is relativistic and open-ended.

Temples and Neighborhoods

A possible solution to the problem of the naming of parts seems to be provided by the system of temples with their territory. Earlier I said simply that every neighborhood had a temple and a patron deity, whose annual festival is celebrated by all the households of the territory. One might then assume that the areas defined by common worship could be taken as social units, that ritual structure, which can be described and mapped with little ambiguity, is a reflection of social structure. The ritual of temple worship and the statements of participants would seem to support this, for both assert the solidarity and community of all worshippers.[18]

However, when in 1967 and 1968 I tried to actually identify such social units, I found it impossible. For one thing, while the households that collectively worship a patron deity form a solidary, corporate whole from the perspective of the deity or temple, the picture changes if one looks at it from the perspective of any individual household. Taiwanese popular religion is, after all, polytheistic and households can worship many deities. While a temple festival does unite a definite number of households around the temple, the festival lasts for only one or a few days. Some of the same households may, perfectly routinely, participate in the festivals of other deities and other temples on other days. The households that unite to worship a deity or raise funds to rebuild a temple do not form a parish; there is no assumption that the cult must be exclusive. If one tries, as I did, to map temple areas, one finds that they overlap. Participation in temple festivals and affairs is not an either/or proposition that can be coded with a plus or minus. It can be a matter of degree, expressed most simply in the amount of money contributed. A household might contribute a large amount to the temple nearest to it, and give smaller contributions to three or four other neighborhood temples, including perhaps the one in the neighborhood that the wife originally comes from. Thus the edges of temple areas are blurred and participation slopes down on a gradient of money and time contributed.

Furthermore, over time temple areas are fluid. Popular religion is a living system operated by human beings for their own purposes. It changes. Temples and their attendant festivals can be founded, refurbished, decline, redefine themselves, or extend their areas of participation. I could see some temples extending their territories and others declining in 1967 and 1968, and I have no reason to doubt that the process has been going on in Lukang since 1700. Temples and cults are, after all, run by men, and the number of people who participate in a cult as well as the amount of money they contribute has something to do with who is on the managing committee and how extensive their social networks are. In the late 1960s temples were involved in local-level factional politics, because factional leaders won prestige and legitimacy through contributions to temples.

The ritual language of popular religion provides ways to assert solidarity, as of an assumed neighborhood, and also to assert alliance and opposition. Some indications of the complexities and problematic nature of the relation between groups defined by common worship and other social groups, such as neighborhoods, is provided by the mutually contradictory origin myths of three neighborhood temples, all dedicated to the same deity.

The first version is that of a temple dedicated to a deity called Su Fu Ta Wang Yeh in a neighborhood called Ship Head (*cunthau*). A fisherman from that neighborhood found a piece of wood fouling his net, and took it home to use for fuel. A set of uncanny incidents including dreams and a strange glow emanating from the wood found at sea caused the fisherman to consult a spirit medium. Speaking through the medium, Su Fu Ta Wang Yeh told the fisherman that if he had the piece of wood carved into a statue and worshipped, the god would grant good luck. The fisherman did this and soon became prosperous, while his family flourished. The neighbors, seeing this, began to worship the god too, for his power and efficaciousness was apparent. Soon the whole neighborhood was worshipping Su Fu Ta Wang Yeh. Word of the efficacious (*ling-kan*) god spread through Lukang, and came to the ears of the rapacious yamen runners.

In Lukang all the yamen runners (the nonofficial underlings, who acted as bailiffs, process servers, or constables for the officials) at the subprefect's yamen, as well as many of the minor military officers, came from the island of Chinmen (Quemoy), which seems to have specialized in the export of such sojourners. In Lukang they had a same-place association (*hui-kuan*). They claimed that the image was theirs, for Su Fu Ta Wang Yeh is a deity peculiar to the island of Chinmen, having been an exceptionally honest mandarin there who was rewarded by being promoted to the position of deity. The yamen runners claimed that they had ordered an image of their patron deity from the original, root, temple on Chinmen, but that the ship had sunk on the crossing, leaving the image to make its own way to its destination at Lukang. (This is all perfectly ordinary, standard Taiwanese religion and folklore, where many deities, like the settlers, had a difficult cross-ing from Fukien.) They claimed that the fisherman had inter-cepted and stolen their image, and sent armed toughs to remove the statue from the humble neighborhood shrine. When they tried, the image became so heavy that they could not budge it. This was a clear signal from the deity that he did not want the image moved. The people of Ship Head did allow the yamen runners, now abashed and contrite, to take some of the ash from the incense burner and so become a branch cult (*fen-hsiang*). They acknowl-edged their ritually subordinate position by coming to the Ship Head Temple every three years to renew the link. Several years after this, a man from Ship Head, a fairly humble neighborhood with many fishermen and laborers, made a uxorilocal marriage, moving into his wife's family in Gu-Thau. He introduced the cult of Su Fu Ta Wang Yeh, who so looked after the lowly in-married husband that soon all the neighbors began to worship the god too. They began a branch cult, housing the image in what was their Earth God Temple (*T'u-ti Kung Miao*), and returning to Ship Head every three years to renew the connection.

In the neighborhood around the temple called the Chinmen Kuan, which was originally the shrine of the same-place associa-tion of Chinmen yamen runners, the story is that an image of Su Fu Ta Wang Yeh was being sent from Chinmen to Lukang when the ship went down.* It was found by a fisherman who took it home and kept it for a while before the rightful owners heard where it was. They took it, but since the fisherman had looked after it properly he was graciously permitted to take start a branch cult by dividing the incense. The residents of Gu-Thau were once at odds with the Huangs who lived around the marketplace, and so wanted to make an alliance with the men from Chinmen. The alliance was formalized by the Gu-Thau people setting up a branch cult of Su Fu Ta Wang Yeh. The residents of the Chinmen Kuan neighborhood claim that the people from Ship Head used to come to their temple to renew the link by mingling the smoke of the incense burners (*kuo-hsiang*), until one year when the spirit mediums of the two temples got into a dispute over which of them should be the first to climb a sword ladder. The people from Ship Head broke off the relation and haven't been back since. Once the

---

*The frequency of foundering ships and floating images in the origin myths of Taiwanese cults might seem to be a poor advertisement for the power of the deities, but is more understandable as a denial of any subordinate, *fen-hsiang* relationship to a mainland cult, or any established cult on Taiwan.

threat from the Huangs had abated the men of Gu-Thau unilaterally abandoned the alliance, and with it the ritual link.

In Gu-Thau they say that their patron god was brought directly from Fukien by someone's great-grandfather. They claim to be the original cult in Lukang, and the root to the other's branches. What I find of interest in the stories is the explicit use of ritual connections to claim subordination and alliance, as well as the assumption that such relations could be initiated and broken off. Temples and their associated ritual provide a language for describing and discussing, among other things, urban social structure, and the temples of Lukang (there were 37 in 1968) form a system with a good deal of internal exchange, cooperation, and opposition. But that system is a dynamic one, undergoing constant change and supporting quite different and indeed contradictory interpretations. It does not simply reflect in a directly isomorphic manner an enduring structure of discrete urban neighborhoods.

The more one looks at Lukang's neighborhoods, the less they resemble villages. Their boundaries are unclear; people make no effort to draw sharp lines and define those beyond them as outsiders. The perceived boundary between Lukang, as a whole, and the rest of the world is quite distinct, but within the city all groups overlap. There is no reason to make sharp boundaries for neighborhoods, for they are not and never were corporate groups. They are composed of diverse populations who earn their living in different ways and whose income ranges from low to fairly high. The same conditions held a century ago. Here I am assuming that the pattern I found in 1968 can be projected back into the past, because I can think of no reason for things to have been different then. Today neighborhoods do nothing in common but get together one or a few days of the year to worship, and in the past they did that as well as, on certain occasions, confronting and opposing other neighborhoods in both symbolic and physical modes.

Neighbors and Neighborhoods

One must distinguish between neighborhoods and neighbors. In Lukang in 1967 and 1968 neighbors were quite important. Much daily interaction was with neighbors, who kept an eye on the children, borrowed and lent small items, and were available to gossip with in the evenings. Residence is quite stable in Lukang, and most families have lived in the same house for years, if not for all the husband's and father's life. People generally knew their neighbors quite well, and the most common reply to questions of who was invited to, or helped out with, weddings and funerals was "friends and neighbors." "Friends and neighbors" were also cited as the people from whom one might borrow money or to whom one could turn for help in emergencies. Fear of what the neighbors would say provided a real sanction, and no one wanted to be branded as a person who didn't care what others thought of him, who didn't mind if "the neighbors laughed at (or perhaps 'mocked') him." Someone who, for instance, refused to contribute to the cost of the festival at the local temple would be scorned and labeled as a misanthrope. Such people became the subjects of cautionary tales, exchanged among neighbors and told to children and visiting anthropologists. Neighbors were described as "people who knew each other" and as those who were "relatively intimate."

Neighbors are not necessarily the people who live in one's neighborhood. A neighborhood (*kak-thau*, which might be translated in some contexts as "segment") must, by definition, have a boundary somewhere. Each household, on the other hand, considers itself the center of a circle of neighbors. If neighborhoods ever did have sharp boundaries, the intersecting circles of neighbors crossed them and so made them rather less sharp.

Neighborhoods and surname groups provided significant categories for the daily life and social relations of individuals. On a few days of the year, under some particular circumstances, they were mobilized as effective groups. They were at least in part defined by opposition to other, equivalent groups, the larger social structure resembling an arch with the forces and tensions of the component blocks (here, surname and neighborhood groups) in balance, and, like the stones of an arch, the shape of each component determined by the need to handle the stresses of the other components. Both surname groups and neighborhoods represented different ways of categorizing and sorting the population of the city. They might be considered, in Fred Gearing's apt term, as "structural poses."[19]

Guilds

The enduring corporate groups that dominated the city's economic and political life were the guilds, which depended on a sorting of the population by occupation. The Eight Guilds of

Lukang were famous throughout Taiwan. There may have been other occupational associations, like the salt workers' surname group cum trade union discussed earlier, but if they existed they left no trace. Old men today sometimes speak of the Ship Guild and the Opium Guild, as well as the Rice Guild, although there is no record of such associations, and they may be referring to trade associations of the early Japanese period. According to a stone tablet commemorating the reconstruction of the Matsu Temple in 1817, the eight guilds of Lukang were the Ch'uan-chou Guild; the Amoy Guild; the South Guild; the Oil Guild; the Sugar Guild; the Cloth Guild; the Dyer's Guild; and the 'Sundries' Guild. It is clear that these do not form a consistent set, for five guilds were organized around trade in a commodity, while three others were named for places in Fukien or for a direction. The Ch'uan-chou and Amoy Guilds began as same-place associations of settlers from those places, and continued as associations of natives whose ancestors had come from there. The South Guild was composed of those businesses that traded with the ports to the south of Amoy, such as Swatow, Hong Kong, Canton, and all the minor ports along the coast of Kwangtung.

The unit of membership in a guild was the business or *hang.* *Hang* had titles and many seem to have gone on over the generations, the names of now defunct *hang* still being visible carved in stone or set in plaster over the front doors of Lukang's old shop houses. According to an economic history of Taiwan in the Ch'ing, the establishments called *hang* appear to have been wholesalers or importing firms, rather than retailers.[20] The guilds of Lukang thus represented large-scale, wealthy merchants rather than the proprietors of small retail shops. The Eight Guilds brought Lukang's wealthiest merchants together in associations that represented the city's upper class and commercial elite. It is simple enough to understand the reasons for the organization of the Sugar Guild or Cloth Guild, but the basis for the operation of the Ch'uan-chou, Amoy, and South Guilds is less clear. A *hang* had to deal in something, and Ch'uan-chou and Amoy are places not products. From everything I could discover, it seems that a *hang* could belong to more than one guild, so that a merchant whose grandfather had come from Ch'uan-chou and was engaged in selling sugar to Swatow could belong to three guilds. Because most of the inhabitants of Lukang stemmed from Ch'uan-chou or claimed to, the Ch'uan-chou association was the largest. A rice guild is notably absent. In the nineteenth century, enterprises engaged in the rice trade to Ch'uan-chou and southern Fukien were probably the most common sorts of business. The Ch'uan-chou Guild appears to have consisted of these businesses, thus serving as a sort of null category or default association, while the other, marked sorts of enterprises had their own specialized organizations. The Ch'uan-chou Guild, which recruited on the most prevalent common characteristic—ancestral place of origin—was the largest, richest, and most powerful of the guilds.

Internal Structure
of the Ch'uan-chou Guild

The Ch'uan-chou Guild is the only one whose internal organization can be described in any detail. The information is based on documents, some collected by the Japanese in the first decade of the twentieth century, and on the recollections of old men whose father's had played active roles in the guild. Like all the guilds of Lukang, the Ch'uan-chou Guild was organized as a religious confraternity dedicated to the worship of the goddess Matsu, patron of seafarers. It sponsored three great festivals during the year, one on the twenty-third of the third lunar month, the "birthday" of Matsu; one on the fifteenth of the seventh lunar month, the hungry ghost festival; and one on the ninth of the ninth, the "Double Yang" or mountain climbing festival. Each year, members of the Guild were chosen for the ritual offices of *lo-cu* and *thau-ke* (Hokkien), the "master of the incense burner" and the "man in charge." These are the usual terms for the men who arrange and manage festivals, and the incumbents were responsible for the guild's celebration of the three great festivals. The men to hold the offices were selected by casting lots before the image of Matsu at the banquet the Guild held in the Matsu Temple on the evening of the twenty-second of the third month. Some old men claimed that the *lo-cu* was the head of the Guild; others that the holder of that office was responsible only for arranging the festivals. The Guild also chose, in some way, a man to serve as a "manager." He had to hold at least the lowest official degree, that of *sheng-yuan*, and if he had a higher degree, so much the better. Being a degree-holding gentleman, an unambiguous member of the gentry, he was more able to deal with the subprefect and other officials as something of a status equal. Some old men said that the manager was simply a hired scholar, rather like a lawyer, while others said that he never really did any work for the guild, but that it was an honorific position awarded to respected and powerful members of the city's resident gentry. The daily and more mundane affairs of the Guild were managed by men called "tally men" or "lot masters." There were two, a head and a deputy, and each received a fixed compensation as a monthly salary. They served for only one month, being chosen from each member *hang* in rotation, so that the responsibility was shared by all the Guild's firms.

The guilds of Lukang, unlike the surname groups, owned land. They held farm land as landlord, and may have held urban real estate as well. The rents were used to pay for the guilds' annual festivals and rituals. The Ch'uan-chou Guild owned the most land. I was told by an elderly man whose father had been an officer of the Guild in the early twentieth century that if the Guild needed money for something and the harvest on its land had not yet come, the Guild could ask its member firms to contribute money as an interest-free loan, which would be repaid after the harvest. In the past the Guild had agents in other parts of Taiwan and in Fukien. Each year the first rice harvest in Taiwan was in the extreme south, on the Pingtung Plain. As soon as the Pingtung harvest was in, a runner would be dispatched to the Lukang Ch'uan-chou Guild with information on the amount and quality of the harvest. This was important because the Pingtung harvest would help to determine the price of rice in Ch'uan-chou. The Ch'uan-chou Guild was also said to have bought ramie up in the Puli Basin and shipped it down to Lukang and off to Ch'uan-chou.

The Guilds and the Officials

The wealthy merchants and their guilds managed the trade that passed through Lukang, and this brought them into contact with the officials who were posted to Lukang to supervise that trade. The guilds, and especially the Ch'uan-chou Guild, had to deal with the officials on an almost daily basis. The guilds clearly held a central position in the political system of Lukang in the Ch'ing period. The merchants were of all the major surnames and lived in different neighborhoods of the city, but were united by their business interests and their dominant position in the local economic and class structure. The guilds were involved in most of the major community projects and services. They, for example, managed the cemetery and charitable association, raised funds for the construction and reconstruction of the city's major temples, played a leading role in the main festivals, and contributed funds to such projects as the construction of the quasi-official Wen-Wu Temple and its adjacent academy, the Wen Kai Shu Yuan. They served the government officially by helping with tax collection and policed themselves, enforcing their own rules for the proper conduct of business. Informally, much of the money the officials skimmed off the trade that passed through Lukang went first through the hands of the merchants, and one may assume a built-in opposition between the merchants and the mandarins over the profits of the trade.

The guilds had connections that extended to other parts of Taiwan and to the mainland, that is, to most parts of the economic system centered on the city. They appear to have aided the government and themselves by raising and paying for the militia, even if they did not directly lead it. One may recall Pickering's account of the arrival of the Lukang subprefect in Wu-ch'e in 1867 accompanied, not by troops of the official garrison, but by the Lukang militia. The militia was either a component of or was linked with the Ch'uan-chou militia of Changhua *hsien*, based on villages both north of Lukang and south of Changhua City. One can also recall Shih Chiu-tuan's rising in 1888, and the accusations by the Changhua district magistrate that the Lukang guild merchants were involved in Shih's plot, and that they had subverted the official garrison and its commander.

The shrine of the Lukang Ch'uan-chou Guild, with its image of Matsu and its incense burner, still exists today (1968), housed in the back room of a drugstore on the main street. (The drugstore is a remnant of a charitable foundation that got the last bit of the Guild's lands when it was dissolved in 1912.) The shrine preserves the wooden eulogy boards presented to the Guild by various Ch'ing officials as tokens of appreciation for services rendered by the Guild. The oldest was presented by the Manchu military governor (the "Tartar General") of Fukien in 1806. 1806 was the year the notorious pirate Ts'ai Chien attacked Taiwan and burned the district city of Fengshan in the south, while militia forces were mobilized all over the island to deal with that threat and with the hordes of local bandits who took advantage of the situation to become more active. Lukang's Ch'uan-chou Guild was involved in helping to raise troops and prepare the defenses of the city and the grain supply that fed the Ch'ing troops in Fukien. Another plaque dates from 1823, when the Amoy and Ch'uan-chou Guilds shipped rice north to Tientsin at the request of the subprefect. Another dates from 1853. The guilds played a major role in governing Lukang, and were the most corporate of the components of its internal social structure. They also played a significant part in the economic and political life of the district and of the entire trading system centered on the city. While the surname groups and neighborhoods of Lukang opposed and even battled each other, the guilds acted in concert to protect the city as a whole. They also acted as brokers between the people of the city and the officials, defending it as far as possible from official exactions and trying to convince the officials of the need for such things as a wall around the city.

The Revised Constitution
of the Ch'uan-chou Guild

The Japanese *Report on Economic Affairs* of the Government General's Temporary Commission for the Investigation of Old Taiwanese Customary Practices includes the text of the revised rules of Lukang's Ch'uan-chou Guild.[21] The rules were drawn up sometime in the T'ung Chih period (1862–1875) when the city's trade had already begun to decline. The text resembles other nineteenth century Chinese guild constitutions, indicating that the structure of Lukang's guilds probably resembled that of guilds in other parts of China more than did the structure of the city's "descent" groups. That is reasonable when one considers the need of the Guild to coordinate its activities with those of the imperial administration, and with its mercantile counterparts across the Straits in Fukien. The document is of interest primarily for its hints on the internal organization and solidarity of the Guild. The first sections of the rules deserve to be quoted at length.

> The rules are established in order to bind us together and to reform the former state of affairs. Under the present circumstances it is of the utmost importance to examine the rules which, since the foundation of our Guild in the Ch'ien-lung period (1736–1796), have been wisely made by our former *lo-cu*. The rules are dignified, glorious and entirely good. Although the national currency is inflated and debased there is still an annual profit.[22]
>
> The Guild's expenses for daily necessities, for collecting and distributing goods, for regulating the weight of commodities and then returning them to the proper people, continually mount. By deciding equitably and without bias, we are able to live together in harmony as moral

people. But the old methods give rise to carelessness, and the old rules do not take into account the cleverness of corruption, which increases daily. Someone must revise the former rules. To do this is very sad. Using this, the general gathering of all members, to decide anew on more satisfactory rules, and relying on the *lo-cu* and general council to manage the Guild's affairs, and on the lot-master to supervise the work with the various ships, we willing members, with united strength assisting, with all in agreement, reverently observe the excellent rules.

1. The *lo-cu* for the year, shall every year on Matsu's birthday (23d of the third month) invite our members to hurry to the Guild Hall and gather together to choose, by lot, a new *lo-cu*. If an enrolled member is not present, first he is to be appealed to on the grounds of sentiment (*ch'ing*), then exhorted by reason (*li*), but if he repeatedly and obstinately delays and makes excuses, intractably disobedient, the general membership will then petition that he be expelled for disobeying the rules, earnestly hoping not to injure good relations. The new head, on hearing himself selected, should accept the seal of office quickly.

Should he delay until the fifth month is past, and on repeated occasions procrastinate, running here and there, and fail to consult with the general membership and settle the matter, then, from the first of the sixth month, whoever has any matter at all will bring it to the new master to settle, and not seek out the person formerly responsible. He should refuse to accept the new master's not yet having accepted the seal of office as a pretext for avoiding his duty. In this way bitterness and joy are mutually shared, each year a turn, and the old order will be changed.

2. A manager is engaged to serve fairly for a year's term. On this matter the previous rules were equitable and good. The manager ought not to, without authority, retain people in positions or hire new ones. Nor should the Guild members, relying on their influence, strongly recommend men for jobs, for using power harms mutual good feelings. If the manager wishes to hire any person, let him first consult the general membership, choose someone of virtue and ability, and then squarely extend the invitation. If there should be a few applicants for employment whose character is not decent, then again make more satisfactory recommendations, and the manager and the members, in

compliance with ordinary sentiment, shall mutually recommend and hire. Those who are shown after investigation to have broken the rules will not be forgiven!

3. In the affairs of the *lo-cu* and the general membership, let them fear only that, through waste and through
advantage being taken of dull wits, there be a deficit. In the
event of a loss, if it be small the *lo-cu* should make it up;
if large, the general membership will be asked to pay. If a
firm (*hang*) has previous commitments, the funds needed
should wait until after the collection of the surplus. The
firm will then receive back a fixed amount, so that those
responsible will quickly take care of the matter. Thus the
prosperity of the guild will continue. If there are two or
three who destructively do not obey, consult the members
and punish them.

4. Should a common enterprise in another place meet
with misfortune, and it be necessary to make a subscrip-
tion for needs, then each firm, great and small, will equitably be asked for a mortgage loan so that the common
enterprise can be saved. Should any unvirtuously make it
a pretext for a legal complaint, procrastinate, and bring
misfortune on this place, then, if his offense is minor the
general membership will be consulted as to the punish-
ment. If the offense is major, then the official (the subprefect) will be petitioned for a judicial investigation.

The rules continue in this vein, with judicial investigation by
the resident subprefect threatened for various sorts of fraud and
cheating of other members. The final rule consists of a lengthy
exhortation to settle everything by public discussion, and urges all
members to be public-spirited and not concerned with only their
own narrow self-interest.

Lukang's Ch'uan-chou Guild, like many of the formal, li-based
associations I discussed in Chapter 2, seems to have been troubled
with internal dissension and with reluctance to assume the burdens of office. No doubt the Guild's common estate helped to hold
it together. And the great rituals it celebrated three times a year
may have helped to reinforce its internal solidarity. But a major
factor in the Guild's solidarity was its relation with the city's
imperial officials. After reading the Guild Constitution, one is left
with the strong impression that the subprefect was willing to back
up the authority of the Guild officers. Since the officials couldn't
supervise or tax the trade, to say nothing of collecting their own

squeeze, without the cooperation of the Guild, they needed the Guild. On the other hand, as the case of the unauthorized voyage indicated, the officials seem to have granted the merchants of the Lukang guilds a monopoly on the lucrative trade across the Taiwan Straits. One can see the wealthy merchants and the imperial officials—who in one sense were antagonists, contending for the profits of the trade—as bound together in a relation of mutual dependence and convenience.[23]

The Guilds, the Officials, and Community-wide Foundations

The guilds and the officials cooperated in other ways as well. Apart from their common interest in the Ch'uan-chou Militia, they acted together to found and manage the city's public institutions. The stone tablets in Lukang's major temples, which commemorate the foundation and periodic reconstruction of those temples, list the imperial officials and the Eight Guilds as responsible for raising the funds and supervising the work. The *Changhua Hsien Chih* contains accounts of temple rebuilding, of the foundation of the Lukang Academy, of the two public cemeteries, and of the trust which managed the estate of the local Benevolent Society.[24] For each of these the officials, the guilds, and the wealthy merchants contributed funds to establish a permanent estate.

In 1774 the deputy magistrate is recorded as having founded the two cemeteries that exist today. In 1778 the deputy magistrate acted together with the guild merchants to found a Benevolent Society called the Ching Yi Yuan. The purposes of this foundation were: 1) to collect and burn lettered paper (that is, paper that had been written on); 2) to collect and bury the bodies of the homeless dead and to provide coffins for the poor; 3) to construct and maintain bridges and paths; 4) to manage the two cemeteries. The foundation's estate consisted of seven tile-roofed shops in Lukang, which paid an annual rent of 264 *yuan* (a *yuan* was an ingot of silver bullion); farm land near the city which paid an annual rent of 300 *shih* of grain; and the groundrent of some land along the edge of the city, which paid 40,000 copper cash per year. In 1817 severe flooding destroyed the bridges the foundation maintained and washed out the road to Changhua City. The subprefect and local military commander headed the fund drive to repair the damage, and the surplus was used to purchase the groundrents of all the shops between two street gates near the northeastern edge of the city.[25]

In 1825 the subprefect, acting with a group of twenty-four local degree holders, (one *chu-jen*, two *kung-sheng*, and twenty-one *sheng-yuan*) raised funds and established an academy, the Wen Kai Shu-yuan. There were already two academies in or near Changhua City, the district capital. The original endowment of the Lukang academy consisted of 89 *chia* of farmland and orchards, scattered all over central Taiwan and held under several forms of tenure; several fishponds; and four shops in Lukang. Its annual income came to 640 *shih* of grain and 395 *yuan* in rent.[26] A stone tablet, erected by the subprefect in 1848, details the individual holdings of the estate, which at that time included two shops in Lukang, and lists the annual income as 1,573 *shih* of grain and 217 *yuan* in cash.[27]

The guilds, the academy, and the charitable foundation held sizeable estates, and the major temples may well have owned a fair share of farmland and real estate. In 1946, after half a century of relative economic decline, the managers of the large Lung Shan Temple gave five *chia* of riceland to the new public middle school and the directors of the Cheng Huang Temple donated one *chia*.[28] In 1912, after trade at Lukang had practically ceased, the managers of the Ch'uan-chou Guild gave what was left of its estate, some 5.8 *chia* of rice land and two buildings on Lukang's main street, to found a charity hospital and drugstore, which still exist. At least some of the city's smaller temples also held urban property. A stone tablet dated 1888 lists the property of the Hsing An Kung, a small neighborhood temple, as five buildings in the vicinity of the temple.[29] In 1856 the Chinmen Kuan, a hui-kuan of minor military officers and yamen underlings from the island of Chinmen (Quemoy), collected funds from their members serving all over Taiwan to renovate the hui-kuan's building in Lukang. The surplus funds were used to buy four shops in Lukang, one in need of major repairs.[30]

In nineteenth-century Lukang the corporate property-holding bodies were not lineages but guilds, temples, and educational and charitable foundations. It is possible that some considerable portion of the urban real estate was held by such bodies. As far as I know, there is no material on property-holding in late traditional Chinese cities, and the case of Lukang suggests that the matter is worth further attention. It might be that as much urban property as farm land was held by corporate groups. The corporate bodies in Lukang were managed by the local mercantile elite, with the resident officials playing at least a supervisory role. The managing boards of the city's major temples, the academy, and the charitable foundation thus brought together representatives of all the major groups that made up the city's power structure. They seem to have functioned in much the same way as the school and hospital boards of directors in overseas Chinese communities, where such bodies often formed the apex of the informal power structure.[31] The Ch'uan-chou Guild, which cut across the other guilds, was the nearest thing to a general guild or the twentieth-century chambers of commerce established in Chinese cites.

Who Were Lukang's Gentry?

Up to this point I have referred to Lukang's "local elite" and to its wealthy merchants, but I have avoided using the term "gentry." By the end of the nineteenth century there were, to be sure, some individuals in Lukang who held imperial examination degrees, and the term "*shen*" appears in documents such as petitions and lists of donors to temple reconstructions. But I have no very clear picture of the world of Lukang's gentry, and I find it very hard to disentangle them from the wealthy merchants. The merchants, as a matter of course, would have owned some farm land as a secure, low-return investment. I suspect that many of the men who held imperial degrees were, if not merchants themselves, then the brothers or sons of merchants and still very much a part of their mercantile families. I also suspect that many of the degrees were purchased, either legally or under the table, rather than earned in the examination sheds. In the decade of the 1860s and after, the central government increasingly raised revenue by selling degrees and the Taiwan examinations had a reputation for being especially corrupt, some Fukien men crossing the Straits only to pass the examinations in Taiwan.[32] Degrees and titles were sold or awarded to those men that the officials wished to reward or whose loyalty they wished to reinforce, and one would think that wealthy Lukang merchants would be likely candidates for such awards. In some cases degrees and titles were granted to distinctly un-Confucian local strongmen, such as the Lins of Wufeng in central Taiwan.[33] Davidson, whose sources for the history of Taiwan were Taiwanese scholars, claims without citing a written source that when Tai Wan-sheng was making trouble in Changhua in 1862, but before he actually rose up, the prefect in Tainan was ready "to bestow upon him a blue button, and furthermore promised to secure an official position for him."[34] The point is that in nineteenth-century Taiwan an official degree did not necessarily indicate a high level of Confucian learning or conduct (Lukang was a long way from the State of Lu), nor an individual of the sort one usually thinks of as a representative of the "Chinese gentry."

Inscriptions and documents from Lukang often refer to *shen-shang*, which I have usually translated as "gentry and merchants," as being jointly responsible for some undertaking. Unless the term is taken as referring to a single composite group, the gentry-merchants, which it may have. The degree-holding gentry of Lukang remain rather shadowy figures to me, but I doubt they were all that distinct from, far less opposed to, the great merchants. In this of course Lukang was not peculiar, for by the late nineteenth century the line between merchants and gentry was a thin or a vague one in many Chinese cities. In his essay on "Urban Social Structure in Ch'ing China," G. W. Skinner refers to "the interpenetration in many cities of merchant and gentry leadership structures. . . . In Chung-king the leaders of most *hui-kuan* included degree holders. . . . A text of 1888 refers to the 'gentry and merchants of the Ten Guilds' in Hung-chiang . . . Can one speak of the consolidation of a new urban elite that transcended the hoary social distinctions between gentry and merchant? Probably not."[35]

The individual firms that made up the guilds competed with each other for profits and commercial success, but such competition was muted by overlapping guild membership, by cooperation in neighborhood and temple affairs, in the joint management of public charitable and educational trusts, and by the merchants' need to maintain a united front against the officials. The guilds competed with each other in the splendor of their ceremonies and in the size of the contributions they made to charity and fund drives. In some ways the guilds may be seen as analogues to the corporate lineages of rural southeastern China. They were corporate groups that owned a common estate of farm land and urban buildings; they were united by common worship; they controlled armed forces; they collected taxes and passed them on to the officials; they were the centers of local economic and political power. They differed from lineages in that they did not include poor men and so lacked the internal segmentation that marked Chinese lineages, and in their relatively close and continuous relations with imperial officials.

The Urban Model

In some ways the political structure of Lukang can be seen as analogous to that of urban overseas Chinese communities. The city's elite consisted of merchants, who were organized in trade and same-place associations, and who cooperated in the management of public institutions. In Lukang the managing committees of the major temples, the academy, and the charitable foundation brought together representatives of all the major groups, functioning much like those school and hospital boards of directors in overseas communities. And the more we learn about the political structure and urban administration of nineteenth-century Chinese cities, the more familiar Lukang looks. The intertwining of merchant and gentry institutions, and the extension to the public of services originally provided by guilds and same-place associations for their membership only were common.[36] It is not clear to me whether Lukang's Eight Guilds formed a single confederation, as did guilds in some Chinese cities, or not. But they certainly cooperated with each other and with the officials, and, as Skinner, drawing on his experience with Chinese communities in Southeast Asia, points out, effective cooperation among associations does not require a separate office or formal charter.[37]

As I see it then, the social structure of nineteenth-century Lukang consisted of overlapping groups, each recruited on a different principle and each acting in a different sphere. Every formal group, in accordance with my model of a li-based group, was united by common worship and had a patron deity. Within each sphere, or frame of reference, groups were opposed to each other, that opposition being expressed in various rituals and competitions. Within any single sphere, such as that of opposition between neighborhood groups, opposition and conflict was limited by the crosscutting ties that bound individual members of the group to individuals in the opposing groups. Any single formal group, whether a surname group, a neighborhood group, or a trade association, was defined not only by opposition to equivalent groups, but by its placement in the total environment of Lukang's society. The merchants of the Ch'uan-chou Guild, who gathered together to celebrate their mutual harmony at the festival banquet on the twenty-third of the third month, were involved on other occasions in throwing rocks at their fellows of different surnames, in telling derogatory stories about the neighborhoods some of their colleagues lived in, and at some point were likely to be involved in negotiations for the marriage of their offspring to those of other guild members. Relations between individuals within Lukang thus could be complex and richly ambivalent, combining concord, calculation of mutual interest, and contention. Relations with groups outside the city were more purely economic or political, and were restricted to straightforward commercial exchange, political negotiation, or open physical combat.

The overlapping and the crosscutting is what we see if we focus on groups and take them as primary. If we think of households and families, we recognize them as the enduring units, and regard the neighborhoods, surname groups, and even the guilds, as short-term (though recurrent) groups, mobilized for short periods, and perhaps for those short periods having priority in the household's loyalties or identity. If we think of Gearing's structural poses, one might think of Lukang's population as like a troupe of acrobats, who make themselves first into one formation, then into another. By combining memory, legend, and laconic official documents, I have presented the social structure of old Lukang as a symmetrical set of balanced exchanges and oppositions. This picture is inevitably rather static and abstract, but it also owes a good deal to the living people of Lukang who told me about their past. One reason they told me about the contests between Uptown and Downtown or about the annual rock fight was that they were contrasting the city as it was with the way it is now. And, as I see it, they find it much more difficult to describe or comprehend the city as it is now. If the past is teams of acrobats competing at forming human pyramids, the present is an amorphous milling crowd within a closed-off square.

Notes

1. *Taiwan Chung-pu Pei-wen Chi-cheng* [Complete Collection of Stone Inscriptions from Central Taiwan] (Taipei: Bank of Taiwan, 1962), pp. 78–79.

2. CHHC, vol. 3, p. 382.

3. The Shihs were by the late seventeenth century the most prominent lineage in Chin-chiang hsien, the central, metropolitan hsien of Ch'uan-chou Prefecture. A late eighteenth-century memorialist accused this lineage of the most arbitrary and notorious behavior. See Ng Chin-keong, *Trade and Society: The Amoy Network on the China Coast, 1683–1735* (Singapore: Singapore University Press, 1983), p. 34.

4. Wang Sung-hsing, *"Pa-Pao Chun Yu Taiwan Chung-pu te Kai-fa"* [The Pa-Pao Irrigation Canal and the Development of Central Taiwan], *Taiwan Wen Hsien* 26, 4 and 27, 1 (1975), pp. 42–47.

5. Jacques Amyot, *The Chinese Community of Manila: A Study of Adaptation of Chinese Familism to the Philippine Environment*. Unpublished Ph.D. dissertation, University of Chicago, 1960.

6. Quoted in Wang Shih-ch'ing, 1968.

7. Amyot, 1960, p. 48.

8. Pickering, 1898, p. 204.

9. Pickering, 1898, p. 207.

10. A brief account of the rock fight was published in the Japanese-language *Minzoku Taiwan* [Folk Customs of Taiwan], published from 1943 to 1945. A Chinese translation of all forty issues of the journal was published in Taipei in 1990. According to that, the Japanese first banned the rock fight in 1911, but it continued to be observed each year around Ch'ing Ming. The author describes the formation as the Shihs as one bloc opposing a unified Huang and Hsu bloc, with other surnames joining in where they pleased. The venue is given as either a river bed, where cobblestones were easily available, or a cemetary, where the grave stones provided some protection. Lai Hsiang-nan, "Lukang te Tui-chen T'ou-shih Chan" [Lukang's Rock-Throwing Battle by Opposed Ranks], *Minsu T'aiwan* (Taipei: Wuling Publisher, 1990), vol. 3, pp. 82–83.

11. George Hughes, *Amoy and the Surrounding Districts* (Hong Kong: Desouza, 1872), p. 89.

12. Chen Sheng-shao (1842). *Wen Su Lu* (Reprint, Beijing, 1983), quoted in "The Decline of Hsing-hua Prefecture in the Early Ch'ing," in Eduard B. Vermeer, ed., *Development and Decline of Fukien Province in the 17th and 18th Centuries* (Leiden: E. J. Brill, 1990), p. 102.

13. Georg Simmel, *Conflict and the Web of Group Affiliations*. Translated from *Soziologie* (1908) by Kurt H. Wolf and Reinhard Bendix (Glencoe, Ill.: Free Press, 1953).

14. Alan Dundes and Alessandro Falassi, *La Terra in Piazza: An Interpretation of the Palio of Siena* (Berkeley: University of California Press, 1975).

15. I was unable to gain access to the household registers in the Lukang town office, and so cannot support my statements about marriage patterns with as extensive data as could be wished. The foundation for this claim is information on the native places

of the spouses, parents, and grandparents of some twenty to thirty individuals, and examination of two handwritten genealogies that contain information on marriages as far back as the mid-nineteenth century and which specifically list the places of origin of in-marrying wives.

16. Yeh Ying-chung, *"Chi Lukang Chung-yuan-te Min-su"* [A Record of the Popular Customs of the Seventh Month at Lukang], in his collection of essays *Hsiao Wu Ta Ch'e Chi* (Taichung: Chung-yung Shu Chu, 1967), pp. 59–66.

17. This point is discussed in some detail in Arthur P. Wolf, "Gods, Ghosts and Ancestors," in A. P. Wolf, ed., *Religion and Ritual in Chinese Society* (Stanford: Stanford University Press, 1974), pp. 170–175.

18. See the papers by myself ("Religion and Ritual in Lukang") and Stephan Feuchtwang ("Domestic and Communal Worship in Taiwan") in A. P. Wolf, ed., 1974.

19. Frederick Gearing, *Priests and Warriors; Social Structures for Cherokee Politics in the Eighteenth Century* (The American Anthropological Association, Memoir 93 [vol. 64, no. 5, part 2, October 1962]).

20. Chou Hsien-wen, *Ch'ing-tai Taiwan Ching-chi Shih* [Economic History of Taiwan in the Ch'ing Dynasty] (Taipei: Bank of Taiwan, 1956).

21. Government-General of Taiwan, *Rinji Taiwan Kyōkan Chosaki: Dai Niibu. Chosa Keizai Shiryo Hokoko.* [Report on Economic Conditions] (Tokyo, 1905), p. 300.

22. I believe this to refer to the debasement of the copper coinage during the mid-nineteenth century, for which see Frank H. King, *Money and Monetary Policy in China: 1845–1895* (Cambridge: Harvard University Press, 1965), pp. 213–215.

23. The role of late Ch'ing officials in mediating commercial disputes is discussed in Rosser H. Brockman, "Commercial Contract Law in Late Nineteenth Century Taiwan," in Jerome A. Cohen, R. Randle Edwards, and Fu-mei Chang Chen, eds., *Essays on China's Legal Tradition* (Princeton: Princeton University Press, 1980), pp. 76–136.

24. CHHC, vol. 1, pp. 53, 63, 106, 148; vol. 2, pp. 152–158; vol. 3, pp. 400, 412, 425, 428, 454, 459, 471.

25. CHHC, vol. 1, p. 63; *Taiwan Chung-pu Pi-wen Chi-ch'eng* [hereafter, Stone Tablets of Central Taiwan], p. 130.

26. CHHC, vol. 1, p. 148; vol. 3, p. 400.

27. *Stone Tablets of Central Taiwan*, p. 130.

28. Changhua Hsien Cheng-fu [Changhua County Government], 1954, *Changhua Chan Wan* [A View of Changhua's Development], Section 9, "Education."

29. *Stone Tablets of Central Taiwan*, p. 117.

30. *Stone Tablets of Central Taiwan*, p. 149.

31. See Skinner (1958); W. E. Willmott, *The Political Structure of the Chinese Community in Cambodia* (London: Athlone Press, 1970); Cheng Lim-Keak, *Social Change and the Chinese in Singapore* (Singapore: Singapore University Press, 1985).

32. Lamley, 1964, p. 73.

33. Johanna M. Meskill, *A Chinese Pioneer Family: The Lins of Wufeng, Taiwan, 1729–1895* (Princeton: Princeton University Press, 1979).

34. Davidson, 1903, p. 97.

35. Skinner, 1977, p. 553.

36. Skinner, 1977, p. 549.

37. Skinner, 1977, p. 551.

Chapter 7

Images of Community

In this chapter, we move from the past to the present (1967–1968) and shift from looking at Lukang from the outside to the inside view. The basic topic is the ways the people of the city perceive it, how they conceptualize and describe their society. After what may seem an excessive amount of time and space devoted to defining the questions and filling in the background, we now arrive at the heart of the anthropological attempt to, first, explicate the ways the people of Lukang describe their own society, and then to suggest some explanations for why they choose to describe themselves in ways that differ from those of outside observers.

Outside Definitions of Lukang

From the point of view of the central government in Taipei, the city of Lukang does not exist. It is simply the built-up portion of the 39.4 square kilometer administrative unit called Lukang *chen*. And that is but one of the 312 nonmetropolitan lowest-level administrative units into which the province of Taiwan is divided. The formal structure of Lukang *chen* is just the same as that of the other 311 townships (*hsiang* and *chen*), and like them it has its elected mayor and council and its Town Farmers' Association. Its people are seen as citizens of the Republic of China, loyal to its leader and obedient to its laws. Internally they are distinguished by occupation, members of each occupation being enrolled in an officially sponsored occupational association. There are no uncontrolled associations or independent centers of power, and the tension between the central, bureaucratic administration and the local elite that characterized imperial China no longer exists, for now the bureaucrats and their state have absolute control.

From the detached point of view of an alien observer, Lukang is a commercial and industrial city that exists in the form it does primarily because of its place in a larger economic system. Its population is marked by extensive division of labor, and economically it consists of hundreds of small, diverse, and autonomous enterprises, each with its own ties to customers and other enterprises. The population is homogenous in terms of place of birth but extremely differentiated in terms of occupation. It is hard to divide the population into any large categories, and it is difficult to observe any enduring corporate groups except individual households, and even they do not endure for more than a few decades. The dominion of the central government is not as absolute as the government asserts; local office holders often use their positions to advance their own positions and harm those of their rivals; and such institutions as the Farmers' Association do not in fact operate in the manner they are intended to. But there is no serious challenge to the authority of the central administration, and local politics consists of mundane competition for offices and attempts to influence the bureaucratic structures that rule the city. From the outside it seems that there is no structure to describe except the administrative organization imposed by the central government, the economic structure of specialized small enterprises, and the replicating structure of households, families, and kin ties.

Inside Definitions of the Community

The people of the city see it differently though. They assert that the city exists as a discrete social unit. They also assert that all its inhabitants share a common identity, and that a well-defined community exists. They have their own model of the city's social structure that ignores both the administrative definition of the Taipei bureaucrat and the economic-statistical definition of the alien observer.

Although Lukang today is a city that in abstract economic and statistical terms differs but little from scores of other small cities, it is sociologically a very distinct and unique place. Its inhabitants are very much aware of their own special identity as Lukang people, and the social boundaries between Lukang and the rest of Taiwanese society are very well defined. There is a clear collective self-definition of the city, and its inhabitants minimize distinctions among themselves and maximize those between themselves and outsiders. The involuted physical structure of the city is matched by its social structure, and the city has a reputation for coolness to outsiders and for a certain degree of xenophobia. For the past century most marriages have been within the city itself, and as a consequence most networks of matrilateral and affinal kin are confined to Lukang. Ritually the city with its thirty-nine temples forms a closed, self-sufficient unit. It is asserted that no outsider could succeed at doing business in Lukang. The emigrants who leave are said to stick together and help each other out in such cities as Taipei, and there are formal Lukang associations in Taipei, Taichung, and Kaohsiung. If one looks at Lukang from the inside, through the eyes of its inhabitants, one will concentrate on what is special and unique about the city and on what distinguishes it, as figure, from the rest of Taiwan or the world, which serves as a somewhat myopically perceived ground.[1]

Distinctive Architecture and Townscape

In fact, Lukang looks different from all other Taiwanese cities. It is the most extensive and best preserved example of Ch'ing dynasty Chinese or Fukienese domestic architecture and urban townscape that can be seen on Taiwan. Before the Japanese colonial government carried out an urban renewal project in 1934 and pulled down many houses to cut several relatively wide streets through Lukang, no street had been more than three meters wide. The narrow lanes were covered with massive timber roofs, which shut out the sky and rain, and Lukang was famous as the "city where you can't see the sky." Today a labyrinth of lanes remains just off the main street, and the natives use a commonly recognized set of shortcuts and rights-of-way that wind through other people's courtyards, gardens, and kitchens. The houses along the main street, which the Japanese widened from perhaps three meters to ten meters, have uniform stucco or concrete facades, but behind those are Ch'ing merchant houses of varying size, opulence, and degree of decay. Some such houses, dank and echoing around their present inhabitants who seem to be camping rather than living in them, are far gone in desuetude, but others, better preserved, are very impressive. They are three stories high and often have internal lobbies that rise to the roof, where a skylight permits beams of sunlight to reach down to the ground floor. The houses are long and narrow and often have a series of open courtyards. They, with the sun coming into the courtyards and throwing the elaborate woodcarvings and decorative tiles and brickwork patterns into relief, retain an aura of a somewhat more gracious life. The people of Lukang are proud of their old houses and temples, and like to show visitors through the best examples, commenting that you won't see anything like this in Taipei. Today the antique architecture is utilized by film companies as a background for historical epics, and the visits of the camera crews, film stars, and directors with megaphones and jodhpurs provide the people of Lukang with even more entertainment than do the films themselves.

Local Accent

The city has a strong and distinct local accent, of which the natives are very much aware. They claim that it is closer to the literary pronunciation of Hokkien than is the speech of other Taiwanese, and that it is therefore more genteel or `cultivated.' It is occasionally said to represent the accent of the city of Ch'uan-chou in southern Fukien. This is a good thing for Ch'uan-chou in the eighteenth and nineteenth centuries had a reputation as a cultivated literary city, as opposed to the vulgar commercialism of Amoy (Hsia-men, Xiamen).[2] The Lukang accent is not, as far as I could tell, restricted to the city itself, for the inhabitants of the surrounding villages and especially of the area north of the city speak in much the same way. The natives of Lukang admit that the accent is "much the same," but claim that the speech of the rustics is less cultivated because of their lower cultural and educational level.

The Lukang accent is perfectly intelligible to other Taiwanese, most of whom are said to recognize it. Taiwanese from outside Lukang describe the Lukang accent as "heavy" or "different" and sometimes as quaint or old-fashioned. There does not seem to be any consistent evaluation of the accent by outsiders, but for Lukang people their accent serves as one way to distinguish themselves from all other Taiwanese, and they regard it as one manifestation of their unique and somewhat superior position in the Taiwanese social universe.

Old Lukang Customs

Lukang is also said to have a set of special "old Lukang customs." While everyone agrees that there are special Lukang customs, people do not, when asked to list them, always agree on just what the customs are. Some people refer to things that used to be done but are no longer practiced, such as the great street processions in which one half of the city competed with the other half, or the annual rock fight between the major surname groups. Other people will think a while, and then refer to things that they have heard about but never themselves done or seen. Several people said that it was a Lukang custom not to help an old lady who fell down in the street to get up again ("but you could put a chair next to her, that she could use to lean on"), but neither they nor I ever saw any old ladies lying helplessly in the dust.[3] Very rarely brides may be carried to their husband's home in an ornate red sedan chair rather than the usual red taxicab, and cases of chair-borne brides are cited as instances of old Lukang custom. There are some lanes so narrow and winding that a taxi might not be able to fit, but there is also claimed to be a special Lukang tradition about the use of sedan chairs by brides. People are said to believe that if the bride in the sedan chair is pregnant she will bear the child she is carrying but will never have any more. Hence if the neighbors are gossiping about a bride's possible pregnancy, her parents may counter the gossip by sending her off in a sedan chair.

Several people cited as a peculiar local custom the refusal of one surname group to use pork when worshipping their ancestors. The Kuos, who mostly live in the neighborhood called Kuo Village in the North End, ordinarily eat as much pork as their neighbors, but slaughter no pigs for their ancestors. They turn out in fact to be residual Moslems, who stem from Ch'uan-chou with its minority of Moslems who trace their ancestry to the Middle Eastern sojourners who resided in Ch'uan-chou when in the Sung and Yuan dynasties that city was China's greatest international seaport. A few people did acknowledge that "their ancestors were Moslems," but more preferred to see them as a local, parochial group, meaningful only in the context of Lukang. The Kuos themselves rebuffed representatives of Taipei's Chinese Moslem (Hui) community who heard of them and sent people to invite them to return to the fold.[4]

I have no way of knowing how many people in Lukang actually practice "old Lukang customs," nor do I know enough about the actual distribution of such customs to be able to say that any are in fact restricted to Lukang. I suspect that a good deal of what is claimed as distinctive and peculiar to Lukang is in fact more widely distributed. What is significant is that the people of Lukang think that their city has a set of special local customs that sets them apart from any other Taiwanese community. And since ordinary Taiwanese are well aware of gross cultural differences and commonly describe them as differences of "custom," ("We eat rice; you eat bread. We eat with chopsticks; you eat with knives and forks. We sit on chairs; the Japanese sit on the floor. We worship *Thi:-kong*; you worship *Thian-cu*.") the people of Lukang may be claiming a distinct subculture for themselves.

The Glorious Past

Local people are very much aware of their city's long history, which provides one of the major elements in their common identity. One is told, over and over, that the city was first settled "three hundred years ago" and that it was the biggest port in central Taiwan, or all Taiwan, or that it was very busy and prosperous. "Lukang then was like Taipei is now." The proverbial saying about the three great cities of nineteenth-century Taiwan "First Tainan; second Lukang; third Bangka (Taipei)" is repeated on every possible occasion. There are many stories about Lukang's past, all of which celebrate vanished glory and emphasize the city's antiquity and connections with great men, usually at the expense of strict historical accuracy. A typical story explains why Lukang has so many people surnamed Shih. It goes as follows:

> After Admiral Shih Lang had conquered Taiwan for the Ch'ing dynasty (1683), he was made governor of the island. He made Lukang his headquarters. The Emperor then decided to come to Taiwan and inspect his new possession and see how Shih Lang was getting on. Shih Lang heard that the Emperor was coming and wanted to show him that the people of the island were loyal to Shih Lang and not likely to rebel. At that time everyone had to have their name up on a board outside their door, so that the authorities could see who lived in each house. Shih Lang ordered everyone to change the surname on their door plaque to Shih. When the Emperor came he would notice that everyone had the same surname as the governor and so would be likely to support him, as well as less likely to support any other governor sent to replace Shih Lang. The Emperor came to Lukang and approved of what he saw. Before the Emperor came, Shih Lang had collected a sum of money from every hosuehold. He said that now that the

Emperor had returned to Peking, everyone was free to change the surname on their door plaque back to the original name. But, he would keep the money of all those who reverted to their original name, while those who kept the surname Shih would get their money back. Most people chose money over the integrity of their surname, and that is why today half the people of Lukang are named Shih.

In fact, Shih Lang was not made governor of Taiwan; the capital was at Tainan, not Lukang; Lukang did not become a major city until almost a century after Shih's conquest; and no emperor ever came to Taiwan, far less Lukang. The Lukang Shihs do count Shih Lang as an ancestor, but this story, which is none too complimentary to them, is not told by people called Shih.

Regardless of historical fact, there are many stories on Taiwan about visiting emperors. Many of them concern the Chia-Ching Emperor (reigned 1796–1821), who is reputed to have visited Taiwan incognito before ascending the throne. In one such story, the emperor's ship was about to sink during a storm when a sailor from Lukang prayed to Matsu, who saved the ship and brought it safely into Lukang harbor. When he returned to Peking the grateful emperor sent a large sum of money and a wooden plaque, but he forgot the name of the temple, and through a bureaucratic error the money and the plaque were delivered to the Matsu Temple in Tamsui instead. Another story tells of this emperor's visit to Lin Pei, Lukang's richest merchant.

> Lin Pei lived two hundred years ago and was the richest man in Lukang. He owned the biggest trading company, the Lin-Er-Mou, and was a big landlord. All his sons became officials, and he used to boast that he had more concubines than the emperor and that his house in Lukang was more beautifully decorated than the Imperial Palace. One day when he was out inspecting his fields some travelers arrived. There were three of them, dressed like well-off merchants. They called at the home of Lin Pei, which was Lukang's greatest mansion and stood close to the harbor. Their clothes weren't cut like those of local people and they spoke an incomprehensible dialect to each other. So everyone wondered who they were and why they had come to Lukang. The household servants invited them in, made them comfortable, and sent for Lin Pei. A servant was curious about the strangers, and after bringing them a basin of water to wash with he peeked in at them through

a curtain. He saw that one of them just sat down, while the other knelt at his feet and, turning his face to the floor, held the basin of water up over his head.

Just then Lin Pei got back from the fields. He heard about the strange visitors, and then the servant arrived with his story of the water basin. Lin Pei immediately realized that such ceremonial meant someone from the imperial family. He remembered his boasts and cried out "Ai-yo, the Emperor!" Without bothering to change his clothes or to wash the mud from his feet he rushed into the guest room and began banging his head on the floor, kowtowing. This pleased the young heir-apparent, who of course had never heard of Lin Pei or his boasts. Lin Pei entertained him well and gave him expensive presents. In return the imperial visitor sent Lin Pei a wooden plaque with the imperial seal on it. The house is still standing, on Ch'uan-chou Street, and you can go and see the plaque.

There was indeed a wealthy merchant called Lin Pei in the Ch'ien Lung period (1736–1796), and the house called the Lin-Er-Mou still stands. Hanging high in the gloom under the rafters in the locked-off front parlor is a wooden plaque that is pointed to as the one the emperor sent from Peking. The family is also supposed to have a piece of the emperor's clothing locked in a trunk somewhere, but since the last male descendant of Lin Pei moved to Taipei some twenty years ago (the Lukang house is subdivided and rented to tenants), the relics can no longer be inspected.

Another set of stories centers on the already legendary figure of Ku Hsien-jung, the Lukang man who invited the Japanese army into Taipei in 1895 and later prospered. Other stories explain the decline of Lukang, attributing it to the Japanese who deliberately discriminated against such a center of old Chinese learning as Lukang. It is significant that the people of Lukang maintain and transmit a body of local legend, and most of them seem familiar with at least some of the stories. The oppositions of the past, as those between surnames and neighborhoods, are echoed in the variants of the stories, which often poke fun at another segment of the city's population.

Claims to Ritual Superiority

Another set of stories and legends concerns the city's temples, and make claims to antiquity and ritual superiority. The great Matsu

Temple, founded by Ch'uan-chou settlers sometime early in the eighteenth century, is today the city's largest and preeminent temple, one of the six large temples regarded by everyone as common to the whole city (*hap-kang-e*) rather than to a neighborhood (*kak-thau-e*). It is claimed that its image was brought directly from the original Matsu shrine on Fukien's Mei-chou Island by Admiral Shih Lang. Some people claim that the land the temple stands on was donated by Shih Lang's younger brother's son. The temple thus claims to be only one step removed from the origin of the cult, to have no ritual superior in Taiwan, and to be the oldest Matsu temple on Taiwan and the rightful "root" of nearly all the other Matsu temples of the island, including the far more popular temple at Peikang.

Such ritual claims to priority and superiority are backed up by no written evidence, and the performance and ritual involved in visiting another temple (groups from one temple frequently take their images and incense burners to visit other temples) can be interpreted as indicating either ritual subordination, of branch cult to its original root, or exchange between equals. Lukang's local leadership has, at least since 1958, been assiduous in pressing the city's claims to ritual precedence, and in encouraging groups to come from outside on pilgrimages. Any important visitor or journalist who comes to Lukang is taken off to the Matsu Temple and told of its significance as Taiwan's oldest Matsu temple. Every year at Matsu's "birthday" (the twenty-third day of the third month), a time of many pilgrimages and organized visits to large Matsu temples, the regional editions of the newspapers carry accounts of the Lukang Matsu and repeat its claims. Pilgrimage groups coming to Lukang are regarded as acknowledging their position as branches to its root, and so demonstrating Lukang's dominant place in the ritual hierarchy.

It is not at all clear that the pilgrims think of it that way though. The pilgrimage trade is not particularly ancient or "traditional." It is the result of improved internal transportation and relative prosperity in the 1960s. What a pilgrimage is, is a group of people, usually associated with a temple somewhere, who have all purchased tickets for an excursion on a chartered bus. It may be a one-day trip or it may last several days, with members of the group being put up for the night in fairly spartan dormitory rooms in large temples. The buses always stop at many temples, and the attitude is often that the more temples visited, the better. When I spoke to such "pilgrims" at the Lukang Matsu Temple I found that they did not think of themselves as demonstrating the ritual subordination of their cult to that of the Lukang Matsu, nor did they seem to regard Lukang's temple as of especial significance. Taiwanese who take a folkloric or scholarly interest in ritual matters and popular religion are well aware of the difficulty of establishing the affiliation of temples to others as branch cults, and of the contradictory claims to ritual precedence that temples make. They joke about travelling down the west coast of Taiwan and visiting ten or fifteen Matsu temples, each of which claims to be the oldest and the source of most of the other cults. To the extent that there is a center to the cult of Matsu, it is at the temple in Peikang, a very old seaport south of Lukang. Far more pilgrims go to Peikang than to Lukang, and many of those who go to Lukang also continue on to Peikang, which is perhaps two hours away by chartered bus. Many people outside Lukang are aware of Lukang's Matsu Temple, or of Lukang as a place with some large and old temples, worth a visit, but the city's claims to ritual superiority are not generally accepted by outsiders.

As one would expect, the men who direct the Lukang Matsu Temple claim that it is the source, the "root" of the Peikang Matsu Temple, and say that once upon a time the people from Peikang used to come to the Lukang temple to acknowledge their ritually subordinate status. A long and not very plausible story explains why they don't come to Lukang any more. It is easy enough to see Lukang in the 1960s claiming in the ritual sphere the central and predominant position it once had in economic and political affairs. And the pretensions to ritual hegemony are in part a public relations campaign, and in part a way for the members of the local elite who serve on the managing committees of the major temples to both demonstrate the extent of their personal networks and to extend them yet further, as they do when they invite the owners of Taipei factories to be their guests at the festivities and domestic banquets that mark Matsu's birthday. But the claims of ritual superiority are not just a public relations device or a cynical excuse for making useful social contacts. They seem to be taken quite seriously by the natives of Lukang, who use the assertions of age and ritual centrality as part of their own definition of the city, and hence of their own identity as "Lukang people."

Contrasting and Comparing

The people of Lukang seem more concerned with the length of their city's history than with the content of that history. If one collects the things that Lukang people say about their history, one ends up with a quite restricted list of simple assertions of past prosperity and great antiquity and with a set of dramatic and charming legends, most of which are just-so stories. The old days before the Japanese, while frequently invoked, seem to be thought of as a static moment, a sort of degreeless noon. The Lukang of 1750 and the Lukang of 1890 are put together in the category of "the old days," which is contrasted with the present. Unlike Taipei or Tainan, Lukang does not support a local historical society, and such things as old documents are few and hard to find, most being tucked away with family papers. (I was, for example, shown a hand-copied version of the constitution of the Ch'uan-chou Guild, which was in the possession of a middle-aged businessman whose grandfather had held office in the Guild.) One finds in Lukang a strong sense that there has been a long history, and a value put on that history, but at the same time a limited view of the past and a general vagueness about dates and details. The past takes its place along with the local accent and the special customs as something which is unique to Lukang, and which contributes to its special identity.

All these elements of Lukang's collective self-image or self-definition stress the city's unique character, and the discontinuities between Lukang and everywhere else. The Lukang of the present is contrasted, usually unfavorably, with the Lukang of the legendary past. It is also contrasted, usually favorably, with other communities in contemporary Taiwan. It is compared to the polar types of the great urban center, such as Taipei, and of the small village. In the eyes of its inhabitants, Lukang lies comfortably in the middle of the rural-urban continuum, in a fortunate state that is "just right."

Lukang is surrounded by villages and many of the people on the streets are villagers. Villages rise out of the rice fields only a few hundred meters from the houses of Lukang, but the social distance between Lukang and the villages is immense. Lukang with its rather relaxed atmosphere, water buffalo in the streets, and ubiquitous chickens, is in many ways rather more like the villages than like the dense and chaotic sprawl of Taipei, but, perhaps for this very reason, its inhabitants make a sharp distinction between it and the villages. From Lukang, the villages are seen as uniformly poor, backward, and uncouth. Country people are said to be very honest and hospitable, but also rather naive and gullible. They have little formal education, so their "cultural level" is very low. They work very hard in the fields, so they are very strong, and their skin, from being out in the sun, is all dark and ugly. Being strong and of a low cultural level they are more likely to resort to blows and crude physical aggression than the people of Lukang. They are unsophisticated, always prefer quantity to quality, and are given to excessive displays of joy and anger. "Country people like to parade around and show off their dowries, and they come and parade them through the streets of Lukang, just to show off." "When they have festivals in the countryside, they have great piles of food. They don't care what it tastes like so long as there's a lot of it." They are said to drink the cheapest sort of rice wine, Big White Wine, in horrendous amounts. When drunk they sometimes fight with knives. The more spectacular and déclassé aspects of the popular religion, such as spirit mediums, trance behavior and self-mutilation, and ghost-raising are said to be more common in the countryside. "They are very superstitious."

The villages, as units, are seen as very tightly organized, highly solidary, and, appropriately enough, very clannish. "In the villages they are all agnatic kinsmen, or else their relations are very close. People are very tightly bound together, and they all support each other in whatever they do." The clannishness of the rustics is seen as going along with their propensity for fighting, for they will all turn out to join any of their fellows who gets into a fight, or will come to Lukang in a body to attack anyone who wrongs one of their kinsmen or co-villagers. "Regardless of right or wrong, all of their kinsmen will turn out to support anyone who gets into a fight. And they aren't afraid of the police either. If someone here in Lukang were sent off to jail he would worry about how his family was to be supported. But, out in the country, if someone is sent to jail, the others in the village will all chip in and support his family. Every household will contribute a certain amount each month, because they are all so thick. So they aren't afraid of going to jail." The supposed solidarity of the villages is contrasted with Lukang, where people all know each other and are cordial, but are not all that deeply involved in each others' lives.

The villages are sometimes described as poor, dull, benighted, and as examples of "the idiocy of rural life." But at other times people in Lukang employ another stereotype, that of the overly wealthy and therefore arrogant bumpkin who goes around with a chip on his shoulder. Lukang shopkeepers comment acidly on the prosperity of the farmers, implying that it is somehow undeserved. "The farmers out there all have new houses. and they all have big motorcycles, whether they need them or not. And they can't even read. Now they all want television sets." "In the past their life used to be very bitter. But the government took the land away from the landlords and gave it to them. Now they're all well-off, because the government supports them. They like to show off all their things. They're very vain and proud now, and they swagger around. They're very touchy, and you have to be careful how you talk to them, or they'll take offense." Some natives of Lukang mockingly refer to the rustics as "Americans." This rests on a pun, Americans in Hokkien being *Bi-kok-lang* and the farmers being called rice-country-people—*bi-kok-lang*. The name is also appreciated by those who are familiar with Japanese, in which the name "America" is written with the characters for "rice country" rather than the Chinese, which uses the characters for "beautiful country." Both farmers and Americans are described as boorish but rich and powerful.

The stereotypes of villages and village life are uniformly negative, and one is left with no doubt that Lukang is a better place. Those that refer to the big cities and to Taipei, which is the prime example, are somewhat more ambiguous. It is acknowledged that Taipei is the place to go to make money or to rise in the world, for "there are no opportunities in Lukang." Taipei is also exciting and interesting, and the best place to go for recreation and a good time. It is always described as very *lau-ziat* (Mandarin, *je-nao*), a term that describes the sort of excitement and pleasure generated by a lot of people, with a lot of different things to do and see, like a carnival. The term has strong positive connotations. Lukang is usually described as suffering from a paucity of *lau-ziat*. "It's dull here, nothing ever happens in Lukang." I was often asked why I had chosen to come to stay in Lukang, where there was no *lau-ziat*.

The big cities are also recognized to have better schools and medical facilities, as well as better shops and restaurants. Educated people in Lukang scorned the town's doctors as poorly trained pill-pushers who treated rustics and the poorer inhabitants of the town. They themselves went off to doctors in Changhua City or Taichung, or perhaps even to Taipei. The major urban centers are regarded as more "progressive, " more "modern" and more "Western" than Lukang. From Lukang, it is easy to overestimate the degree of "modernity" and of foreign influence to be found in Taipei.

Modernity and progress are not, of course, unmitigated blessings, and people in Lukang also comment on the dirt and chaos of Taipei. They are well aware of the higher cost of living in the capital, and of the problems of finding a place to live and of getting around the sprawling conurbation. The usual remark is that while you earn more in Taipei, you have to spend more too, and it's so inconvenient. Life there is well known to be hard for poor people or for unskilled migrants. People may mention the unhealthy conditions in the slums and assure each other that not everyone who goes to Taipei ends up rich. "You know, a lot of people from Lukang aren't well educated and don't have any skill. They have no choice but to work with their bodies, use their strength, like carrying things. If they do it at home here, everyone will know, and it will be embarrassing. So they go to Taipei where no one knows who they are. Their families will say to the neighbors that he's gone off to Taipei to do business, but really he's just being a construction laborer or digging ditches."

Taipei and the other large cities are also seen as hotbeds of vice and crime. People exchange stories about the pickpockets and thieves of Taipei, and the newspapers, published in Taipei, devote a lot of space to axe-murders, rapes, and suicides, most of which appear to happen in Taipei. "Once I was up visiting my relatives in Taipei, and I was walking by the Central Market. There were two men fighting in the street, with big knives, like cleavers. And nobody did anything, nobody paid any attention. It frightened me. You'd certainly never see anything like that here in Lukang." The big cities are also known as the home of organized gangs of criminals and extortionists, the *liu-mang*, who are either stronger than tho police or in league with them. "There are no *liu-mang* in Lukang."

Life in the big cities is usually summed up as *luan*, which may be translated as "confused, disorderly, all messed up." It has in Chinese a strong negative connotation. This term is applied to urban heterogeneity, to the rapid and unplanned growth of Taiwan's major cities, and to the traffic of Taipei. "I didn't dare cross the street. It was all so *luan*." It also refers to the quality of human relationships in the big city, to the constant presence of strangers, and to the anonymity of urban life. People contrast Lukang, where people are more intimate and take an interest in each other, with the big cities and their impersonal and atomistic society.

My father's sister lives in Taipei, by Ch'ang-An Street, not far from the Circle. It's a four-story building and each tenant owns a floor. Somebody else owns the ground. Any time they want to do anything to the building, all the tenants have to agree. The people who live there don't really know each other at all, or have anything to do with each other, so it's very difficult for them to agree. They don't know the neighbors on either side at all. People keep coming and going. Everyone keeps big locks on their doors because of the thieves. It's not like that here. Our family has lived on our street for a hundred years, and we know everybody else who lives there. We don't worry about thieves.

Taipei is often characterized as a place where there is no *jen-ch'ing-wei. Jen-ch'ing-wei* is another value-laden term, with no direct English equivalent. It could be glossed as something like "an atmosphere of human feeling." A proper translation would include the notions of cordiality, or some minimal intimacy, of taking an interest in other people regardless of their station or the role they happen to be playing, and of functional diffuseness. It implies taking people for what they are, and making allowances for their individual natures. It is not quite the same thing as friendliness, nor does it necessarily demand perfect accord, but it is the opposite of impersonality and of devotion to abstract rules and principles instead of to living people. *Jen-ch'ing-wei* usually has a good connotation, although people sometimes point out that if carried to excess it may result in favoritism and corruption, which are bad things. Lukang is agreed to have a lot of *jen-ch'ing-wei*, which is a good thing. Life in Lukang is characterized neither by the antlike mechanical solidarity of the villages, nor by the impersonality and suspicion of the big cities. In this, as other ways, Lukang sees itself as occupying an ideally fortunate, median position on a scale of variation, both extremes of which are bad.

Categories and Boundaries

Lukang as a community possesses a high degree of self-awareness and a well-defined self image. The boundaries between it and other places are clearly defined, and the category of "Lukang person" is quite unambiguous. Every possible aspect of life in the town is utilized as evidence of the ways it is counter, original, and strange. People prefer to talk about the ways in which Lukang differs from all other places, rather than the ways in which it resembles other places. The most usual categories are "Lukang people," "Taiwanese" and, when speaking to foreigners like myself, "Chinese." Other categories that could be used, such as "Changhua

County people" or "Central Taiwanese" or "small-scale shopkeepers and workshop proprietors" or "inhabitants of dull provincial towns" are seldom or never used. People in Lukang also prefer to stress what all inhabitants of the town have in common, rather than the ways in which they differ. Little public attention is paid to distinctions within the population of 28,000, and there are no large categories or stereotypes that apply to segments of Lukang's population. People are aware of distinctions that can be made within the category of "Lukang people." Some are rich, some poor; some live in one neighborhood, some in another; some have one surname, others another. But these distinctions are not too important. One might say, though no one in Lukang ever expressed it in such explicit terms, that while it is possible to divide the population of the town into distinct segments, based on such criteria as neighborhood or surname, such segments are qualitatively equivalent, while there is a qualitative difference between "Lukang men" and all others. To its inhabitants, the most significant categories or boundaries are those that separate everyone in Lukang from everyone outside. Every other distinction is secondary.

Personal Relations
Within the Community

Within the boundary of Lukang there are no further categorical distinctions. At this point people usually shift from talking about "Lukang people" in general to discussing specific, named individuals. The names, significantly, are nicknames known only within the community, rather than the formal, legal names recorded on everyone's ID card. The city, at this point, is described either as an undifferentiated, pure community, or as a background, a field within which personal relations can be established by autonomous individuals. Shopkeepers and businessmen kept responding to my questions about the significance of common schooling or common surname by insisting that such categories were totally irrelevant, and that within Lukang anyone could do business with anyone else. People are seen as free to initiate relations with anyone else, and such relations are described in a vocabulary that recognizes their inherent variability along the dimensions of intimacy and confidence. They are "good" or "very good" or "not bad" or "broken off" or they are "thick" or are characterized by a lot of "mutual interaction."

Within the city a normal adult male will "recognize" or "be acquainted with" hundreds of other men, and be able to give brief sketches of those men he recognizes. He may describe any of these men, as long as he is of comparable age and generally comparable status, as his "friend," and feel capable of approaching him directly without a go-between to request a minor favor or suggest some mutually beneficial arrangement. Some, maybe a hundred, of these men he will see more often and regularly, as at domestic banquets given for temple festivals or as a fellow guest at a wedding. He may, if pressed to talk about it, refer to these relationships as "relatively more intimate." Some of these men in turn he will have quite a lot of interaction with, either in his work or in the neighborhood. He may feel capable of being less formally polite with such men, and may be able to give to and receive substantial favors from them, because he can trust them. If he is fortunate, he will have a few truly intimate friends, whom he may have been close to since adolescence, with whom he can exchange confidences and let his guard down.

Although, if he is willing to play the role of informant, one can elicit from such a man an ordered set of kin terms that make a large number of precise distinctions, he will describe his social, business, and local political relationships, which generally loom larger in his life than those with distant kinsmen, with a much smaller and less precise vocabulary. Furthermore, he will resist making fine verbal distinctions and saying who is close and who is distant, or who he trusts more than another. The terms he uses to talk about his social relations are just as vague and imprecise in Chinese as are such words as "relationship" and "contacts" in English. He demonstrates the extent of his trust for someone else when he agrees or refuses to join a rotating credit society with him, or does business with him, or contributes money to his campaign for election to local public office. But he does not make such decisions public knowledge, and if one should be so rude as to ask how many rotating credit societies he belongs to and who all the other members are, he won't tell. This poses some difficulties for anthropological inquiry. One might infer something about his social relationships by following him around and recording whom he greets and how, and with whom he spends his leisure time. But such techniques of behavioral observation, useful for looking at small children in a nursery school or baboons on a savannah, are not practical in a city whose inhabitants conduct their affairs behind brick walls and who are well aware of when they are acting in public, "on stage."

To approach such a task one would have to be far more sensitive to the Goffmanesque nuances of face to face interaction than any foreign anthropologist could hope to be. In speech and in his general demeanor, the Lukang citizen will avoid making sharp distinctions between people, and will present himself as affable and on good terms with everyone he meets. In a paper on business relations I described the ideal Lukang small businessman as having "a lot of amiable, matey, but not too intimate ties with as many people as possible," and said that they felt it better to have limited relationships with a lot of people than very close ties with only a few.[5] A native of Lukang must greet, if only by eye contact and a slight smile, hundreds of people every day, and possess a large repertoire of verbal greetings and polite phrases that are exchanged when meeting others. Men are condemned for being aloof or stuck-up, and when people wanted to flatter me they praised me for speaking with and being polite to everyone I met. The prevailing assumption is that within Lukang everyone counts as a friend or a neighbor, and that it is not done to make distinctions within these categories.

That people do not willingly make verbal distinctions within the broad category of fellow townsman does not mean that they don't or can't tell the difference between close and reliable bonds and those which are more distant or more explicitly instrumental. The small businessmen probably have a cash limit on how far they are willing to trust each other. The assertions of solidarity and mutual good fellowship are far from mere hypocrisy—nobody talks that way about people from outside Lukang—but they are not all there is to local social life either. The city's small businessmen are well aware that at least some of their fellows are out to profit at their expense, and that appeals to common sentiment and affect may conceal traps for those who are too innocently trusting. A certain degree of wariness and calculation of one's own best interests is considered a normal part of any mature person's social skills. When natives of Lukang describe villagers as very honest, they are paying only a partial compliment, for the term usually translated as "honest" (*lao-shih*) carries connotations of gullibility and social naiveté. Young adults in their twenties sometimes comment that life "in society," as they put it, is more "complex" (*hok-cap*. Mandarin, *fu-tsa*) than it was at school, and that they have had to learn not to take everything people say or do at face value.

At the same time, it would be crude in the extreme to go around publicly questioning other people's motives or intentions, or drawing attention to differences of opinion or opposition. The dramatic public expression of mutual opposition that was so common in

Lukang in the past century has no counterpart today. Neighborhood temples play down any elements of competition or one-upmanship, and people of different neighborhoods use the occasion of festivals to exchange polite invitations to share wine and meat rather than to exchange blows and insults.[6] Tension, struggle, and opposition exist, but now they all take place offstage, and the moves and motives of the contestants are shrouded in clouds of gossip and rumor.

In one way the frequent assertion of Lukang as an undifferentiated community and the bland and undiscriminating affability with which its inhabitants treat each other in public settings can be seen as compatible with the Confucian picture of bounded and highly solidary groups, as well as with the value of *li*, of rationality and equity. Even though contemporary Lukang has none of the formal, corporate groups of the sort I described as based on *li*, and its social structure can only be described in terms of extensive and overlapping personal networks, which are in my terminology *ch'ing* groups, the values of fairness, equity and rationality are certainly recognized and held up for emulation. The city's small businessmen with their insistence that anybody can make a deal with anybody else and that affect is affect but money is money, struck me as the incarnation of pure economic rationality. And temples and temple ritual, which are inclusive and serve all residents equally, are organized on a foundation of *li*. Indeed, temples are the closest approximation to a formal group based on *li* to be found in contemporary Lukang. They are run by committees, and the members of the committees as well as the holders of the ritual offices of *lo-cu* and *thau-ke* are elected or chosen by lot or by strict rotation, and hold office for a definite term. Their financial matters are open and explicit, and the accounts of expenses and income for festivals or rebuilding are always posted on the temple wall, along with the name of every donor and the amount of the donation. The members of the cult gather once a year for a formal banquet. And what could be a better symbol of the definition of the members as functionally equivalent and interchangeable persona than the temple's incense burner, in which the identical sticks of incense presented by every household burn down to a common residue of ash and each line of smoke mingles in a common cloud?

Ritual and Models of Community

Taiwanese popular religion can be analyzed or interpreted in many ways. One of these is as an idiom in which to talk about or think about the composition of society and relations between people. Taiwanese popular religion asserts the solidarity and community of all those united by common worship. It also provides ways to describe the relations between groups that are united by common worship, such as temple groups. A major component of Taiwan's popular religion consists of exchanges between temple groups, each of which represents a community of some sort, usually residential. The exchanges can be interpreted as expressing everything from ritual dominance and subordination to recognition of historical links to alliance to competition.

If we look at Lukang's internal ritual exchanges, those between the neighborhood temples (of which there were 31 in 1968), we see a symbolic representation of the community, a model of Lukang's internal structure. The neighborhood temples are a disparate lot, with different origins, ages, and deities. They could be interpreted as evidence of the historical specificity and uniqueness of some elements of the city's population, such as settlers from Hsing Hua, assimilated Chao-chou Hakka, or the one-time yamen runners and minor military officers from Chinmen. But they are not. Rather, the neighborhood temples are equated and regarded as equivalent. As far as public discourse and symbolic expression go, one is much like another. The message seems to be, first, that neighborhoods exist and are significant, but, second, neighborhoods are equivalent units, related through reciprocal exchanges.

The point I want to make here without a lengthy repetition of the ethnography of Taiwanese ritual, is that of the many things that the people of Lukang could do in ritual, things that are within their cultural repertoire, that other Taiwanese do, and that they are perfectly well aware of, they chose to do only a limited set, and that this choice conveys a message.[7] Lukang has a lot of temples, most of them small neighborhood temples that are usually unfrequented. Many people did not even seem to know the name of the deity in their neighborhood temple, referring only to "the neighborhood god" (*kak-thau sin*). The large temples common to all Lukang, such as the Matsu Temple, provide the city's inhabitants with access to deities of proven power and responsiveness and with such religious services as divination, healing and personal protection on an individual, retail basis. I found it difficult to understand why the people of Lukang supported (with money and time and effort) such an inordinate number of small neighborhood temples which appeared to have no religious purpose.

In one of the frequent small-scale and low-key rituals a magician
of the popular religion (*huat-su*), who is cleansing a neighborhood, pauses to spiritually purify a well with fire and sword.

What the neighborhood temples, some of which actually were
used as workshops or living quarters, did do was celebrate an
annual festival. (The Hsing Hua Matsu Temple, possibly the city's
oldest, was being used in 1968 as a workshop to assemble television cabinets and the stone tablets in the walls commemorating its
various renovations were inaccessible behind piles of timber
guarded by a chained watchdog.) Some temples housed more than
one deity and so had more than one annual festival, and some festivals were celebrated in multiyear cycles. The result was that
Lukang was the scene of fairly frequent, small-scale temple festivals. There were several each month. These featured public entertainment, in the form of puppet shows or Taiwanese opera, and
extensive domestic banqueting. The point of a banquet is that
guests are invited. In Chinese culture generally, social relations
are established, maintained, and strengthened by sharing food,
and the principle of reciprocity requires a return invitation. When
a neighborhood is celebrating the festival of its temple, every
household will be hosting a banquet. One cannot invite one's
neighbors, as they too are acting as hosts, so one invites members
of one's social network from outside the neighborhood. Typically
these include some matrilateral and affinal kin, workmates, old
friends, and those to whom one owes a social debt or whom one
intends to ask a favor of. Thus the festival of the neighborhood
temple that asserts neighborhood solidarity is also the occasion on
which individuals or families mobilize part of their social net-

works that extend beyond the neighborhood. One may invite as many guests as one can afford, and all the neighbors know who invited how many guests and therefore have information on how well one is doing financially. In Lukang, people do not invite guests to banquets in their homes without an occasion, and the only occasions for hosting feasts are weddings, funerals, and temple festivals.

From the perspective of individuals and individual families, one of the purposes of the frequent neighborhood temple festivals is to provide an occasion for feasting, which is intrinsically rewarding and provides a holiday to people, many of whom ordinarily work seven-day weeks and put in long hours each day. The feasting also provides an occasion on which to repay and create social debts, maintain and extend individual social networks, and show off one's wealth and success in a culturally appropriate manner. (The Chinese norm of frugality was in evidence in Lukang, and people would and did gossip about frivolous and excessive consumption. Spending a lot on weddings, funerals, and popular religion brought esteem; such self-indulgence as gambling, frequent trips to Taipei for the night life, and even buying too much meat in the market brought negative gossip.) Acting as a ritual officer and organizing the annual festival gives ordinary householders a chance to win prestige through an activity defined as one of public service. Deciding to rebuild the decrepit neighborhood temple and heading the committee that collects the funds and manages the project brings prestige to individuals, and may even be a springboard to public life and a role in local politics. From the perspective of the city as a whole, the frequent celebrations of the festivals of neighborhood temples increase interaction and mutual hospitality between the residents of Lukang, and so, in a fairly straightforward way, promote Lukang's solidarity and sentiments of community.

From a more analytic perspective, if one takes the ritual as a statement about society and social relations, one sees the city as divided into neighborhoods. No other possible subgroup receives any public or ritual recognition. Having been defined by ritual, the neighborhoods are further asserted to be internally solidary and to be equivalent and interchangeable with each other. The system of neighborhood temples provides a model for the internal organization of an otherwise undifferentiated community. If one first asserts that Lukang does exist as a community, that within its boundary all residents are equivalent "Lukang people," then the community can be subdivided into essentially arbitrary and equivalent units, which can then exchange gifts and so bind themselves even more closely together in mechanical solidarity. Some of the nineteenth-century distinctions, such as that between Uptown and Downtown had this arbitrary character, but they were offset both by other equally arbitrary distinctions, such as those of surname, and by distinctions such as those of occupation and guild membership which reflected real differences of interest. In the past, the picture was one of balanced opposition and limited contention, but today it is one of almost saccharine amity and mutual hospitality. Neighborhoods in contemporary Lukang, I repeat, are not corporate groups, have no readily apparent boundaries or distinctive features, and correspond in no regular way to such distinctions as those of occupation or class that an outsider might consider significant. Sorting the inhabitants of Lukang into thirty or so neighborhood temple groups makes a little more sociological sense than dividing the inhabitants of an American city into twenty-six groups by the initial letter of their surname, but only a little more. What arranging the people of Lukang by neighborhood temple does do is to provide a way to include everyone, a way to ignore such awkward matters as distinctions in class, or education, or personal compatibility, and a way to sort the populace into equivalent categories that can then interact with each other in well-defined and amiable ways.

When one reflects on the picture of Lukang's social structure that emerges from the residents' assertions of sharp contrasts between Lukang and everywhere else, of the undifferentiated quality of its populace, and its internal division into equivalent neighborhoods, one ends up with the rather odd spectacle of a commercial and industrial city of 28,000 people, in a rapidly growing economy, whose inhabitants consistently describe it as if it were a closed corporate community. The model of the city's society provided by the ritual structure bears a remarkable resemblance to Robert Redfield's "Little Community," which he describes as distinctive, small, homogenous, slow to change, and self sufficient.[8]

This doesn't strike me as a very good model of contemporary Lukang, but it is at least a model of something, and communities can do far worse than to find ways that permit their people to interact in well-defined and amiable ways. The great advantage of the ritual model is that it is, in a well-worn phrase, "good to think." The disadvantage is that it leaves out so very much, both Lukang's position in the larger society of Taiwan and in the international economic and political system, and the city's complex structure of internal social relations. Here one may note a resemblance (perhaps a family resemblance) between the Confucian model of society, discussed in Chapter 2, and the model expressed in the idiom of popular religion, which although not canonically Confucian is certainly the product of Chinese civilization and culturally distinctive patterns and categories of thought.

That which is excluded from the model of society provided by ritual is very difficult to summarize or to represent as a simple and coherent model. Professional anthropologists and sociologists haven't come up with any neat, simple ways to represent what I take to be present-day Lukang's social structure. One can hardly fault its inhabitants then, who, although they are interested in describing their own society, also have other interests like earning a living and providing for their children, if they have not come up with a comprehensible and consistent picture of their own social organization. If one puts temple and cult groups to one side, all one sees when one looks for Lukang's social structure is an untidy, only partly visible, conglomeration of personal networks, which overlap and intertwine in ways so subtle as to defy description. The customary textile metaphors—fabric of society, multi-stranded relations, webs of kinship, and folded fishing nets of Norwegian villagers—used by social anthropologists strike me as excessively simple and two-dimensional for representing Lukang's society. Metaphors that have come to my mind have been more three-dimensional, and have included a can of worms, a kelp forest, and the mycelium that links what are at first glance separate and individual mushrooms.

In the last chapter I described the social structure of nineteenth-century Lukang as consisting of enduring corporate groups and of the patterned relations between such groups, thus following the model of social structure set out in such classic texts as Evans-Pritchard's *The Nuer*. In this chapter I can see no way to describe the social structure of contemporary Lukang but as "the set of actually existing relations, at a given moment of time, which link together certain human beings," to use Radcliffe-Brown's phrase.[9] If we take 28,000 people, or only, say, 14,000 adults, and assume that each of them probably knows and has some sort of social relation with 100 other people, the size of the set of actually existing relations is clearly unwieldy. Even if people were willing to tell inquiring anthropologists all about their social networks (which they are not), no single anthropologist could record all the data or make anything of it. I have thought of a sort of sociological Maxwell's Demon, who could know every person's social ties to every other person and so produce a monster sociogram, but short of that we will have to make do with metaphors and a few examples to suggest what the metaphors rest on.

Notes

1. Lukang is well-known within Taiwan, having a reputation for being a very "traditional" and a very "Taiwanese" sort of place. Some indication of its distinctive atmosphere and local color is provided by the Lukang-born novelist Li Ang's famous novella *Sha Fu* [Slaughtering the Husband] (Taipei, 1983). This was translated into English by Howard Goldblatt and Ellen Yeung as *The Butcher's Wife* (San Francisco: North Point Press, 1986).

2. George Hughes, *Amoy and the Surrounding Districts* (London, 1872): "The city is by no means fully occupied, and retired mandarins, acting government officials, and an innumerable host of literary men, or rather aspirants to office, form a very large proportion of its inhabitants," p. 82.

3. This custom provides the foundation for a scene in Li Ang's novel *The Butcher's Wife*, in which an old woman who may have suffered a stroke is left sitting in a courtyard late into the night. "I've heard that when old people fall down, you're supposed to let them get up on their own. Here, somebody bring a rattan stool over for her to lean on." Li Ang, *The Butcher's Wife*, p. 56.

4. See Barbara Pillsbury, *Cohesion and Cleavage in a Chinese Muslim Minority*. Unpublished Ph.D. dissertation in Anthropology, Columbia University, 1973. See also Dru C. Gladney, *Muslim Chinese: Ethnic Nationalism in the People's Republic* (Cambridge: Harvard University Press, 1991), pp. 279–282.

5. D. R. DeGlopper, "Doing Business in Lukang," in W. E. Willmott, ed., *Economic Organization in Chinese Society* (Stanford: Stanford University Press, 1972). pp. 321, 323.

6. D. R. DeGlopper, "Ritual and Religion in Lukang," in A. P. Wolf, ed., *Ritual and Religion in Chinese Society* (Stanford: Stanford University Press, 1974).

7. This point is elaborated in my 1974 paper on ritual in Lukang, ibid. On the ethnography of popular religion in Taiwan, see the papers in Wolf, 1974; and in Emily M. Ahern and Hill Gates, eds., *The Anthropology of Taiwanese Society* (Stanford:

Stanford University Press, 1981); David K. Jordan, *Gods, Ghosts and Ancestors: Folk Religion in a Taiwanese Village* (Berkeley: University of California Press, 1972); and Robert P. Weller, *Unities and Diversities in Chinese Religion* (Seattle: University of Washington Press, 1987).

8. Robert Redfield, *The Little Community and Peasant Society and Culture* (Chicago: University of Chicago Press, 1960), p. 4.

9. E. E. Evans-Pritchard, *The Nuer* (Oxford: Clarendon, 1940). A. R. Radcliffe-Brown. 1940. "On Social Structure," *Journal of the Royal Anthropological Institute*, vol. 70. Reprinted in Radcliffe-Brown, *Structure and Function in Primitive Society* (London: Cohen and West, 1952), p. 192.

Chapter 8

Personal Networks
and Ch'ing-based Groups

In contemporary (1968) Lukang what at first glance look like effective formal associations, such as the Farmers' Association or the Credit Cooperative or the occupational associations, turn out to be imposed on the community by the fiat of the central government and to be best regarded either as, like the Farmers' Association and the Irrigation Association, effectively branches of the government with some local participation or, like the Trade Associations (*Kung Hui*) or the local branch of the Kuomintang Youth Corps or of the Association for the Revival of Chinese Culture (Taiwan's answer to China's Great Proletarian Cultural Revolution), to be organizations that exist only on paper, facades with form but no substance. As soon as one begins looking at how things work, at local economic and political organization and action, one comes up against shadowy but very important personal networks, usually nameless *ch'ing* groups with substance but little form. Such groups animate the body social, but are usually invisible or transparent, and do not form an element in the public image of local society or in public discourse on local affairs. Their existence and operation are topics that are not discussed in public, for reasons best left till later, and they are generally regarded as either illegitimate, as private and confidential, or as so taken for granted that there are no words for them.

Such ectoplasmic groupings are more difficult to isolate and dissect than formal groups such as lineages, but they are certainly important, and they are far from amoeboid blobs. If the term structure is taken to mean that the object under consideration is not "wholly amorphous," as Kroeber once put it, then *ch'ing* groups have a structure and can be described. Chinese culture may not have elaborated a vocabulary for discussing them, but for anthropologists they fall into the category of "that which can be said." How clearly it can be said is another matter, but the only way to find out is to try. As examples of *ch'ing* groups in Lukang, I will present the relations of small businessmen, of the skilled artisans who make furniture, and of participants in local political factions.

Business Relations

The owners of the thousand or so small enterprises on which Lukang's economy rests pursue their calling in a booming national economy with a stable currency, little arbitrary interference with markets by government bodies, and have access to fairly adequate if not ideal sources of capital, credit, and goods. Most commercial and manufacturing enterprises are small-scale, rarely employing more than twenty-five employees. It is not too difficult to start up a new business, to change one's occupation or line of business, or to fail and go bankrupt. Over the course of a five to ten year period there is a fairly large turnover in the city's businesses, as some owners sell out, try a new line, or fail. In general, Lukang as a business environment resembles the textbook example of a free market with free competition.

Businessmen insist that they can do business and establish what they call "business relationships" (*sieng-li kuan-he*) with whomever they please, regardless of such categories as surname, native place, or common schooling. They also assert that they do not do business with total strangers. This is reasonable for almost all business dealings except for retail sales are done on credit and so involve some degree of mutual trust and confidence. Everyone, with striking unanimity, agrees that the most important thing in business, a firm's most valuable asset is *hsin-yung. Hsin-yung* refers to informal credit rating, to a reputation for meeting one's obligations. A man who can't pay his debts, who for whatever reason fails to meet his obligations, immediately loses his *hsin-yung*. People say that to start a business one must have capital but that capital alone isn't enough; one must have *hsin-yung* too. *Hsin-yung* provides credit and custom, and with it all things are possible.

To have *hsin-yung* one must know people and have a good reputation with a set of other people, most often the other people in the same occupation, the *nei-hang-jen,* "people on the inside of the line (of business)." *Hsin-yung* in the narrow sense is predicated on performance in business, and is earned by satisfactory performance in a series of transactions. It is always achieved, never given, assumed, or ascribed. All transactions take place before an audience or chorus of *nei-hang-jen*, who continually observe and comment on each other's doings. Within the confines of Lukang, where it is claimed with some exaggeration that "everyone knows everyone else," the reputation of most businessmen is known to others in the same line, and, less accurately perhaps, to many other townsmen as well.

Success in business does not come from staying within one's shop, from sticking to one's last. One does one's job of course, as well as one can, but success comes from the confidence that others repose in one. That confidence is earned by participation in local social life, by the satisfactory performance of business and social transactions, and by being tuned into local communications networks, so that one can accurately estimate other people's *hsin-yung*. In Lukang, confining yourself entirely to the network of other people in the same trade is a bad strategy. Given the exigencies of business life and such things as seasonal variation in trade, it is often necessary to get credit to meet already established obligations and so maintain *hsin-yung*. The summer months, for example, are the slack season in the furniture trade, a time of few sales when the larger firms try to build up their inventory. To do this they must pay their workers and pay for their wood, which is usually purchased from local sawmills on thirty days' credit. They borrow money to get over the summer.

Banks are not a common source of operating credit for Lukang's small businesses. It is important to remember that a firm's *hsin-yung*, its credit rating, is a matter of public concern but not of public information. There are in Lukang no certified public accountants or credit rating firms or centralization of record keeping. Businesses routinely try to conceal their profits from the tax collectors, and those with the requisite acumen and time are reputed to keep several sets of books. Information is a resource, and it is not given away freely. The most reliable estimate of a man's or a firm's reliability can be made by the people he deals with, by the insiders, but one must be an insider to have access to that information. The banks, which are all owned by government bodies, make loans to government-owned corporations and invest a substantial portion of their funds in government bonds, which are secure and pay fairly high interest. They are in no position to make rational economic decisions about which of scores of small businesses, a few of which are certain to go bankrupt in the course of the next year, are good risks. They therefore make loans only on substantial collateral, a process one foreign critic described as more like pawnbroking than banking.[1] For their part most small businessmen express distaste for the red tape and general fuss, such as two guarantors, necessary to obtain a bank loan.

Informal Credit

Instead, they prefer to meet their needs for operating credit through informal, private channels. Much credit is extended by wholesalers and suppliers, who accept postdated checks, which are technically illegal.[2] Such suppliers as sawmills will accept 30-day or sometimes 60-day postdated checks from furniture firms. They only do so, of course, when they know the proprietor of the firm and feel able to assess his *hsin-yung*. The general term for informal credit arrangements is *min-ch'ing*, which translates as something like "popular sentiment." Rotating credit societies, sworn brotherhoods, and unsecured personal loans are all examples of *min-ch'ing*. People say that *min-ch'ing* depends on verbal agreements; nothing is written down. The obligations of *min-ch'ing* are, they explain, thus not legally enforceable, as there is no properly witnessed and sealed piece of paper to present to a court. The arrangements of *min ch'ing* are sanctioned by reciprocity and appeal to community opinion. There is always some risk in such arrangements, but it can be minimized by dealing with people one has known for a long time, people who are committed to membership in the community, and who have a reputation for satisfactory performance in the past. In Lukang, this means primarily natives of the city, for even if one has not previously met a man who is, say, organizing a rotating credit society, his reputation can be checked out fairly easily. One would be more wary of a salesman from Taichung or one's brother-in-law's old army buddy from Chiayi. Many people told me that there was quite enough risk involved in joining rotating credit societies within Lukang, and that they would not consider joining any involving people from outside the city.

In this regard Lukang forms a moral community. Lukang people are regarded as, on the whole, more trustworthy than outsiders. This is not because they are more moral or more honest than outsiders, but because there is more information available on them and they have more motivation to live up to their commitments.

The repeated assertions of community and intimacy that one hears in Lukang do not necessarily mean that its inhabitants particularly like each other, but they do feel that they know each other. The incessant gossip about each other's doings, affairs, and character that so preoccupies the natives of the city (and leaves at least some of them feeling oppressed) has a clear role to play in maintaining the city as a moral community. And while it is true that *hsin-yung* is earned only by a history of satisfactory business exchanges, a man's moral character is judged on more than business transactions. A man who participates actively in local society, which includes everything from sitting around noodle stands in the market and meeting friends of friends, to attending funerals in the neighborhood, to joining rotating credit societies, to contributing time and money to temples and making occasional personal contributions to charity, as when old Mr. Huang from down the street comes by collecting money for a neighborhood family whose father is ill and unable to work, will be known to a large number of people, and will establish himself as a moral man, concerned with other people and with the common good. He will also be a desirable candidate for a rotating credit society and for any relation based on *min-ch'ing*. When he needs help, as for meeting a payroll or covering the check he gave to a Taichung supplier, help will be forthcoming. For these reasons alone the city's small businessmen strive to keep on amiable terms with as many people as possible, to extend their social networks widely, and to know many people moderately well rather than a few very well.

Wide Networks Preferred

The businessmen have other reasons for extending their networks. Success in business is generally attributed to cleverness, which means being able to look at a situation and adapt one's own behavior so as to take advantage of it. The most success comes from seeing an advantage where no one else does. There are many exemplary tales of rich men who perceived opportunities no one else did, such as the Lukang migrant to Taipei who bought garbage dumps and profited when the price of land rose. Perceiving the opportunity in a situation does no good if one can't take advantage of it. Taking advantage of an opportunity (*ch'en ji-hui*) was something that Lukang businessmen talked about a lot, and they were clear that to do so one had to be personally autonomous, beholden to no one in particular. Personal autonomy and freedom to make one's own decisions are highly prized. Thus, whenever possible, they prefer to spread their patronage, to obtain the same commodity from several suppliers. Cloth retailers may deal with fifteen to twenty wholesalers; woodworkers purchase timber from several sawmills. The basic strategy is to keep one's options open.

In the same way, businessmen prefer to obtain credit from a large number of sources, like the people in twelve different rotating credit societies that a shopkeeper or owner of a handicraft enterprise may belong to, rather than be indebted to one source, like a bank or a rich man. If one man gives another a large personal loan or arranges one from the bank, then he has done the recipient a large favor, and the favor as well as the loan must be repaid. If one is obligated to one other person, one's freedom of action is diminished. In Lukang it is possible to get a personal loan from one of several wealthy men, but this is to be avoided if at all possible. Not only is the interest fairly high, but the men who make such loans are in many cases local political figures who use moneylending as one way to extend their influence. Once indebted to such a man, a small businessman may find himself under pressure to deal with associates of the moneylender or to extend favors or support to them. In contrast, all the members of a rotating credit society are formally defined as equals, rather than as a dominant donor and a subordinate receiver. Having to beg a rich man for a personal loan is embarrassing and rather shameful, while participating in rotating credit societies is a mark of good standing in the community. While under some circumstances it is to the advantage of Chinese businessmen to cultivate close, "thick," (*mich'ieh*) particularistic relations with those they deal with, in the circumstances prevailing in Lukang they prefer to spread their nets widely, and to put more trust in the size and spread of the network than in the strength of any particular strand.

Networks in the Furniture Trade

Workers as well as the owners of businesses aim for wide personal networks, and at least some of them value personal autonomy very highly. Lukang is known throughout central Taiwan for its high quality, handmade wooden furniture, and people come from a wide area to buy it for dowries or new homes. The city had, in 1968, nineteen firms making and selling expensive furniture, as well as six firms that made and sold stools, simple tables, and chairs. Furniture firms employed from four or five to as many as twenty-five workers. The furniture trade employed 200-odd workers. Taiwanese houses and apartments do not usually have closets, and clothes are kept in large wooden wardrobes (for which the common local name is *khe-hia: tu*, (adulterous) lover cabinet, the implication being that a wife's paramour can hide in the wardrobe.) A set of furniture would include a wardrobe, perhaps another chest of drawers, a mirrored dressing table, a bed, a dining table, and perhaps a sofa and large chairs. A dowry usually includes a complete set, which furnishes the room allocated to the new couple in the home of the groom's family. It is considered appropriate to furnish a new house or apartment with new furniture as well. In addition, most homes contain a formal parlor with a high wooden altar table that holds ancestral tablets, images of deities, and family heirlooms and mementoes. If the family can afford it, the parlor will also be furnished with carved hardwood tables and chairs. It is this sort of major, expensive items and sets of furniture that the Lukang furniture shops sell.

With the exception of one shop whose owner was experimenting with mechanization, each piece of furniture is made by hand, by a single artisan. The owner of the shop provides the wood, the order, and the place to work. The craftsman provides his labor, his skill, and uses his own tools. He is paid by the piece and usually gets about 20 percent of the item's retail price. The unit of production is the firm, not the household, and the owner of the firm does not provide lodging or meals, even to apprentices.

Sales are seasonal, as are the weddings that provide the largest share of the demand for sets of new furniture, and vary from a high point in the first two (lunar) months of the year to a low point in the summer. Employment is also seasonal, for many of the firms are small and their owners cannot borrow enough money to keep buying wood and paying craftsmen throughout the summer. The rise in incomes and living standards in Taiwan has led to a vastly increased market for the products of such "traditional" craftsmen as cabinetmakers. The result has been an increase in the number of craftsmen, in the number of furniture firms, and probably in the proportion of craftsmen who succeed in opening their own firms. Every year a few new firms are opened by craftsmen, a few are sold, some move to Taichung or Kaohsiung, and some go bankrupt. The craftsmen are quite mobile and can easily leave Lukang and work for a while in Taipei or Taichung or some other city. Some establish their own firms in other cities where their shop signs and their accent identify them as Lukang furnituremakers, which is to say, as the real, first-rate, thing. There is therefore a fairly high rate of labor turnover, especially in the smaller, less adequately capitalized firms, and many artisans, who can be thought of as rather like independent subcontractors, work for several different employers during the course of a year.

Artisan Networks

The craftsmen have a strong sense of vocational identity and solidarity, and the values of personal independence and self-reliance play a large part in their collective presentation of themselves. Many say that they are in a "floating trade" and describe themselves as moving easily and often from employer to employer. They are proud of their craft skills, and will tell one that it takes ten years to master the craft and twenty years' experience to be a real expert, able to make anything at all. Although they have a strong sense of common solidarity, they have no formal organization, and nothing like a trade union or a guild. What they do have is an extensive social network, which is important in hiring and in determining wages. Every owner selects workers by asking those already working for him to recommend someone. All hiring, except for apprentices, is done on the basis of recommendation by those already employed. The artisans claim that they all know each other, all keep in touch, and that they know what's going on in every firm in Lukang. They also keep in touch, though less intensely, with comrades working outside Lukang. Their common information includes just how much is being paid for any particular job, such as making a wardrobe or altar table of a certain size. No one will accept less than the going rate. They claim that the way wages are determined is that one artisan in one shop bargains with the owner. He refuses to do the job for the amount offered, and points out that the price of rice and pork and of cloth has gone up since the New Year. "The boss tries to find someone else to make it at the old price, but we artisans all stick together, and no one will. So they bargain and finally agree on a new amount. The next day every artisan in Lukang knows about it, and no one will make a wardrobe for less. That's how wages are set." This doubtless oversimplifies what must in practice be a very complex process, and it may well idealize the solidarity of the craftsmen, but seems an accurate way of the general way wages (or perhaps fees or compensation, since these are not hourly or weekly wages but piece-work rates) are determined.

Although there is no formal trade union or employers' association, the worker and his boss are not described as confronting each other as isolated individuals. Each is aware of his membership in a larger category. Since the workers, through their recommendations, control, or at least have a major voice in, hiring, they have, even without a formal union, considerable power to discipline those of their fellows who might work for less than the going wage. The necessity of being recommended by other workers also provides a considerable incentive for an individual craftsman to participate in the informal network. An artisan who offends his employer of the moment has a lot of other employers to pick from, but one who seriously offends his fellow craftsmen is in real trouble. The individual artisan making a complete object at his own workbench with his own tools is in fact just as dependent on his reputation with his community of artisans as is the small businessman who describes a reputation for trustworthiness—*hsin-yung*—as the most important element in business.

This system, a functional alternative to a trade union or a guild, operates in a small city within an occupational community of no more than a few hundred craftsmen. They work for, and negotiate with, the owners of small-scale enterprises, almost all of whom have risen from the ranks of artisans. The situation in a large city or within a large-scale enterprise is probably quite different.

The artisans, in conversation, present themselves as men who take nothing from anybody, especially their employers. Shop owners often described their workers as highly skilled but difficult to get along with, touchy and unpredictable. Several owners of small firms complained that during the height of the busy season when a firm whose survival is in doubt must make its money, the workers would take advantage of the situation by demanding extra pay for coming in at night to finish orders, or would be lured away by the owners of other firms. Workers demand from their employers the respect they feel themselves entitled to. If they don't get it, they leave. Nor do they like to commit themselves to their employer of the moment, as they would be if they accepted favors or borrowed money from him. They make a point of not doing these things, and try to keep relations limited to a "business is business" approach. They find their long-term security in their ties to the network of artisans and in their relations with their kinsmen, friends, and neighbors who are not in the furniture trade at all. Employers are not paternalistic nor are workers dependent.

The seasonal quality of the business, the annual variation in demand for labor, the high degree of labor turnover, the practice of hiring through recommendation by workers, the importance of artisan solidarity and their informal network, and the value of independence and personal pride the artisans claim for themselves all fit together to form a functionally integrated system. If business were steady throughout the year, workers would not be let go in the slack season or lured away by other employers during the busy season. If employers hired new workers less frequently, recommendation and the good opinion of other artisans would be less important, as would the network of artisans. If the informal network were not so necessary to secure work, there might well be less feeling of craft solidarity. If workers were let go less often and did not have so many opportunities to be hired by other employers, they might not make so much of their independence and take such pride in being in a "floating trade." Those aspects of artisan identity and values that they claim as inherent characteristics may in fact represent accommodations to a particular structure of business and employment opportunities. Nevertheless, if we are looking at descriptions and conceptualizations of society in Lukang, the furniture makers provide one more example of a stress on solidarity within a category, of a claimed absence of structure and hierarchy, and of a world of autonomous individuals, free to negotiate and bargain with each other within an assumed community where their reputation is known.

Networks Less Than (and More Than) Total Communities

Within Lukang, occupational groups provide a relatively objective and clear way to sort the population into meaningful subcategories, and those of skilled artisans such as the furnituremakers, which have a pronounced identity and collective self-consciousness, look like exceptions to or modifications of the image of the city's population as an undifferentiated mass of "Lukang people." But, while I, following the words of the artisans, have spoken of a "community" of artisans in the furniture trade, the limited and functionally specific nature of that community must be made clear. The cabinetmakers do not live together; they do not marry each other's daughters; they do not even collectively worship the patron deity (Lu Pan) whom they all recognize and who has a small shrine in every workshop. Recruitment to the trade is through apprenticeship, and apprenticeship is open to any young male who wants to try or is told by his father to try. Cabinetmaking requires many years to master and the pay, while adequate, is not especially high. There is not much competition for apprenticeships, and the dropout rate among fifteen- and sixteen-year-old apprentices, who are expected to work for a year and a half without pay, is quite high. The trade is in no sense hereditary. Few of the fathers of the artisans I talked with had been cabinetmakers and they did not necessarily expect their sons to follow them. One elderly artisan explained that it was not a good idea to have all your sons learn the same trade unless you planned to open your own shop. The sons of the owners of successful furniture shops entered middle school and went on to university rather than entering apprenticeship. Some Lukang artisans leave the city to work or set up shops in other settlements, and their relationships with the community of artisans in Lukang, while not usually broken off, do over time become attenuated. The goal of every artisan is said to be to open his own shop and become the employer of his fellow artisans, and some do succeed at this. The capital for such a venture will come from personal savings and from *min-ch'ing*, which requires active participation in social circles besides the network of artisans. While cabinetmakers do work long hours, they are also members of neighborhoods and of families, and their long-term interests lie with their families rather than with the other cabinetmakers. Their "community" is one whose members also belong to other "communities" and reference groups, and some members move out of the "community" during the course of their lives.

Networks and Political Factions

The city's political factions demonstrate the significance and power of informal organizations, as well as the limits and deficiencies of that form of social organization. All of local politics takes place within a context of factional alignment and opposition, and one can't understand what's going on without knowing who's in what faction and what the relations between and within factions are. Factions are real and they are important, but over time they are ephemeral and their solidarity is low. They have no legitimacy; are not publicly recognized or acknowledged; and people never admit that they themselves belong to a faction. The ideal community is just that—a community whose members work together for the public good—and people sometimes regret the existence of factions, regarding them as unfortunate evidence of human weakness. On the other hand, factions are very interesting, and the same people who on one occasion or in one mode of discourse will deny that their community has any factions will on other occasions or modes eagerly tell tales of factional intrigue and speculate on the real reasons behind some recent event. Community solidarity is an ideal, but if it were ever achieved there wouldn't be very much to say about it. There is always something to say about factions though. Their struggles, besides determining who gets some public job or which roads are paved, also provide a good deal of entertainment and serve some of the same functions as professional sports in the West.

Taiwanese local-level factions (*p'ai-hsi*) compete for the control of elective offices and the allocation of public resources. While some people trace the origins of the present factions to the Japanese colonial period, and I wouldn't be surprised if factions had played a large part in the politics of nineteenth-century Lukang, the present factions, which are the only ones on which information is available, compete in the arena of local government and such quasi-governmental bodies as the Farmers' Association and the Irrigation Association. Like octopuses in jars they take the form of their containers, so that to understand them one must know something of the structure of local government and elections, for these set the limits within which the factions operate.

Administrative and Electoral Structure

Every citizen above the age of twenty has the right to vote in local elections. Farmers also vote, indirectly, for the heads of the Farmers' Association and the Irrigation Association. Local people elect (as of 1968) the mayor (*hsiang-chang; chen-chang*) and town council (*tai-piao hui*) in every township (*hsiang* or *chen*). They also elect a county head (*hsien-chang*) and members of the county assembly (*hsien yi-hui*). They elect representatives to the provincial assembly (*sheng yi-hui*), the highest office filled by election. The provincial governor is appointed by the central government. The elections are staggered and not all officials are elected on the same day. In January 1968 people in Changhua County elected mayors and members of the county assembly. In April they voted for county head and for Changhua County's five members of the Provincial Assembly. In May the members of the various town councils were elected for their three-year terms. In all these elections turnout was quite high, with over 80 percent of the registered voters (who are the same as the registered citizens) casting ballots.

The official powers of local governmental bodies are few, and in all cases their budgets are set by the next highest administrative level. The Provincial Assembly, the highest-level elective body, is legally empowered to criticize and to pass, but not to amend, the budget for the provincial government (the amount of which is determined by the central government), to make "suggestions" and "proposals" to the central government, and to investigate problems and make recommendations. Town mayors may transfer but not hire or fire the employees of the town office. The official sphere of town government is very limited, being restricted to population registration, local public works, the health station (public health and inoculation), and supervision of the market and the town slaughterhouse. At least half the budget of the town government goes for the salaries of public employees, and the Farmers' Association usually has a larger budget than the town government. One wonders why anyone would want to be elected to such limited and powerless posts.

Acquaintance with the central government's regulations on elections and campaigns leads one to further wonder how anyone ever gets elected in the first place. The central government feels that elections should not be disruptive, or lead to unrest, and that underhanded or vicious electioneering should not be permitted. Therefore campaigning is limited to a ten-day period before the election day, and candidates are warned not to break the law by indulging in personal attacks on their opponents, or anyone else, or by making potentially disruptive statements. (The central government considers itself in a state of war and, although this is not obvious in daily life, ultimately the country is under martial law.) The Kuomintang, the ruling party, nominates candidates for offices as low as (rural) town mayor, and its candidates almost always win. Candidates run either as Kuomintang candidates or as independents (nonparty candidates). Kuomintang candidates for local posts are chosen by the Party Secretariat at the next higher administrative level. Electoral districts are large. Lukang *chen* has some 65,000 people, and candidates for the county assembly run at-large in an electoral district consisting of several administrative towns, with a population of about 125,000. Candidates can thus hardly hope to be elected by asking their friends and relatives to vote for them, and few voters ever meet the person they vote for.

Elections, then, are held under very strict limitations on campaigning, for positions in relatively powerless assemblies or for largely ceremonial posts as heads of local administrative units. Decision-making and fiscal powers remain in the hands of the central government, whose members are not elected. Doubt as to the significance of local elections is increased by the knowledge that there is often but one candidate for a post. In Lukang in the 1968 elections there was only one candidate for mayor, one candidate for county head, and five candidates for the five seats the second electoral division filled in the county assembly. Six people, five Kuomintang candidates and one independent, ran for the five seats allotted to Changhua County in the Provincial Assembly. Only in the race for town council was there significant electoral competition, with about twice as many people running as there were seats. Yet men are eager to be elected, and they do compete for public office, and join together in factions to try to ensure the election of one of their fellows.[3]

The Rewards of Office Holding

Elective offices, for one thing, do have significant powers of patronage and influence. The Provincial Government decides how much money Changhua County can have each year to pave roads, but it does not stipulate which roads will be paved. Farmers' Associations have larger budgets than most town governments and rather more discretion on how the money is spent. Patronage is of extreme importance in the Credit Bureaus of Farmers' Associations. Loans need not be made only to farmers, and nonfarmers may join the Association as nonvoting associate members, who are entitled to loans. The Marketing Bureau of the Farmers' Association, designed to market crops and cut out profiteering middlemen, can give out, sometimes in conjunction with the County or the Provincial Farmers' Associations, contracts for the production of such cash crops as asparagus or mushrooms, offering a guaranteed price.

It is not impossible then for a businessman who has good relations with the head of the Farmers' Association to get a substantial loan at low interest from the Credit Bureau and use the money to set up a canning factory that will then receive a contract from the Marketing Bureau to process the asparagus the Marketing Bureau has contracted with farmers to have grown. This can be quite profitable, and the businessman would be expected to reciprocate the favor by supporting the man that the head of the Farmers' Association wants to see elected to the county assembly. He might also introduce the head of the Farmers' Association to an old friend and classmate who now works in the taxation bureau of the Provincial Government. The men would meet at a banquet in the private room of a winehouse in a nearby city, a banquet whose guests would include other businessmen and public administrators from the region.

When a muddy road is paved or an irrigation ditch improved and lined with concrete it is only reasonable for the local member of the county assembly to claim credit for persuading the public works department of the county government of the urgent necessity for such work. Nor would it be too unlikely for the work to be done by a building contractor whose sister is married to the head of the town council, and who hires a truck belonging to the brother of the head of the town public works department. And should the cement on the new road turn out to be only half as thick as specified so that the road soon begins to break up under heavy rain and heavy truckloads of stone and gravel being removed from the riverbed and sold to a private construction company, then the leader of the town's opposition faction would not be likely to go to the district court in a nearby city and charge individuals with corruption, misuse of public funds, and sale of the cement that should have gone into the road to a certain merchant in a nearby town. For the daughter of the head of the opposition faction might well have just obtained from the County Assemblyman an introduction to the principal of a good school in Taichung City. With this introduction, the daughter, newly graduated from Taiwan Normal University, would not have to teach rural children in some leaky-roofed school out in the sweet potato fields, but could live and work amid the bright lights of the big city (and be on hand to do a little baby-sitting for the family of her mother's older sister with whom she will be staying). And the present, the red envelope, she would present to the school principal (school principals do have the power to hire and fire their staff) would not have to contain the equivalent of fifty to one hundred U.S. dollars customary for teachers getting such a prized post. And if, in spite of this, charges were pressed and the affair of the missing cement were to get into the newspapers, then the matter of the land held by the opposition leader's family, some five hectares more than the limit allowed by the Land Reform Law, might come up.

These examples are deliberately fictitious, but, as would be obvious to any reader of Taiwanese newspapers, this is the stuff of local politics—patronage and favors shading off at some ill-defined point into graft and corruption. Apart from such rewards there are other reasons for seeking election to public office. There can only be, it is obvious, one mayor in a town, and only a very few can be members of the County Assembly. Such men have a position; they are known and visible; they are prized guests at weddings and temple festivals. Some of the aura of the Mandarins seems to linger on, and the holders of such offices as town mayor get more prestige and public deference than do elected officials of comparable units in the United States. And although they may be the targets of much vicious gossip, they do not have to face the public opposition and personal slurs that are the lot of similar office holders in the West. They greet important visitors and get their names and photographs in the newspapers, and people constantly call on them, asking favors that may or may not be granted. They are invited to many banquets and can extend their personal networks yet further. In the rhetoric of public speaking, banquet hosts, and newspapers they are public servants, motivated by dedication to the common interest. Along with such public flattery they also have the advantage of being on the inside, privy to secrets and gossip, and knowing what's really going on behind the scenes—where the new factory will be built, who will get the contract to renovate the local temple.

Factions Mobilize Support and Votes

Such things as the desire for patronage powers, the chance of making some money, the glory of office holding, and the joy of defeating one's rivals motivate at least some men to seek election. But the controls on electioneering and the limits on candidates' ability to appeal to the interests of special categories of the population, such as farmers or industrial workers, make it difficult for any candidate to win the votes of as many strangers as he must to be elected. These problems, which face every candidate for local office, are dealt with by political factions. Such factions are groups of people, recruited in diverse ways, who unite to elect a man to an office in the expectation of benefiting from his election. One of the prizes that factions compete for is the Kuomintang nomination. From the perspective of local factions the Party nomination is an object of struggle, committing those who gain it to very little save public repetition of the same rhetorical statements that are presented in the newspapers, on the radio and the (1968) recently available television, in all public schools and a variety of public media ranging from wall slogans to matchbooks. From the perspective of the Kuomintang, the nomination is a reward that it can use as a lever in the local political arena. It is useful in ensuring unanimous support for the party and the central government, and also in winning the commitment of some of the local elite to the central government. It can also be used to influence, if not to completely control, the careers of ambitious local men. In some areas of Taiwan the Kuomintang appears to follow a policy of playing factions off against each other, giving the nomination to first one, then the other faction and so preventing the growth of any unified local group or a locally based political figure with strong popular support.

Factions, so long as they are localized and center on personalities rather than policies, do not interfere with the role of the Kuomintang as the sole organized political party. Nor do they threaten its power. The men in Taipei who control the party don't really care who is elected to such offices as those in the Changhua County Assembly, so long as such people don't publicly question the legitimacy of the central government or its leader. And if local officials are identified as leaders or members of factions, which connote the pursuit of selfish and private rather than common and public ends, then the higher-level administrators and power holders, who are never identified in the newspapers as members of factions, look even better by comparison.

No local faction could be said to control even a township branch of the Kuomintang, but factions do control votes. The simplest and most effective way to persuade a citizen who is, perfectly reasonably, quite indifferent as to which of a number of total strangers becomes mayor or town assemblyman to vote for one rather than another candidate is to pay him, and this is the way most votes are obtained. That votes are bought is no secret; newspapers discuss the going price for votes in particular contexts. The necessity of raising money to buy votes is an important element in the structure of factions and local elections, and one of the things that makes local politics a system with roughly predictable behavior and outcomes.

Costs of the Electoral Contest

It is immediately obvious that buying enough votes to win election in a large district requires a very considerable sum of money. The cost of votes runs (1968 figures) from U.S. $.25 (NT $10.00) up to

U.S. $1.25 (NT $50.00) or even higher depending on the locality and the degree of competition. In 1968 NT $10.00 would buy two-plus *chin* (2.6 pounds) of rice or one-third of a *chin* of pork or one package of expensive cigarettes, while NT $60.00 was an adequate day's wage for a skilled cabinetmaker. A rough estimate of election costs is U.S. $700 for the Town Council, U.S. $5,000 for Mayor, U.S. $3,750 for County Assembly, and U.S. $37,000 for Provincial assemblyman. It costs money to go into local politics. This restricts serious involvement to the local rich. In a country town like Lukang very few men could supply all the cash necessary to buy votes from their own pockets. A group of wealthy men can contribute funds though, and this is another pressure for the formation of factions.

Personal Networks Guarantee Votes

It takes money to go into politics, but money is not enough. Votes are bought, but the relation between buyer and seller involves more than a simple cash nexus. The problem for the vote buyer is insuring that the votes he pays for are actually delivered. If it were a straight cash transaction between strangers, people would cheerfully sell their votes many times over, and no one is naive enough to stand around on the street handing out money. Vote buying is delegated to individuals who buy up the votes of those people with whom they already have a social relation of mutual trust. Vote buyers, who are the agents of the factional leaders, usually buy the votes of from twenty to perhaps fifty people, all members of their personal networks. Vote buyers typically deliver their own families, some of their close kinsmen, and anybody who owes them a favor. It is the responsibility of the vote buyer to see that the votes are actually delivered. The vote buyers make up the bulk of the active membership of the faction, but they are functionaries, foot soldiers who have little say in decisions. They are, in the first place, the candidate's and other leaders of the faction's close kinsmen and friends. They are also, and more importantly, anyone over whom the leaders have any sort of authority, as employers. In rural Taiwan employees of the Farmers' Association, who owe their jobs to the head of the association, are routinely expected to deliver the votes of their families and as many other people in their home communities as they can. Some men can, by virtue of their personal relations and personal authority, guarantee the votes of, say, an entire village. They will be allies or subordinate leaders of the faction. Faction leaders may sometimes contract the services of the *lo-mua* (Mandarin, *liu-*

mang), local petty hoodlums who get along by shaking down shop-keepers, acting as bouncers in whorehouses, and running gambling games. They can deliver some votes, and may be used as a strong-arm squad to deter rival vote buyers, sometimes putting a cordon around villages or neighborhoods the night before the election and so keeping out agents of rival candidates. In cases of extreme competition, which are rare, they may be employed to beat up rival vote buyers, faction leaders, or candidates.

Vote buyers, who are the rank and file of factions, differ in their degree of loyalty and commitment to the leaders. Some, like employees, are quite reliable, while others, like village big men, are only conditionally loyal and may well shift allegiance from one election to the next. The task of the faction leader is to bind such persons to himself in any way possible, to somehow put them in his obligation. He tries to manipulate any recognized category of mutual solidarity, such as common surname or common devotion to the same deity. He will use his influence to do favors for people, especially for people who may control votes or other sources of support. Successful faction leaders, whether in office or out, maintain a perpetual open house to which all those with problems are welcome. An ordinary person might approach such a leader for help finding his son a job. The jovial big man will hear the case and then write a short recommendation on his name card, which the petitioner then takes off to the potential employer. He will usually refuse the proffered gift or red envelope (the polite way to pass money, as one does at weddings), for he prefers the obligation, which can be called in when and in the form that he most needs.

In the manner common to local politicians in all countries, Taiwan's factional leaders often serve as intermediaries between citizens and the state bureaucracy, cutting through red tape and securing benefits such as planning permission for new ventures, tax abatements, decisions in long-delayed appeals and disputes, and so on. These were traditional roles of China's gentry, and the faction leaders, local big men, are to some extent simply continuing this traditional role. The more successful ones however, do more than simply help citizens deal with an unresponsive bureaucracy; they actively interpose themselves and try to make their approval and recommendation necessary for any interaction. As an example, a new employee in a clerical job in a public office was failing to receive his salary. It was necessary to appeal to a local leader, who himself had no formal role in that administrative system, before the pay envelopes began arriving. The leader was not interested in anything so crude as a cut of the fairly low salary and refused any present for his "help," preferring the gratitude of the worker and his family. The person telling the story clearly felt that the leader had seen to it that the salary did not arrive, and public circulation of the story, the truth of which could not be verified, served to enhance the reputation and hence the power of the leader.

Factions' Solidarity is Low

Factions have no ideological element at all and do not correspond with distinct subgroups in local society or with territorial distinctions. There is no firm foundation for a faction in local social structure nor any way to predict which faction a wealthy man will support. It is true that the leadership core of a faction usually has relations based on kinship, common schooling, or residence, what J. Bruce Jacobs, a student of Taiwanese local politics, has called a "kuan-hsi base," but the same sorts of ties can be traced between such leaders and neutrals or leaders of opposing factions.[4] It is not unknown for brothers or neighbors or former business partners to support different factions. Not only is the allegiance of the lower level vote buyers conditional, but members of the inner circle can and do fall out and change from close allies to bitter enemies. After all, the only thing that binds them together is their pursuit of self-interest, and if a man thinks he can get a better deal from another leader or another faction he will calculate his costs and benefits, and if the benefits outweigh the costs he will transfer his allegiance. Over time, the membership of factions changes and factions split and form new alignments. There is a host of stories that go, in summary," A and B used to be good friends and close allies. Then X happened, and the relation was broken off. Now they're enemies." The relatively low solidarity of factions and the brittleness of the bonds that link the leaders help to limit the intensity of the opposition and struggle. The character of factional conflict can be seen most clearly in its best defined aspect—the electoral struggle.

Factions Negotiate

The simplest form of electoral contest consists of wealthy men gathering support and supporters and spending money to win elections. Such a contest is a zero-sum game with one candidate winning all and the other or others losing entirely. Such simple contests rarely occur. What is more common is for factions to enter men for all posts open and then begin a set of negotiations that result in the withdrawal of all but one of the candidates for each post. This process of negotiation, which is how most elections are decided, is the core of Taiwanese factional competition, and one of considerable general interest. If a man loses a local election he has lost everything he risked on it and the money he and his friends raised is wasted with nothing to show for it. If he withdraws, after making a judicious estimate of his chances of victory, he will save the money that would have gone for votes. But he will not withdraw simply because he has no hope of winning. Even if he doesn't control enough votes to win himself, those votes may well be enough to block someone else's victory or to guarantee victory to a third contestant. Such actions should not go unrewarded, and negotiations are opened to see what the reward is liable to be. No serious candidate withdraws unless he is promised something to compensate him for abandoning any chance of being elected. The simplest form of such a negotiated agreement would be that faction A withdraws its candidate for the county assembly, ensuring victory for faction B, while faction B withdraws its man from the race for mayor, thus giving the post to faction A's candidate. For each, half a loaf is better than none, but a more important pressure for mutual accommodation rather than total and unrestrained conflict lies in the problem of money and of guaranteeing votes.

A candidate and a faction that loses a contested election has wasted money. The money itself is not spent until the voters are paid off on the eve or the morning of election day, and one who negotiates withdrawal saves money. The price of votes, like anything else, responds to demand, and goes up in a contested election, thus raising everyone's costs. Voters expect at least a token sum for going to the polls and casting a ballot, even when there is only one candidate for each post, but this sum is only a fraction of the amount paid in contested elections. Furthermore, as competition rages, the chance that money paid out will actually bring in a vote goes down. In cases of severe electoral competition the vote buyers are pressured to bring in more and more votes and to try to get the votes of those who are not so closely bound to or obligated to them as those whose votes they normally deliver. Ordinary people are perfectly willing to take money from as many people as are willing to offer it, and if the price is high enough a vote buyer might switch his allegiance from one leader to another. It was estimated that vote buying normally guarantees the vote in 75 to 80 percent of the cases, but that with severe competition the reliability goes down to only 30 to 40 percent.

In contested elections, individuals who as a matter of course try to extend their personal networks widely and to avoid committing themselves too deeply to any single person outside their immediate family, find themselves approached by more and more vote buyers, each appealing to some culturally recognized base of solidarity and trying to call in a social debt. Personal networks always overlap, which is one of the most useful things about them, but in these circumstances the costs of multiple allegiances become evident. People are caught in the middle and find themselves in the uncomfortable position of being unable to satisfy one "old friend" without offending the others. With competition the use of hoodlums (who may be imported from the big city as leaders activate that part of their networks) to deter rival vote buyers and bring in votes increases. Violent clashes become more likely and the seamy side of local life is exposed to public view. Under the strain of electoral competition the allegiance of supporters, always somewhat conditional, becomes more and more questionable. Each faction tries to win over members of the opposing side, or to buy off smaller factions or minor candidates. Betrayal lurks in the camp of even the strongest candidate.

Thus, in the fiercely contested campaign for Changhua County head in 1964 there were five candidates. One of them, the leader of an exceptionally strong local faction, was sure of victory because he controlled a large bloc of votes while the other four split the remaining votes between themselves. But at the last moment two of the weaker candidates suddenly threw their support to a third man, up until then their bitter rival. He went on to win by the narrow margin of 4,000 votes.

The line between a faction and a coalition is not clearly drawn. By their nature, factions have no membership rolls and no public existence. In the case of the 1964 Changhua County head election the winner and his two last-minute supporters might form a new faction, at least at the county level. Or, they might only have made a one-time agreement, a short-lived coalition. The only test would be that of long-term cooperation.

Limits on Conflict

Everyone involved in local politics is well aware of the dangers and uncertainties of unrestricted competition. There is pressure on candidates to negotiate an agreement, since limiting conflict is to everyone's benefit. Arranging negotiations is not difficult. The candidates and leaders of factions are all members of a small, relatively well-off elite. They are for the most part middle-aged or elderly men who have spent their whole lives in the parochial worlds of their home communities and are certain to have common acquaintances who are not directly involved in the contest. Meetings are easily arranged, and usually take place in private rooms in restaurants or winehouses, the normal haunts of the local rich and the common venue for all sorts of negotiations. Negotiations may stretch out over a period of several weeks, with many plenary sessions and much coming and going of messengers and go-betweens.

Agreements usually involve a balancing of offices, so that each side gets an uncontested seat. Another common item for negotiation is jobs. The factions that withdraw their candidates can demand that their men be hired by the town office or the Farmers' Association, or that the other side use its influence with superior authorities to secure an appointment or a contract. Agreements can take any form and since they are verbal, the possibility of betrayal and broken promises is always present. Many people besides the candidates themselves are involved in the process, and it is nearly impossible to satisfy everyone. Since every local political figure claims more influence with the bureaucratic bodies that govern the region than he probably possesses, men sometimes make promises that they cannot really fulfill. Even the most successful negotiation is liable to result in some resentment and some people who feel that they have been overlooked, slighted, or been taken advantage of. Such feelings set the stage for the next cycle of breach and schism.

The candidate who withdraws does not demand money for himself. That is too crude and there is always the possibility that he might use any money received to buy votes in the next election. The usual stipulation is that the winner of the election (because he will run unopposed) will donate a large sum for local good works, to the school, or charity, or temple. The amount of money donated is of course an item to be negotiated. Such an action, apart from guaranteeing that the money will not be used against the donor, also shows his concern for the community at large rather than for his narrow personal advantage, and so helps to boost his reputation.

In the election for Changhua County Assembly in 1968 the field in the first electoral district was finally narrowed down to eleven candidates for ten seats. One of the eleven offered to withdraw if the others would each contribute NT $100,000 (US $2,500.) for poor relief. He would himself contribute half that sum, making a grand total of NT $1,050,000 (US $26,150). However, one of the ten candidates was a woman, who was guaranteed a seat in the assembly by law, for each electoral district must elect at least one woman, and she was the only one running. Sure of election, she would not contribute. Three of the others were from towns outside Changhua City and would not contribute to a fund intended only for the poor of Changhua City. That was negotiable, but the woman was the great problem. In the end a settlement was reached, for the man withdrew, assuring all the others of an uncontested election.

Similarly, in a town to the north of Lukang a former member of the county assembly was running for mayor. He offered to withdraw if the other candidate would give him a voice in the selection of personnel for the town office, agree not to interfere with the political arrangements of the villages that supported the former assemblyman, and agree to contribute NT $200,000 (US $5,000) to build more classrooms for the local junior middle school. The first and second conditions were readily agreed to, but the other candidate thought that NT $200,000 was too much to ask, especially in a poor rural town, and tried to bargain down the price.

Negotiations between factions are entered into and proceed on the basis of a shrewd estimate of the resources and support available to each side. Many of the offers to withdraw if the opposition puts up a certain sum can be understood as bargaining gambits, tests to see just how much money the other side can raise. If they can't come up with NT $200,000 to pay off their rival they may well not be able to raise the cash to buy enough votes either. Registration for an election is often the initial bargaining ploy, though to be worth buying off a man must have some credible support. A candidate who entered with no backing, with no factional support, might find that no one took him seriously enough to buy off, and he would lose all the expense of the election, including his deposit, and become a laughing stock as well. This helps to limit participation in local politics to a small fraction of the total population, one small enough that arrangements can be made and benefits traded off.

Deception and Uncertainty
Characterize Factional Struggle

Negotiations for withdrawal as much as elections themselves are the arena for local political struggle and accommodation, but negotiations depend on estimates of one's opponents' resources and intentions. They offer splendid opportunities for bluff and counter-bluff, and deception and mystification are integral parts of the negotiating process. A certain degree of uncertainty surrounds all estimates of strength, both one's rivals' and one's own. In part this is due to the relatively amorphous nature of the factions and to the conditional loyalty of supporters and allies. Close allies may suddenly switch allegiance and subordinates may be found to have been acting as double agents. In the world of local politics, sudden reversals of fortune are common and the innocent do not prosper.

Some of the uncertainty is the result of deliberate policy. Long ago Sun Tzu in his classical treatise, *The Art of War,* said that all war is based on deception. Factional leaders are well aware that this also applies to politics, and go to some lengths to confuse their opponents and try to keep even their supporters and allies, none of whom is wholly reliable, from being privy to their intentions and stratagems. Of course this in turn reduces solidarity within factions, for why put your trust in a man who does not trust you? It also leads people to look at every action in terms of secret, ulterior motives, and helps to generate a lurid gossip world whose basic assumption is that things are never what they seem. Information is, along with money and influence, one of the most important weapons in the factional struggle. Successful faction leaders are usually described as exceptionally shrewd, well-informed, and astute men, who are very good at manipulating other people, predicting their behavior, and winning their support. Ideally they know what is going on and what will happen even if no one else does.

Given these conditions, it can be seen that negotiations cannot always be relied on to arrange matters smoothly and achieve mutually acceptable accommodations. The negotiations depend on estimates of strength and support, and no one, not even the leaders of factions, can ever be certain about these things. No matter what devious ploys and cunning stratagems are used in private, back room bargaining sessions, all depends on the number of votes and the influence with administrative bodies that various men command. Since these cannot be taken for granted, they must be demonstrated, and control of votes is only demonstrated in actual elections. The utility of the frequent, staggered local elections becomes clear. Were all local officials to be elected at once, on one day every three or four years, pre-election negotiations between factions would become more difficult. Elections are important not so much because they directly determine who gets what, but because they provide an objective, quantifiable assessment of the strength of factions, and force their shadowy, potential structure (even if only for a moment) to become more manifest.

Local factions compete very seriously for office and influence, but their conflict is limited, and there are strong pressures for accommodation. This is in part explained by their nonideological goals, their focus on persons and parochial affairs, and by the restriction of active membership to a small, wealthy segment of the population. It is important to point out that a man's wealth and social position are not at stake in local political competition, and that it is not necessary for most wealthy men to play an active part in local politics to guarantee their position. One who loses a round in local factional politics is perhaps less well-off than he would have been had he won, but he retains his property and social standing and is in a position to try again. Those who succeed in local politics gain a relative advantage but they do not get complete control over local power and resources. The watchful eye of the central government, which sets the rules within which local factions compete and can change them whenever it pleases, along with the differentiation of the local economic and social structure mean that no one man or group of men can monopolize power and influence.

Identification with Factions Varies by Community

The degree to which ordinary citizens identify with factions and use factional allegiance to guide their social relations is difficult to determine. Those knowledgeable about Taiwanese local politics generally agree that local factions are more salient in some regions of the island than in others. My colleague, Lawrence W. Crissman, whose fieldwork in the market town of Erhlin, some 18 kilometers south of Lukang, partially overlapped with my stay in Lukang, feels that there, in a country town populated largely by recent migrants from the immediate countryside, many people's choice of which shop or restaurant or doctor to patronize is determined by factional allegiance. My impression of Lukang is that relatively few ordinary workers or small shopkeepers are personally identified with a faction. This may be another facet of the difference between settlements such as Erhlin or Kaohsiung City that have grown very rapidly and contain populations of migrants with few ties to each other, and that, like disturbed ground to weeds, offer a favorable niche to factions that can offer a quick and accepting social network, and those settlements like Lukang whose inhabitants with their deep local roots, like the unbroken sod of a prairie, have a more diverse and individuated set of networks. Seen in this perspective, the local factions in such communities as Erhlin are the functional equivalents of the speech group and regional associations of migrants and the associated secret societies that organized the early settlers in Taiwan and the cities of Southeast Asia. The local level factions operate within populations that share the same dialect and subethnic identity, and so cannot, as their ancestors did, use these distinctions to organize themselves.

What I saw in Lukang was a quite complex and differentiated social field, which contained a set of wealthy and relatively powerful men, each trying to extend his net of people dependent on him and obligated to him. Doing favors and making loans were the most obvious way to do this. At the same time, the bulk of the populace was trying to resist being caught up in a big man's net and striving to retain their own autonomy and freedom of action. Big men want clients, but smaller men do not want patrons. They prefer sets of "friends" with whom they exchange favors.

The behavior of men who engage in local politics and negotiations is not difficult to understand—they are actors out to maximize their own benefits through making and breaking alliances with other equally self-interested actors. The game takes place within limits, and no one is seriously hurt by losing. Still, in spite of one's knowledge of the powers of patronage and the prestige of office, one wonders if the payoff is really worth all the effort and money that some men put into local politics. There is some graft and corruption, but in a place like Lukang nobody is going to get rich out of local politics, and it is likely that even with graft thrown in some men are doing little better than breaking even. Of course no one familiar with academic politics should doubt people's ability to put far more time and energy into parochial struggles than rational calculation, to say nothing of common sense, would dictate. And not every Taiwanese businessman who can afford to play a part in local politics does so, and it may be that the minority of their class who do devote themselves to factional struggles do so to assuage personal psychic needs in much the same way as their peers who devote their leisure to playing bridge or mah-jong. It is also possible that factional leaders aren't really putting any more time and effort into their professions than their fellows who work long hours and devote much of their attention and cunning to such matters as selling cloth to farm women, raising ducks for the market, or treating respiratory complaints. Taking one's job seriously and devoting much attention to it are aspects of generalized Chinese economic culture, as is the willingness to work hard for a small immediate return.

Local Politics as a Cultural System

One difference of course is that cloth-selling and duck-raising are not subjects for public discussion, while local politics and the activities of local leaders are. It is worth noting the attention ordinary people give to local politics and the fascination that factional leaders seem to hold for them, a fascination matched only by that of possessed shamans. Politics and religion are the favorite topics of gossip, and someone who refused to talk about them would brand himself as either unsociable or excessively interested in money or sex, the other major topics of gossip. A group of men whiling away an afternoon in a shop are liable at some point to trade stories about local political figures, or to exchange increasingly implausible stories that they themselves only half believe. Such stories are usually marked by the introductory phrase "I don't know if it's true or not, but some people say (*U lang kong . . .)*. My favorite example of the *genre* is the one explaining why the non-Kuomintang candidate, Kao Yu-shu, defeated the Kuomintang candidate for mayor of Taipei in the spring of 1964. (After that the position was made appointive.) After an earlier mayoral term, Kao was sent to the United States for a year of study, and happened to study public administration at Duke University. This made him a fellow alumnus (*t'ung-hsueh*) of then Vice President Richard Nixon, who graduated from Duke University Law School. Vice President Nixon therefore ordered the United States ambassador in Taipei to see to it that his fellow alumnus be elected mayor of Taipei. (That Mr. Nixon was not in fact still vice president in 1964 was either unknown to the narrator or considered irrelevant, as in Chinese political life powerful men often hold no formal office.) As mentioned before, it is commonly assumed that things are never what they seem, that there is an inside story, and that all events in politics result from schemes and stratagems. Common themes of the stories about politics are misplaced confidence and its betrayal, cunning and counter-cunning, and the downfall of men who think themselves master strategists but are undone either by sheer chance or by one small factor they have left out of their calculations.

These topics are also common in many folktales and in the operas and puppet shows presented at Lukang's temple festivals.

When I first heard the accounts of local political events I was unsure whether to regard them as inaccurate reports or as folklore. From a more distant perspective, I doubt that anyone except the participants could be expected to take an interest in the fine details of such mini-cycles of Cathay as those of Lukang politics. The way people think about or talk about local politics and politicians is of more significance than the details, unknowable anyway to an alien ethnographer, of just who is taking advantage of whom in any particular month. The stories do have a folkloric element, and it is not impossible that the better of them may eventually enter the canon of local oral tradition. One reason the stories have the form they do is that they are the products of minds predisposed to think of political matters with models from such sources as the *San Kuo* (The Three Kingdoms), that epic historical novel and source for hundreds of plays that offers a garden of stratagems and successful deceptions. Another reason is the desire to attract an audience for one's stories and to do so by making local life seem more colorful and dramatic than it is.

The local pages of the newspapers also fill many column inches with stories about the purported plans and negotiations of political factions and accounts of the going price of votes. These make for interesting reading and help to sell papers, and reflect the normal journalistic tendency to make much of local trivia and ephemera. They permit what is after all a controlled press in a one-party state to produce colorful and overwritten accounts of a sort of pseudopolitics, in which there are no serious issues at stake, while the factional politics of the ruling party and the serious issues confronting the central government are either ignored or treated much more circumspectly. And if the reporting of local politics in the newspapers produces the impression that Taiwan's only freely elected representatives and local officials are a set of self-serving and untrustworthy scoundrels and buffoons, that impression only reinforces the aura of dignity and high seriousness surrounding the state's unelected central leadership.

To some extent people regard local politics as a performance, a drama, and the stories about it reflect this perspective. Arthur Smith in one of his offhand remarks mentions the "extravagant fondness of the Chinese for theatrical representations," and claims that they tend to see themselves as actors on a stage.[5] In Lukang everyday life is a social drama, and one could regard much of its social life as a performance staged for the other citizens. The local factional struggle, like the old rock fight, combines serious contest with a distinctly dramaturgical quality.

The Balinese, we are told in a famous essay, use cockfights to "tell themselves about themselves."[6] The Taiwanese, whose imagination is less taken with beasts, tell themselves about themselves in many ways, one of which is factional contests. If one puts aside who gets what and attends to the commentary on the contest, one finds a discussion and elaboration of the themes of trust, confidence, autonomy, subordination, and calculation in human affairs. The protagonists of the stories are political actors, autonomous, self-directed and free to wheel and deal with whomever they will. Their orientation to their fellow men is wholly instrumental and calculating, and they look at life as stratagem and counterstratagem. By being so presented, they serve as exaggerations of what everyone is doing in their everyday lives. In the social world of contemporary Lukang, where there are no effective corporate groups beyond the household, and where everyone is free to establish relations of mutual trust and reliance with everyone else, and where some degree of calculation and self-interest is assumed, the faction leaders stand out as supremely skillful. They are virtuosos of social relations, who carry favors, influence, and the manipulation of *ch'ing* and of *kuan-hsi* to their practical extremes. What has been called the "relationship game" is an art, and the faction leaders do it very well, as a sport and a pastime.[7]

The attitude toward them is ambivalent, for they are superb performers and can get away with things, like writing worthless checks to cover their indulgences in the fleshpots of Taipei, that are beyond the reach of most people. At the same time, they are not nice men, nor are their lives uniformly or consistently successful. In contemplating their performances and the sort of world they live in, some of the limits and costs of so exclusively self-interested and calculating an orientation to social life become more clear. Ordinary people derive some satisfaction from considering and retelling their defeats and downfalls. If you want to know how far is too far to go in pursuing private advantage, you have only to look at some local political leaders or would-be leaders. I doubt that many people want their sons to become local-level politicians.

Spirit Mediums as the Antitheses of Political Leaders

Even less attractive but even more fascinating are spirit mediums (*tang-ki*), who are also the topic of many stories, much comment, and rapt if uncomfortable attention when they perform in public.[8] Spirit mediums, as a topic of discussion and commentary, are the opposite of factional leaders and provide another example of what not to be. While politicians are selfish, spirit mediums in trance are literally selfless, their "soul" temporarily displaced by the deity who uses their body as an instrument and speaks through their mouth as through a microphone. Stories about spirit mediums emphasize both their bizarre and bloody self-mutilations (which are nothing if not theatrical and give rise to a fair amount of superficial bleeding, but are nowhere near as grave or dangerous as popular stories make them out to be), and their total lack of volition and consciousness. It is usually alleged that nobody wants to be, or chooses to be, a spirit medium, but that the god arbitrarily picks someone and makes them ill or possesses them until they agree to serve as medium. If the relation between a medium and his patron god is compared to an ordinary relation between two humans, it is one in which the patron is totally dominant and forces the relation on an unwilling client who loses not only his autonomy but his very personality. One is told again and again that *tang-ki* remember nothing of what they have said or done while in trance, and people seem fascinated but appalled by such absence of self. Political leaders are too manipulative and calculating; spirit mediums are too passive and manipulated. Although spirit mediums are useful to have around the community, nobody would want their son to become one or their sister to marry one.

I am arguing that ordinary people, the bulk of the population, who neither play an active role in factional politics nor are possessed by deities find those of their fellow citizens who do to be worth thinking and commenting about because they bring to mind, personify, issues and problematic areas of everyone's lives. The issues are those of autonomy, subordination, partnership and alliance, the line between trust and gullibility, and the balancing of obligations. Most of the population of Lukang work in small enterprises or head their own small enterprises, and find security in wide ranging social networks that cut across ascriptive categories. Success, or just breaking even, requires them to be able to initiate new relationships of mutual confidence, to limit their commitment to and liability in specific social relations, to gracefully turn down invitations to deepen relations with or extend trust to certain others, and to look out for their own interests. Furthermore, this must all be done without explicitly verbalizing it, within a prevailing ethos of affability and community solidarity.

A possessed spirit medium attracts a large crowd.

This is some of what young adults have in mind when, having left school and, as they put it, come out into "society" (*sia-hue*) they find it "complicated," (*hok-cap*). The lines separating what might be considered normal tact and politesse from dissimulation from outright deception are not easy to draw. Everybody has to be instrumental and calculating to some degree, but what that degree is, is not always clear. Stories and gossip about local public figures examine these issues and help to frame their discussion.

As one example, it was alleged that one local political leader, Mr. X, was carrying on an affair with the wife of another leader, Mr. Y. Mr. Y was said to be aware of the liaison but to be doing nothing about it. Both men were part of the leadership of the same faction. Mr. X had a reputation for audacity and outrageous behavior, which included drinking, gambling, and womanizing at other people's expense, which he also used to demonstrate that he was above the law. Mr. Y, on the other hand, was more of a behind-the-scenes operator, with a reputation as an astute strategist. The question that came up was why Mr. Y was apparently acquiescing to a situation that could make him seem a dupe, a cuckold, and a laughingstock. Both men held public office, and one explanation was that Y needed the cooperation and support of X, at least for the short term, and so was cold-bloodedly ignoring the provocation. Such self-discipline shows some of the qualities necessary for success in the political arena. Mr. Y was also known to be a strategist and schemer, and indeed was reputed to read a chapter of the *San Kuo* (The Three Kingdoms) every night. He may have initiated the relation, using his wife as the bait in a scheme to destroy Mr. X, whose generally flamboyant behavior posed a threat to the interests of the faction. (I heard these stories from men, and they focused on the relation between the two men, paying no attention to the situation or conduct of Mrs. Y. Women, if they were discussing the same story, would presumably have a different perspective.) Another possibility was that X had initiated the affair, and that Y was biding his time, preparing a particularly subtle and devastating revenge, while acting in public as if nothing was amiss and he and Mr. X were the best of pals.

This story, like many others, is gossip, and may well have had no truth to it at all. But it is a fair sample of gossip, and illustrates what I meant when I said earlier that local politicians were not nice men, and by the standards of their community, not mine. Nobody comes out looking good, and the group of seven or eight men sitting about in the drugstore (Lukang does not have such public places for sociability as the teahouses described in accounts of older communities in China, and small groups of male acquaintances habitually gather in certain shops to drink tea, smoke, and chat) can agree that they would never act like that, and then volunteer yet another story about deception, or misplaced trust, or breach of norms.

The Relation Between Local Politics and Popular Religion

If one is fascinated by both local factional leaders and by spirit mediums, the place to go is a temple festival where one will have a good chance to observe both. On the face of it, temple cults and factions are antithetical organizations. Factions rest on *ch'ing*, affect, while temples are based on *li*, rationality and equity. Factions are private; temples, public. Factions exist for conflict; temples celebrate concord. Factions are ephemeral; temples endure. Yet in Lukang, as in every other Taiwanese community I am acquainted with, the religious and factional structures interpenetrate and influence each other in many ways. Their personnel overlap, for it is the wealthy and prominent men who hold ritual offices and contribute money to temples who also participate in factions and hold positions in their shadowy structures. Participation in temple affairs confers prestige and social identity as a man concerned with the welfare of the community as a whole. It can be seen as conferring legitimacy on men who gain no legitimacy from buying votes. Local political figures are aware that people do not respect or trust them in their persona of faction leaders, and they gain prestige and publicity through their involvement with temples and festivals.

On the other hand, the religious sphere benefits from the large contributions of those motivated less by faith than by face, from those who seek the respectability that can be obtained only from participation in community ritual. Religious cults themselves gain in reputation by association with important and powerful men, and the largest and best known Taiwanese temples proudly display tokens of recognition from Ch'ing emperors and officials. Lukang's great Matsu Temple is decorated with carved plaques presented by Admiral Shih Lang (who conquered Taiwan for the Ch'ing in 1685), the Ch'ien-lung Emperor (r. 1736–1796), the Kuang-hsu Emperor (r. 1875–1908), and the previous governor of Taiwan, and a photograph of the visit of the United States Ambassador in the early 1960s is prominently displayed. Such men as county heads (*hsien-chang*), provincial assemblymen and local mayors are honored guests at temple festivals, and the temple, its ritual office holders, and the guests benefit from the visit. Everybody gets a bit of prestige and a chance to meet important people and extend their range of acquaintance.

In one sense religious activities provide a field of action in which political figures act for their own, nonreligious, ends. Such political activity has a distinct effect on the organization of temples and their festivals. It is possible for a group of political allies to work together to build up a temple and make its festival a glorious event, reflecting glory back on those who sponsor it. Various temples may become associated with factions who try to exclude their rivals from prestige-generating ritual offices, or to use the ritual offices to lure rivals or the uncommitted into their camp. The rivals may respond by building up another temple and trying to extend its constituency. The political struggle is thus transformed into a different sort of struggle, one carried out not so much for votes as for contributions to a temple, and justified by claims to ritual precedence and antiquity.

The notion that common worship reinforces social solidarity is an old Chinese idea, and people will sometimes bring it up when discussing the cult of the ancestors or neighborhood temples, but no one ever suggested that factions were held together by common worship. If any solidarity is generated by common worship, it seems easily outweighed by individual ambition and self-interest. In

Lukang the city's largest and most popular temple is the old Matsu Temple (so called to distinguish it from the New Matsu Temple, founded in 1787 by the Manchu general who landed at Lukang to suppress the rebellion of Lin Shun-wen). Its management was generally associated with the dominant faction, which in 1967–68 controlled both the town office and the Farmers' Association and managed to contain, for the time being, its fissive tendencies. (More often, the local government and the Farmers' Association are controlled by rival factions, and a situation like that of Lukang is probably unstable over the span of a few years.)

Members of a rival faction, the out of office group, responded by taking over the cult of a moderately popular deity from one end of the city and investing a good deal of money in the construction of a most imposing new temple, directly opposite the Matsu Temple. They, or some of them, were reported to have previously tried to use the Shih surname association as a vehicle for their ambitions, trying to extend their influence through it. That failed, so they turned to the temple, and began putting money into its festival, hiring opera troupes, and hosting large banquets in their homes. Eventually they were able to win enough support to be able to start a fund-raising campaign and reconstruct and enlarge the temple itself. They dedicated the new temple with a magnificently extravagant festival, attended by temple groups from all over Taiwan, who were invited, along with their deities, as guests. Thousands of people came, and the procession was so long it took two hours to pass. The temple managers were making a determined effort to claim for their temple the status of a pan-Lukang temple, common to the whole city and supported by all its inhabitants (in practical terms, pan-Lukang temples tend to be supported by a small, relatively wealthy segment of the populace of the whole city) rather than a neighborhood temple, which is what it had been.

Still, the relation between political factions and religious cults is not one of complete identification. Not every member of a temple managing committee or a festival's ritual officers is deeply committed to a faction or its leaders, and it is possible, if not always easy, for well-to-do and prominent men to resist attempts to recruit them to factions. Such men may remain on relatively good terms with members of opposed factions and serve a useful role as intermediaries. They may hold ritual office in several cults, and their presence along with the association of temples and cults with social solidarity helps to limit the effects of political competition. Some of these men participate in temple affairs because they believe in the gods or take the ideals of community solidarity and good fellowship seriously. The popular religion is a force in and of itself, and cannot be described as a mere epiphenomenon or as nothing but a reflection of other structures.

Cults and Factions as Ideal Types

One can contrast religious cults and factions as ideal types, seeing them as distinct and structurally opposed forms of social organization. Religion stresses the long term; factions the immediate. Temples include everyone, symbolizing wholeness and harmony, and distribute supernatural benefits to everyone equally. Factions are restricted to the wealthy and influential and exist for strife, trying to concentrate rewards in as few hands as possible. Temples represent continuity; factions, schism. Each provides a model of society and man in society, and each model is, taken by itself, inadequate. Lukang is fairly obviously not a pure community, a *gemeinschaft*, as is asserted by the ritual model, but equally obviously there is more to local life and society than an aggregate of totally free and uncommitted individuals making temporary, contingent contracts with each other and arranging themselves in various ephemeral, loosely knit groupings.

The Third Element: State Administration

To see local society only as a contrast between faction and temple, or, to be more abstract, network and corporate group, is itself inadequate for it ignores the third image or model of local society, which is that provided by the state and its administrative structure. Anthropological studies of villages in what are called "complex societies" have too often, in their enthusiasm for community and microsociology, either ignored the state or considered the community as in some vague way causally prior to the state. This will never do, especially when the community being considered is a Chinese one. Lukang has been part of a centralized state since its foundation and state policies have had a tremendous influence on the city's economy and social organization for the past two hundred years. The people of Lukang, who after all are legally required to carry personal identification cards and who register changes in their household composition with the household registration office of the town administration, are well aware of the administrative structures that in some ways shape their lives. Under some circumstances they identify themselves as citizens of the nation, the province, or the administrative township. They choose to make much of the distinction between Lukang and its people and the rest of the island or the world, but this does not mean that they think of Lukang as self-sufficient or that they want the city to become an independent, sovereign state.

The best way that I can think of to sum up and characterize Lukang as a community, or as a social structure, is in terms of a triad of forces, or organizational principles, or structural poses, or models of society. These are temple cult, faction, and unit of a centralized bureaucratic state. The relation between the three principles of organization is one of mutual opposition, but not necessarily of contradiction. Although each is spoken of in its own frame of reference as if it were all that mattered, each is in fact part of a larger whole. None is all-embracing or self-sufficient, in and of itself, and each is defined by the others and dependent on them for its operation.

The Triple Contrast

As ideal types, the three-way contrast can even be set out in a little table, which may help to make clear what, in terms of local, culturally specific understanding, each principle represents or connotes.

Administration	Faction	Temple
Outside	Inside	Inside
National, World	Local	Local
Legal Public	Private Group	Local Public
Li, rationality	*Ch'ing*, affect	*Li*, rationality
equity	partiality	equity
Distance	Suspicion	Trust
Long-Term, Future	Short-Term, Present	Long-Term, Past
Morally Indifferent	Bad	Good
Rational Planning	Scheming	Spontaneous Action
Armed Force	Influence	Public Opinion
Legitimate	Illegitimate	Legitimate

As sources of power, factions are illegitimate, but the principle of which they are the political expression, that of affect or sentiment is, in its proper place, a perfectly normal and legitimate form of social interaction. The three principles are equally based in Chinese culture and practice. Each represents a different way of looking at society and men in society. The bureaucratic rational way is to make logical distinctions and apply them in an even-handed way, so that taxes, say, are proportional to the amount of land held or, better yet, to the size of the average harvest. The factional way, that of private sentiment, is to take human relations as foremost, and try to use a special tie or influence to have one's taxes reduced or even canceled altogether. The way of temple cults is to consider what people have in common rather than what distinguishes them, and, as a pure type, it would aim to equalize holdings and taxes or to hold everything in common. What is emphasized when a temple collects funds for its annual festival is that everyone in the neighborhood contributes, even if only a tiny sum. That some in fact contribute much more than others is equally obvious, but that is a different matter, relevant in a different context or frame of discourse.

As ideal types the three principles are clear enough, but in the actual world, "on the ground," as the anthropologist puts it, they mingle and intertwine in actual groups and in the behavior of real individuals. Factions live and operate within local government and administration. In one way they represent the sort of interstitial, supplementary, and parallel structures that, as Eric Wolf puts it, are "allowed to function in the entrails" of the state.[9] But Wolf sees such organizations or networks as "supplementary to the system . . . which is logically if not temporally prior to them." It is true that if the structure of Taiwan's central government were to change, or if it were to change some of the rules on elections, then the form of the factions would change. But it is also true that factions of some sort have been around in China and in the Chinese bureaucracy for a very long time. Several people told me that contemporary Taiwanese factions went back to competing alignments of Taiwanese landlords under the Japanese, and if it were possible to do a history of factions one might be able to trace a continuous succession back to the middle of the Ch'ing dynasty.

I am uneasy with arguments that ascribe priority to the State with a capital "S" or which consider most of local level politics or social organization to be no more than a response to the policies of central governments or to the impersonal workings of world systems.[10] As I see it, both the bureaucratic state and the personal networks, here labeled as factions, that thrive in its interstices and mediate between it and local societies, are equally Chinese, equally valid modes of social organization, and it seems simple-minded to describe either as no more than the shadow of or a response to the other. As recent history has made clear, the Chinese Communist Party, which was once presented to credulous Westerners as a pure case of a bureaucratic and managerial organization, turns out to be thoroughly factionalized at the top and clientilist at the bottom, and it is impossible to understand much of recent Chinese political history without raising questions about factions.

The Three Principles Represented and Refracted in the Ritual Idiom

Factions also influence local religious activity. It seems clear that one reason for the persisting vitality of popular religion in Taiwan during the 1960s and the 1970s, in the face of the central government's opposition to what it considered "wasteful" religious festivals, was the mutual relation between politics and religion at the local level. As long as local political figures gain publicity and some legitimacy from their sponsorship of festivals, they will continue to promote local festivals. And as long as festivals and banquets are good places to meet new people and reinforce one's relations with old acquaintances, political figures will, just like small businessmen or cabinetmakers, invite their friends to banquets on the occasion of the local temple's festival. Before Taiwan's political system opened up in the late 1980s, some of the resources that went into sponsorship of temples and their festivals were those that in a more open political system might have gone for advertisements and campaign expenses. As long as one did not push the point too far, it was possible to see in the popular religion certain muted and largely implicit political themes, which included assertion of Taiwanese identity, symbolic opposition to the government and its definitions of citizens and their roles, and the ratification by communities of their own leadership.

Yet another reason for the persistence and growth of temple festivals may be a desire to assert the existence of local communities and systems of communities in a different way than the government's definition of them as no more than parts of centrally imposed administrative units. The regional systems represented by the various community festivals, cycles of festivals, and pilgrimage routes overlap and spring into life only for a few days every year or every twelve or sixty years, and they combine the impress of long-vanished economic and political structures with the shifting alliances and personal networks of their current sponsors, but they certainly offer a different definition of communities and linked sets of communities than that offered by the hierarchy of current administrative units. It must be understood that Taiwan's popular religion in and of itself offers no challenge to the centralized state, and it has no ideological content. Folk religion takes the centralized bureaucratic state for granted, for the gods themselves are the supernatural bureaucrats of a counterpart shadowy (the *yin* world) celestial empire. People in contemporary Taiwan are, as Arthur Wolf has pointed out, quite ready to compare the gods to modern officials and administrators.[11]

When people collectively worship the gods enshrined in temples, they present themselves to themselves as an undifferentiated community who share and exchange food and drink. I was told over and over again that neighborhood temples had no managing committees for "in our neighborhood everyone knows everyone else and we're all intimate. When something has to be done, like repairing the temple, why we just get together and do it." By defining themselves as temple congregations, all those "under the incense burner" (*lo-kha*), communities can describe their relations with equivalent communities in the ritual idiom of exchange and reciprocal invitation to festivals. But people can also worship the gods in the temples, or any gods at all, as private individuals. A single man or woman may establish a special relation with one god or with as many gods as they please. These are private, dyadic relations in which the human partner offers incense and food in return for special favors, information, and influence. If the god fails to come through, the relation is broken off, and the person looks for another, more responsive, god. A farmer from the nearby countryside asked the deity in Lukang's New Matsu Temple (the one founded by Fu K'ang-an in 1787) to preserve the health of his aged father. Through the divining blocks the god agreed, and the farmer, keeping his end of the bargain, sacrificed a pig. Two months later the father died. The farmer came in to the temple with an axe and cut off the head of the statue, and suffered no ill consequences. That particular god, who in one sense is Matsu but is not the same as the Matsu in the great (old) Matsu Temple, lost face and any reputation for efficacy and responsiveness. In consequence, the temple had very few individual worshippers and was usually deserted except on the day of its annual festival, when the neighborhood demonstrated its solidarity. Like much of the symbolism of Chinese ritual, the model of human social relations provided by individual relations with deities, who gain or lose a reputation for being useful and responsive (*ling-kan*) needs little explication or comment—we have a *ch'ing*-based tie with a social superior who can grant or withhold favors. Ritual and religion provides an idiom for representing and discussing all three of the models of social organization.

How the People of Lukang
Describe Themselves to Themselves

If one asks how the people of Lukang describe their own society, the first answer would be "inconsistently and not all that completely." Some aspects of local society such as the extensive division of labor receive no public attention at all. Nor does the continuing relation with the emigrants or the city's character as an emigrant community. Sometimes the city is described as part of the administrative unit of Lukang *chen*, or of the Republic of China, but more often it is characterized as a closed corporate community, either totally undifferentiated or divided into equivalent segments that exchange dinner invitations and entertainment. If the city is taken for granted and becomes figure instead of ground, the picture becomes one of atomistic individuals who build and maintain extensive personal networks, and who have to constantly gauge the reliability of the other members of their networks. There is no single, comprehensive image of the community, and the same individuals will describe it in different ways in different contexts.

To some degree this is a function of what has become known as the ethnography of speech, that is, of what sort of speech is appropriate or customary in a given social context. The various images of the community are not intended only as pure description or model. They are used, employed by people in concrete situations, and represent, among other things, social strategies. A relative stranger who goes into a long speech about the great solidarity of Lukang people is asking for trust, and may want a vote or another recruit to a rotating credit society. Someone who tells a long story about the perfidy and bad character of one man may be justifying his own tie with another. The people of Lukang, while some are quite intelligent, are not intellectuals and are not concerned with intellectual consistency. They are neither social scientists nor philosophers. My impression was that they tended to operate on any single occasion in one frame of discourse or in another, but to keep the frames of discourse distinct. That is, they would discuss Lukang either as an undifferentiated community, or as a backdrop for interpersonal ties, or, less often but sometimes, as part of the Republic of China or of "China" in general, and tended not to acknowledge contradictions between the various frames of discourse or models. Conflicts of principle (how much *jen-ch'ing* is too much) were recognized, but not in the sort of abstract discourse that I have employed in this explication. Rather, they were handled in stories and gossip, a narrative mode that combined a rich awareness of complexities of motivation, character, and context with a very close focus on individuals and on minute particulars.

The puzzle is why so much that must be obvious to the people of the city is left out, and why they should so insist on their collective peculiarity and solidarity. Why all those neighborhood temples, which meet no obvious social function? Why the near-obsessive repetition of a very limited set of characteristics supposedly peculiar to Lukang. Why, to repeat, should the inhabitants of a fairly prosperous if not booming small commercial and industrial city, with economic (and therefore personal) ties reaching to all parts of Taiwan and beyond Taiwan to the whole world, describe itself in terms reminiscent of Durkheim's notion of an Australian horde, as a case of almost pure mechanical solidarity?

Notes

1. Edward Tenenbaum, *Taiwan's Turning Point* (Washington: Continental-Allied, 1963).

2. On the place of postdated checks in Taiwan's commercial sectors, see Jane Kaufman-Winn, "Decriminalizing Bad Checks Should Help to Rationalize Taiwan's Financial System," *East Asian Executive Reports,* vol. 8, no. 6 (August 1986), pp. 9, 19–22.

3. On Taiwan's local factions in general, see J. Bruce Jacobs, "The Cultural Bases of Factional Alignment and Division in a Rural Taiwanese Township," *Journal of Asian Studies* 36 (1976), pp. 79–97; Jacobs, "A Preliminary Model of Particularistic Ties in Chinese Political Alliances: Kan-Ch'ing and Kuan-hsi in a Rural

Taiwanese Township," *China Quarterly* 78 (1979), pp. 237–73; Jacobs, 1981; Edwin A. Winkler, "Roles Linking State and Society," in Emily M. Ahern and Hill Gates, eds., *The Anthropology of Taiwanese Society* (Stanford: Stanford University Press, 1981), pp. 50–86; Lawrence W. Crissman, "The Structure of Local and Regional Systems," in Ahern and Gates, eds., 1981, pp. 98–116.

4. J. Bruce Jacobs, *Local Politics in a Rural Chinese Cultural Setting: A Field Study of Mazu Township, Taiwan* (Canberra: Contemporary China Centre, Research School of Pacific Studies, Australian National University, 1980).

5. Arthur H. Smith (1899), *Village Life in China* (New York: Revell) (Reprint, Boston: Little Brown, 1970), chapter 8, "The Village Theatre," p. 37.

6. Clifford Geertz, "Deep Play: Notes on the Balinese Cock Fight," *Daedalus* (Winter 1972). Reprinted in Geertz, *The Interpretation of Cultures* (New York: Basic Books, 1973).

7. On the relationship game, see Mayfair Mei-hui Yang, "The Gift Economy and State Power in China," *Comparative Studies in Society and History* 31, 1 (January 1989), pp. 25–54.

8. The public fascination with the performance of spirit mediums has been noted by David Jordan who labels it "morbid curiosity." David K. Jordan, *Gods, Ghosts and Ancestors: The Folk Religion of a Taiwanese Village* (Berkeley: University of California Press, 1972), p. 82.

9. Eric Wolf, "Kinship, Friendship and Patron-Client Relations in Complex Societies," in M. Banton, ed., *The Social Anthropology of Complex Societies* (A.S.A. Monographs No. 4) (London: Tavistock, 1966).

10. On this point the treatment of the Mafia of Sicily by Blok and the Schneiders is exemplary. See, Anton Blok, *The Mafia of a Sicilian Village: 1860–1960* (New York: Harper and Row, 1974); Jane and Peter Schnieder, *Culture and Political Economy in Western Sicily* (New York: Academic Press, 1976).

11. Arthur P. Wolf, "Gods, Ghosts and Ancestors," in Wolf, 1974.

Chapter 9

Using the Model

The Absence of Formal Associations

One way to address the question is to go into it more deeply and to concentrate for the moment on those characteristics of Lukang's population and society that all observers, native and alien, would agree on. One of the most salient of these is the extensive division of labor within the city. Over the past fifty or twenty years the city's population size has remained almost static, while the occupational and economic structures have become more and more differentiated. Men who live and work in Lukang have less and less in common with each other. A man who unites with the other members of his occupation ends up with but a small number of fellows, and remains isolated from most of the people he lives among. Furthermore, while Lukang has obviously never been economically isolated or self-sufficient, the increasing division of labor and the increasingly effective transportation and communication links with the rest of Taiwan mean that people will share more direct, economic interests with those outsiders they sell to or buy from or from whom they seek employment than with the neighbors down the lane whom they greet every day. The owner of the small workshop making shears has more to do with the steel firm he buys from and the Taipei trading company he sells to than with the owner of the concrete casting yard and the maker of mirrors who are his immediate neighbors. There is no logical reason why the cabinetmakers should not identify themselves with the cabinetmakers of Changhua City and of Taichung. Lukang is not at all like a farming community where people take turns with the irrigation water and help each other bring in the harvest. It looks

as though the forces of technical progress and improved transport
are, in a familiar fashion, pulling the community apart and leaving
its people with less and less in common.

The combination of a fairly small population with considerable occupational diversity means that each occupational group
contains relatively few people—not many people make fish nets
or sell Chinese drugs or repair motorcycles. In each occupational
group the numbers are small enough for the sorts of informal
groups and networks that I discussed with reference to the furnituremakers to operate effectively. There must, one assumes, be an
upper limit to the size of a diffuse, informal group, and at some
point the advantages of formal organization and regular procedures become overwhelming. But do the twenty-one druggists or
the eight photographers of Lukang need a formal trade association? In Lukang, the combination of economic growth, which has
increased occupational differentiation, with a stable population
has made the growth of formal associations organized by common
occupation less likely than one might initially have expected.

The argument can be extended. Do the few score men who
dominate public affairs require a formal political association? Do
the hundred and twenty-five households on one street require an
elaborate organization to manage the annual festival when the
older men of the neighborhood who have lived there all their lives
and so "know each other very well" can get together and take care
of it. If most of the people of Lukang made their living in the same
way or at least worked in the same industry, then a formal occupational association would probably be useful. But then, like the
Farmers' Association or the Irrigation Association, it would most
likely be co-opted by the government.

Occupational Flux and Mutability

The city's economy rests on a foundation of several hundred
small-scale and extremely differentiated enterprises. Over the
space of a few years many of these fail, are sold, or shift into new
lines. The growth of Taiwan's economy means that many completely new sorts of enterprises are opened up by hopeful entrepreneurs or their subcontractors. Some cabinetmakers now assemble television cabinets for firms in Taipei; some metal workers
now repair power tillers and make fittings to attach small carts to
them; a manufacturer of household mirrors shifts to producing
rearview mirrors for motorcycles; former grain merchants become

agents supplying hormone enriched and antibiotic laced feed for battery hens. Just as many craftsmen move from firm to firm, many small businessmen have changed their line of business many times. The man who is a soap wholesaler this year was dealing in peanut oil the year before, and before that worked in Taichung for a Lukang emigrant who has a small factory making patent medicine, and before that was a clerk in the office of the Farmers' Association. Many small family enterprises purvey odd combinations of goods and services, such as tea and men's tailoring. If at any single moment the picture is one of great division of labor, over time it is one of flux as individuals, attempting to seize opportunities, move from employer to employer and trade to trade. The movement from one calling to another is aided by the general expansion of Taiwan's economy, which increases the chances of success, or at least of getting by, means that failure at business can be lived down and recovered from, and rests on the unquestioned assumption, which seems to be common to Chinese culture, that anyone can learn to do anything as long as they work hard at it and have someone to imitate.

The Utility of Wide Social Networks

The small size of enterprises and occupational groups and the frequent changes of employer or occupation all encourage people to extend their social networks beyond the limits of their occupation of the moment. As explained in an earlier chapter, small-scale businesses rely on informal sources of credit, and these in turn rest on wide networks of personal acquaintance and estimates of a person's overall moral character. Any single rotating credit society of twelve or fifteen members will have many different occupations represented, and any single small businessman or middle-aged housewife will be participating in several rotating credit societies at any single time. A shift in employer, as from one furniture shop to another, or a shift in line of business, as from selling cloth to running a beancake press, depends on an estimate of chances of success in the new niche and on personal contact with someone already established in that place or trade. The wider one's personal contacts, the better one's chances. This applies to both one's fellow Lukang men and to people from outside the city, but the odds on knowing someone well enough to trust or take advice from are higher for Lukang people. Maintaining a wide-ranging network of acquaintance and trying to keep on good terms with as many people as possible is therefore only good sense, and economic self-interest if nothing else would dictate such behavior.

The peculiarities of Lukang's demographic structure make such a social strategy easier to follow than it might be in another sort of community. Since almost everybody in Lukang was in fact born and raised there, as were their parents, people have had a good long while to get to know each other, and the complex overlapping of circles of acquaintance mean that it is not too difficult to learn the reputation of those Lukang people one has not actually met. With three primary schools and near universal attendance, the odds are one in three that one will have known a contemporary since age six. Those who attended the city's single middle school are more likely to remain in Lukang than their contemporaries who attend the more highly ranked middle schools of Changhua City or Taichung, and all graduates of the middle school can at least claim common acquaintance. The relatively frequent changes of employer or of occupation mean that occupation does not form so significant an element of personal identity as it does for, say, middle class Americans, while position in a community is a more significant element. This in turn means that occupational diversity, while not insignificant, does not have all the social consequences one might at first assume it would.

Relations with Lukang's Emigrants

While the owners of many of the city's small shops or factories have important business relations with suppliers or customers from outside the city, it is possible that a good many of those outsiders are in fact Lukang emigrants or the children of Lukang emigrants. The economic role of the emigrants and their contributions to the city's economy are topics about which I have, regrettably, little detailed information. It is public knowledge that the largest contributors to the rebuilding of Lukang's temples, including small neighborhood temples, are often emigrant businessmen who reside in Taipei or Kaohsiung. Many of the pilgrimage groups that come to Lukang are in fact composed of emigrants or their children, who support temples in the cities where they reside and bring those deities back with them when they visit their old home. It is equally public knowledge that many families are supported either entirely or in part by money sent back by emigrants, and occasionally a well-to-do emigrant returns to Lukang either to retire or to open some sort of business. The latter situation, which is rare, results in gossip that he must have failed in the big city, else why come back to Lukang (where everyone knows there are no opportunities) to earn money. It seems likely that emigrants who leave Lukang are aided by being able to appeal to successful earlier emigrants in terms of the sentiments of common place of origin, and it also seems likely that many of the businessmen who stay at home in Lukang are aided by their contacts with the emigrant communities. If this be so, then there is an additional reason for casting one's net widely and trying not to offend anyone unnecessarily, for you never know when his brother or uncle in Kaohsiung may be in a position to be helpful to you.

If Lukang is considered as an emigrant community, a city that, among other specialties, produces human talent for export, then its claims to internal solidarity and to generalized traditionalism take on a new significance. In his book on the emigrant community of San Tin in Hong Kong's New Territories, James L. Watson suggests that emigrant communities are often conservative.[1] While San Tin, practically all of whose adult males are working in restaurants in the United Kingdom or western Europe, is so conservative as to be anachronistic, Lukang only thinks of itself as conservative, and little hard evidence of traditionalism can be adduced. My impression is that few of the Lukang emigrants ever come back, even to retire, and that for most purposes they are absorbed into the society of Taipei or Kaohsiung. They are after all the majority population, Hokkien-speaking Taiwanese, and thus in a very different position in Taipei than Cantonese restaurant workers in London or Hokkien merchants in Jakarta. Many of them probably consider themselves more as migrants than as sojourners. It is to the advantage of the people back in Lukang to define those who leave as sojourners, and so retain a claim on their loyalties, in order to keep the money flowing, to maintain the communication channels and the business contacts, and to be able to find jobs for those who continue the tradition of out-migration.

One can hardly expect the migrants, some of them gone for twenty or thirty years, or the sons of migrants (often by non-Lukang mothers) to continue to identify themselves as Lukang men and to give special consideration to strangers with no more claim on them than their common status as Lukang men if the people back in Lukang no longer claim to share something in common or to be a distinctive group. If the community dissolves, there's no reason to expect anything from those who left earlier. The solidarity and distinctiveness of Lukang may well be a myth, but it is a useful myth. And since in the culture of contemporary Taiwan, or in the prevailing social idiom, the way people assert solidarity and community is through ritual, Lukang goes in for a lot of temples and claims to ritual antiquity and precedence. The temple festivals are occasions for the migrants to return and to invite their non-Lukang friends and associates from the big cities. They are occasions, and indeed invitations, for the successful migrants to return and show off their wealth and success. G. W. Skinner has pointed out that in overseas Chinese communities in Southeast Asia it is often those Chinese who have the most extensive ties with the host populations and are in some ways the most "assimilated" who are the leaders of the Chinese community.[2] One could argue that those Lukang men who are most successful in Taipei and Kaohsiung are probably those who have the most extensive ties with the economic and political elites of those cities, and of all Taiwan. I would guess, by the Southeast Asian analogy, that such men would most likely be the heads of the Lukang associations that flourish in those cities, and, on a smaller scale, the same would hold for those emigrants who head not a formal Lukang association but a temple in Puli or Taitung, which is a branch of a Lukang temple. If by emphasizing or overemphasizing the social boundary between Lukang and Lukang people and the rest of Taiwan, Lukang is able to keep claims on the loyalties of some members of the commercial and industrial elite of the country's largest cities, as well as on the loyalties of some well-educated, middle-ranking members of the national bureaucracy, then the city has done fairly well for itself, and can serve both its pride and its pocketbook.

Networks and Lukang's Ritual Style

The increased division of labor and the consequent need to maintain wide networks of potential allies and creditors also serve to make some sense of the muted and low-key quality of the celebrations of the neighborhood temples' festivals. In the past the complex web of crosscutting ties and overlapping formal groups that bound the city's inhabitants together permitted the open expression of forthright though limited opposition. But today the only recognized subcategories of the population are those of neighborhood. If the relations between different neighborhoods were overtly expressed as opposition and competition there would be no compensating loyalties to cut across and limit identification with neighborhoods, and the result could well be real bitterness or else severance of relations. Individuals would lose if they no longer had the possibility of doing business with or recruiting to rotating credit societies members of certain other neighborhoods, and they would gain nothing from severing relations. So, the people from different neighborhoods are careful not to give offense, and are very polite to each other, and this in itself can be interpreted as evidence of a decline in common interests.

The Logic of the Situation

So far, in my attempt to account for the wide gap between Lukang's economic and social structure and the way its people describe it, I have concentrated on the economic rationality of their style of personal network, their refusal to publicly discriminate within the category of "Lukang people," and their assertion of community. I have done this not because I think economic rationality to be the only cause, or because I believe men to be motivated only or primarily by economic interests, but because I wish to show how, in the proper context, those things people say and do that originally puzzled me make sense. I have begun with economic rationality because the logic of the situation here seems the most clear and straightforward. I believe there are other reasons for the people of Lukang to describe their society as they do, but my arguments for those reasons rest on assumptions about what is going on inside the heads of the people, assumptions that cannot be backed up by such specific evidence as lists of factories or employment histories.

To elaborate a point initially made in the last chapter, I think that the people of Lukang do want to make sense of the place they live in, to feel that they inhabit an orderly community. But, I also think that the city's present social organization, which rests on an economic foundation of hundreds of small, diverse, and often ephemeral enterprises, and which takes the form of what can very loosely be described as a complex array of overlapping personal networks, is hard to sum up or make a neat model of. It is not "good to think." I am a professionally qualified social anthropologist who is familiar with attempts to describe such "complex" or "loosely structured" societies as that of contemporary Lukang. I took a business census, have quite complete data on the occupational distribution of the city's work force, and investigated a few sorts of occupations in detail. I still find it difficult to sum up Lukang except with vegetable metaphors. How much more so the people who live there, who discuss different aspects of their communities social organization in different contexts and don't seem too concerned with overall consistency.

Describing Communities

A flux of diverse small businesses run by independent owners whose goal is to grab the main chance and maximize their medium-term returns is not easy to picture to one's self. Nor are the many ways the city is connected to the larger world of Taiwan or to the world as a whole. Few of the usual ways employed by social scientists to dissect communities, especially those of comparable size and complexity, can be applied very easily to Lukang. Ethnicity and even subethnicity are uniform. So, for all practical purposes, is religion. There is no structure of formal associations to be analyzed. If anybody in the community has political opinions or goals that differ from those of the party in power, they very prudently keep them to themselves. I have already mentioned the difficulty of trying to take occupational categories as significant subgroups. Not only are there very many occupations, but people change from one occupation to another with relatively high frequency. The significant basic units are families and households, whose members often pursue several different occupations and have multiple sources of income.

Class

In the abstract, my favorite candidate for the intellectual tool most likely to be useful for analyzing the community would be class. To have any validity or persuasive power though, a description in terms of class must be grounded in the details of the community in question; it cannot consist of the loose application of a set of taken-for-granted and European-derived categories that fit all societies ("petit-bourgeoisie"). It proved very difficult to do a halfway adequate analysis of Lukang's class composition. For one thing, households often have multiple sources of income and it is difficult, though not impossible, to estimate the annual income of any single household. It is hard to go beyond one's initial impression that there are some rich people, some poor people, and that most of the population falls somewhere in the middle. Working for yourself and working for someone else, and working in a small business whose future is uncertain and working for a large-scale organization are obvious distinctions to make, but in Lukang itself very few people have white collar, salaryman jobs and very few employers employ more than ten other people. The old class structure of landlords, merchants, and tenant farmers is gone. My impression is that at least from about 1953 to 1968 social mobility was fairly common and the class structure fairly fluid. Taiwan's overall economic growth, which was accelerating during the mid and late 1960s, raised living standards generally, provided full employment, promoted occupational diversification, and provided opportunities for entrepreneurship and speculation. Since the eighteenth century the economic interests of Lukang's elite have extended beyond the city's streets, and that remains true today. Men residing in Lukang may have shares in factories, shops, or real estate in Kaohsiung, Taichung, Taipei, or almost any other community. Sometimes this is done through a family economy, with a brother or brother-in-law managing the Taichung operation, and sometimes it is done through trusted business associates who are not kinsmen. But there is no way to tell this by looking at the brick or stucco facade of a family's house, and the value of the holdings in other places is not public information. The consequence is that the extreme top and the extreme bottom of the class structure are easy enough to identify, but the vast middle range is much murkier.

And, all of this applies as much to the people of Lukang as to foreign observers. A good deal of gossip revolves around how much a given family is really worth, and common themes are that many people who look poor are really rich and many people who act rich are really poor. Many people are quite skilled at impression management and at controlling information on their finances. Hints and clues, but no more, emerge from the size of contributions to temple festivals and rebuildings (these are listed on posters on the temple wall), and from the amount spent on weddings and funerals, which are, however, infrequent events for any given family. As of 1968 there was very little new residential construction in Lukang, and the size and condition of a family's house indicated little about its current income. Conspicuous consumption is not really an element of life in Lukang, which offers few venues for it, and spending on banqueting and other indulgences is usually done in Changhua City, Taichung, or Taipei. Showing off one's wealth within Lukang is more likely to invite negative than positive comment (with those doing so labeled either as spendthrifts, not too intelligent, or, with the Minsk/Pinsk logic of assumed misrepresentation, to be acting rich to conceal financial loss or trouble).

On top of this, the government discourages talking about class, and usually prefers to see its citizens as uniting their efforts for the common good. Talking too much about class or suggesting that people in different occupations but with similar life situations have something in common and should think of themselves in those terms is not prudent, and is not commonly done. Probably the closest most people come to talking in terms of class is discussing educational levels or "cultural levels." The more formal education someone has, the better, and someone who is a senior middle school graduate is, everything else being equal, distinctly one up on someone else who is only a junior middle school graduate. Residents of Lukang justify their disparagement of farmers by the "low cultural levels" of rustics. But categorization by educational level is usually applied only to discrete individuals, such as prospective marriage partners, and people do not generalize about all junior middle school graduates or all primary school dropouts. Beyond the superficial awareness of differences between rich and poor, the people of the city don't publicly use class to place themselves or to categorize others.

Community Goals and Direction

Nor is there any simple way to characterize Lukang and where it is going. The past is clear, but the present and the future are obscure. If Taiwanese communities were in the habit of announcing themselves with roadside signs, like some American communities (Sauerkraut Capital of the World), I can't imagine Lukang's sign doing anything but referring to the past (Lukang: Once Second Only to Tainan. Lukang: Taiwan's Oldest Matsu Temple. Lukang: City With That Old-Time Atmosphere.) Although its people enjoy a higher standard of living and their lives are different from those of their parents and grandparents, the city itself has not grown appreciably or changed in any striking way in the past twenty years. Very few new buildings have been constructed, and there is still no public water supply or sewer system. The factories are small and most of them are tucked away on back alleys or on the edges of the city. Temples are much more conspicuous than factories. There is little feeling that the city is progressing much or going anywhere in particular. Local political figures are regarded more as faction leaders or local big men who dole out individual favors than as leaders who can define the future of the community. After a while one gets the impression that all the most significant things about Lukang have already happened, and that the past constitutes a real burden. If the present resists definition or description while the past is all too clearly (which is not to say accurately) defined, then the easiest way to describe the present is in terms of the past.

Ch'ing and Li, Markets and Temples, Networks and Communities

An exercise of the sociological imagination permits one to see the repeated assertions of Lukang as a community that is, in Redfield's phrase, "distinctive, small, homogenous, slow to change and self sufficient," as the necessary corollary or obverse side of the stress put on independent actors, free to establish short-term relations and transact exchanges with whomever they please. In terms of Chinese culture, the field of those willed and inherently variable relations described with terms for "affect"—*ch'ing*, cannot exist alone. They must be balanced by the predictable, regular, enduring ties of *li*, reason or rationality. And groups, or even communities, based on *li* are also characterized as internally homogenous. Although such formal corporate groups as the guilds with their patron gods and annual banquets no longer exist to permit their members to generate enough mutual trust to do business with each other, the whole city could be considered, in its structural pose as a set of temple cults exchanging hospitality, as one big *li* group. If so, then like other *li*-based groups such as lineages and guilds it will ignore, play down, or forbid its members to establish social relations that cross its boundaries (see collections of lineage rules); insist on considering its members as equivalent and interchangeable; and constitute itself as a religious group, united by common worship and commensality. Lukang is not only an industrial city that is pretending to be a Central American Indian village (a closed corporate community); it is a Chinese city pretending to be a lineage or a guild. Not surprisingly, the pretense is not wholly convincing.

In more general logical or sociological terms, short-term transactions between independent strangers cannot serve as the foundation for a social order, nor can they themselves generate a social order, because the actors must trust each other before they can begin exchanges, and they must have confidence that contracts will be enforced. The trust and confidence that underpin the exchanges and the wide-ranging personal networks must come from somewhere. In narrow terms this is a question of sanctioning contracts, but it has a general application to all of social life. A treatise by an economist on the limits of the market principle points out that: "In brief, the principle of self-interest is incomplete as a social organizing device. It operates effectively only in tandem with some supporting social principle. . . . Informal social controls in the form of socialized norms of behavior are needed to allow the market process itself to operate. These range from personal standards such as telling the truth to acceptance of the legitimacy of commercial contracts as a basis for transactions."[3] He also points out that the social prerequisites of markets have been studied by sociologists rather than by economists.

For Lukang the point is that the business relations, the extensive personal networks of *ch'ing* ties, the overlapping circles of rotating credit societies, can only operate among people who believe themselves to belong to a community of moral humans who honor their obligations. In their culture, the way to indicate the existence of such a moral community is to form themselves into temple cults, burn incense, exchange dinner invitations, and do a lot of gossiping. In the short run the necessity for small businessmen to donate money to temple festivals and to spend quite a lot of time in diffuse social interaction could be seen as irrational, or as a cost. The burden of the central government and the Kuomintang's low-key but continual effort to discourage the practice of folk religion is that it is "wasteful," and that if people want to donate money they should build schools rather than temples. But in a larger perspective or in the long run, the activities of small businessmen are perfectly rational and reasonable, since that is the way basic trust is obtained. Refusal to participate in community affairs means no *hsin-yung*, and without *hsin-yung* no business can succeed. A study of overseas Chinese businessmen in South Vietnam in the 1960s argues that one reason for the relative success of Chinese businessmen is their access to cheaper credit, that is, lower interest rates, than their Vietnamese counterparts, and that the lower cost of credit is a direct consequence of the ability of the Chinese to extend relationships of mutual confidence within their network of same-place and speech-group associations.[4] Fred Hirsch, the economist quoted above, goes on to point out that "individuals can obtain their self-interested objectives only if they behave as if they were altruistic."[5] One might argue that the more Lukang's economy is based on small and diverse firms, and the more social relations consist of dyadic bonds, the more stridently its people will assert their special identity and solidarity, what strikes the outsider as evidence to the contrary notwithstanding.

In most of the Taiwanese communities I am familiar with, temples are physically adjacent to markets, and this is, as they say, not accidental. Temples and markets are the physical manifestations of the two social principles, calculation and communitas, that guide the social life of the people beyond the confines of the family and kinship. To have a Chinese community you need a temple and a market; each implies the other and together they form a whole. Every market has an adjoining temple, but not every temple has a market. The response here is that there is more to social exchange and transactions than selling cabbages and fish, and that commercial transactions are simply the most visible subset of the larger category of transactions and relationships that make up social organization, what Morton Fried called "the fabric of Chinese society."

Notes

1. James L. Watson, *Emigration and the Chinese Lineage: The Mans in Hong Kong and London* (Berkeley: University of California Press, 1975), pp. 217–218.

2. G. W. Skinner, "Overseas Chinese Leadership: Paradigm for a Paradox," in Gehan Wijeyewardene, ed., *Leadership and Authority* (Singapore: Singapore University Press, 1968).

3. Fred Hirsch, *Social Limits to Growth* (Cambridge: Harvard University Press, 1976), pp. 12, 121.

4. Clifton A. Barton, "Trust and Credit: Some Observations Regarding Business Strategies of Overseas Chinese Traders in South Vietnam," in L. A. Peter Gosling and Linda Lim, eds., *The Chinese in Southeast Asia*, vol. 1, *Ethnicity and Economic Activity* (Singapore: Maruzen Asia, 1983), pp. 46–64.

5. Hirsch, 1976, p. 139.

Chapter 10

Varieties of Conscious Models

To the extent that this work has been a community study focused
on the city of Lukang, it owes such significance as it may have to
its contribution not to Taiwanese local history or memoirs but to
larger issues of Chinese society and culture. Behind all the details
of neighborhood structure or its absence, of local self-images, and
of the terminology and concepts applied to commerce and the disreputable activities of political factions lies a concern with both
the patterns of Chinese social life and with the categories, the
models if we will, that the members of that society use to describe
it and, hence, themselves. Less fully articulated, but nonetheless
present, is my concern with the ways that foreign observers conceptualize and study Chinese society and culture.

Echoes of the Classics

On the face of it, nothing would seem more alien or distasteful to
the Confucian persuasion than a city full of small-scale businessmen, all motivated by self interest and the pursuit of profit. And
yet, when one listens to those merchants and artisans talk about
their lives, one discerns certain echoes of or affinities with the
Confucian model of society. Most obviously, instead of talking
about profits, or advantage, or competition, they talk about character and morality and do so using a term, the *hsin* of *hsin-yung*,
that is one of Confucian Five Virtues.[1] Like good Confucians they
deny the legitimacy of contention and prefer to speak of everyone
in the same occupation as trying to suit an impersonal market or,
even more vaguely, "conditions," rather than trying to beggar their

neighbors. They describe social life in terms of "sentiment," as based on two-person relations. When they do refer to a category of persons, such as all those who follow the same trade or all those who live in the same neighborhood, or all the inhabitants of their city, they, like the author of the colloquial version of the Sacred Edict, assume that membership in the same category necessarily corresponds to membership in a social group, and that the group must be homogenous and highly solidary. They also take for granted that all humans are inherently social and sociable, and equate morality with participation in social, community life. Men frequently described women as selfish and "narrow-hearted," and explained this as a consequence of women's greater confinement to the narrow world of the household and dearth of opportunities for participation in what they called simply "society" (*sia-hue*).[2]

There is no need to push the point too far. If one hears echoes of Confucianism in the vocabulary used by petty capitalists or in the rhetoric associated with popular religion, they are no more than echoes. Most of the shopkeepers had never read the Confucian Classics. In their descriptions of the need to adapt one's behavior to a complex and constantly changing set of "business conditions," I heard strong echoes of Taoism. But, again, few if any of the artisans or shopkeepers had read *Chuang-tze* or *Lieh-tze*, and none belonged to any identifiably Taoist sect or group.

To flatly label Lukang's cabinetmakers or drapers as Confucianists or Taoists would be to distort the situation and invite the scorn of sinologists who know what real Confucianists or Taoists are. (Or, who think they do. An article by Nathan Sivin draws our attention to the very loose way the term "Taoist" is in fact employed and the record of a 1989 conference on Confucianism revealed a surprising lack of consensus on the content of that familiar term.[3]) But, to ignore the parallels between the ways Taiwanese shopkeepers and artisans describe their world and the classical texts of their civilization seems shortsighted and distorting in its own way. In a very general way, all I am saying is that the Lukang businessmen and artisans share a generalized Chinese culture, which contains elements that can be labeled as Confucian or Taoist. This, however, is neither particularly original nor particularly enlightening.

Muffled Echoes

It is somewhat more enlightening to argue that the apparent discontinuities between the classics and Confucianism on the one hand and the concepts people use to describe personal relations, networks of "connections," and the worlds of commerce and electoral politics on the other hand are only apparent. One could argue that, properly understood, the Confucian tradition and its tenets underlie, or underpin, or constitute the deep structure of the concepts employed to conceptualize such superficially non-Confucian relationships as those of commerce and politics. In this mode of argument one would say that the cultural heritage of Confucianism gives the economic organization and the state structure of Sinitic societies their peculiar and distinctive character. This offers a way out of the sterile and superficial distinction between the traditional and the modern, or between tradition and high culture on the one hand, and economic rationality on the other. As an anthropologist describing the economic utility of the "conservative" and "traditional" practices of Hausa merchants in West Africa put it, "It is quite true that Hausa organization of long-distance trade is "traditional" but what (critics) overlook is that in the present circumstances this organization is the most rational, the most economic and hence the most profitable."[4]

Commerce and economic rationality have, after all, been part of Chinese culture for over two thousand years, which is certainly long enough for gross conceptual contradictions to be reconciled and smoothed over.[5] A recent study of ancient Chinese history pushes the notion of relations established through "pacts" (*yueh*) or contracts back to origins in the Warring States period.[6] Studies of Chinese family structure made in the 1970s and 1980s have emphasized the compatibility between the "traditional" Chinese family system and the demands of economic growth and development.[7] Specialists in the "statecraft" school of Confucian thought, which flourished in the Ming/Qing period, argue that "there was a great deal more flexibility in the Confucian economic tradition than has often been thought."[8]

Maurice Freedman once wrote of the politics of an old state,[9] and one could equally well write of commerce, contracts, and personal networks in an old society. For China, extensive commerce, division of labor, and widespread recognition of what we call economic rationality go back at least to the Han dynasty. The Confucian tradition has thus had ample time to come to terms with them, and those doing business and establishing extended social networks and formal associations have had equally long to find ways to cloak their activities in the prestigious nomenclature of Confucianism. The presumed discontinuity between them with which this exposition began can be seen, I now feel, to be consequence of regarding these subjects in isolation, in foreign libraries and seminar rooms, rather than in the proper context of a living Chinese community. Within Chinese culture people commonly refer to acculturation with the metaphor of cooking, distinguishing "cooked" and properly civilized Chinese from "raw" barbarians, and it is perhaps not too far-fetched to regard Chinese culture as like a very long-simmering stew in which all the original ingredients have had a chance to swap flavors around, and in which it is very hard to say which single taste or ingredient is the base or substratum.

Weber and Confucius

The striking economic success of Hong Kong, Singapore, Taiwan, and South Korea in the 1980s, as well as the economic take-off of China's Kwangtung (Guangdong) province have generated a scholarly reevaluation of the Confucian tradition. They have also given the academic literature of the 1940s and 1950s, which assumed a conflict between the requisites of economic development and general "modernization" and the dead hand of traditionalism, familism, and particularism a distinctly dated and musty quality. The air of patronizing condescension toward the traditional economic practices of East Asian societies has been replaced by admiration, baffled insistence that it can't possibly work, or attempts to save earlier conceptualizations or explanatory schemes by reducing the success of some small East Asian polities to epiphenomena of the capitalist world system or the short-term gains of "self-exploitation."

Efforts at reinterpretation of the Confucian legacy have ranged from fairly vulgar treatments that reduce Confucianism to valuing education, hard work, and saving to sophisticated scholarly works that point out the presence within indubitably Confucian and traditional texts of such aspects of rationality and supposed modernity as a concern for education and for a "fiduciary community" whose citizens have overcome egoism, nepotism, and parochialism.[10]

Historian Thomas Metzger, a specialist in the internal structure of the Ch'ing bureaucracy, has consistently stressed the rationality, adaptiveness, and initiative of Ch'ing officials, whose values included industry and thrift, dedication to the responsibilities of their positions, universalism, and respect for law. He condemns Western characterizations of Confucianism and Chinese civilization as flawed by traditionalism, particularism, and submission to the authority of the past as misconceptions based on inadequate understanding of Confucianism. Metzger's neo-Confucians are an active, dynamic lot, quite as intent on changing, as opposed to only understanding, the world as any Marxist, and possessed of a functional equivalent to Max Weber's Protestant ethic.[11] Hence, anyone accepting Weber's link between religious orientations and the prerequisites for the development of capitalism would find that Confucianism would serve as well as Calvinism. Indeed, Ronald Dore has argued, with special reference to Japan but in terms that could be extended to Chinese culture as well, that the habits of "relational contracting" common to chopstick-using East Asia are not only compatible with the demands of capitalism and the mechanisms of sustained economic growth, but that they are actually better suited to producing that growth than the institutions of the Western societies which began the process.[12]

Benjamin Schwartz argues that although Confucianism itself was not oriented toward wealth and power, it was not necessarily an impediment to modernization, and indeed many practices and institutions associated with Confucianism proved favorable to economic growth.[13] Acceptance of the subordination of individual interests to those of on-going social groups, the stress on education and the long-term individual effort required to master knowledge that is properly used in transforming the world, and acceptance of a role for the state in the management of what some in the West would define as "the economy" are Confucian orientations that have benefited the economic performance of many East Asian nations.

Interpreting the Echoes of the Classics

As a field anthropologist well aware that the community I was looking at was a small part of a larger society and civilization and as one modestly acquainted with the classic texts of that civilization, I expected the statements of the people of Lukang to have some relation to the larger culture and the heritage of China's high civilization. My study of small businessmen and artisans was motivated by Weberian questions of relations between culturally specific systems of values, including models of and for society, and behavior in the marketplace and beyond the confines of the family. I found it difficult, though, to draw any convincing link between any specifically Confucian term or concept and the statements of my informants. Nor did I see, as I had suspected I might, evidence of any great discontinuity between the values and vocabulary of the marketplace and those of the home and the community. Students of religion in Taiwan have described the difficulties of identifying specifically Taoist or Buddhist practices or statements in religious behavior in Taiwanese communities, or of understanding why Taiwanese informants labeled some religious practices as they did.[14] In a similar way, I found it difficult to distinguish Confucian values, norms, and statements from the larger matrix of Chinese culture in general. In fact, I was unable to do this and wrote instead of concepts and categories used to describe business relations and those between people not linked by the ascriptive bonds of kinship. That the terms, like *hsin* and *ch'ing*, were complex words with referents in the classic tradition was a point acknowledged only in passing. With this experience in mind, I do not, on reflection, find the argument set out in section two above, on the Confucian tradition "properly understood" serving as the underlying foundation of contemporary modes of economic or political organization to be convincing. It's not a bad argument, but I don't think it really works. It rests on the assumption that there is an unambiguous, clearly understood Confucian tradition that can be demonstrated to "underlie" or serve as the "template" for contemporary economic and political-economic organization and action.

Confucianism, Culture, and the Community

It turns out that trying to distinguish Confucianism from Chinese culture in general is not a problem afflicting only anthropologists who are, at best, half-educated in the Classics and trying to record and interpret the often poorly articulated concepts of people who are even less well-educated in the Great Tradition of their civilization. With hindsight now it is more evident that in trying to describe aspects of Lukang's society I was grappling with a conceptual problem that continues to confound everyone who tries to write about economically successful East Asian societies and their supposed Confucian heritage. The motivation for invoking the Confucian heritage is, I feel, in part the lingering influence, often unacknowledged, of Max Weber, and in part an attempt to find some factor common to the otherwise disparate societies of Japan,

South Korea, Hong Kong, Taiwan, Singapore, and perhaps Kwang-tung and Fukien as well. Confucianism, which was self-con-sciously adopted into Korea and Japan and is today explicitly taught in the public schools of Singapore, looks like a good candi-date for the Weberian source of values and the common factor.

However, when one reviews the literature, journalistic, higher journalistic, trendily scholarly, and simply scholarly, that speaks of the Confucian heritage, one finds little agreement on what that Confucian heritage actually consists of. Each writer glosses Confu-cianism in a different way, and it would prove instructive to sim-ply list all the qualities that Confucianism is taken to connote. Some reviewers have taken to task authors for whom Confucian-ism becomes indistinguishable from traditionalism, from any-thing nonmodern, and from culture in general.[15] I was most impressed by the intellectually high level of the discussion reported in the East-West Center's volume on *The Confucian World Observed: A Contemporary Discussion of Confucian Humanism in East Asia.* I was also impressed by the general fail-ure of the distinguished participants, all far better acquainted with the content of the Confucian tradition than I, to come to any agree-ment on what Confucianism was or is, or how it is to be distin-guished from Chinese civilization or culture. When so many seri-ous and knowledgeable scholars fail to agree on the content of what would appear to be a fairly well-defined intellectual system, the problem would seem to lie not with the individual writers and their shortcomings but with the way the issue is framed.

Reinventing Culture?

As I see it, though concern for the effects of the Confucian heritage on contemporary societies and their economic systems demon-strates a commendable recognition of the significance of values, culture, and history for understanding social life, it is in practice impossible to disentangle Confucianism from culture, whether Chinese, Japanese, or Korean. Calling it Confucianism instead of Chinese culture doesn't really aid understanding. The anthropo-logical concept of culture or of "a culture" is a difficult one, and anyone trying to use it as an explanatory concept is risking many conceptual pitfalls, dangers, and subtle confusions. In a nutshell, the most apparent of these include circular reasoning (the culture can only be inferred from behavior, which means that it can't be used on the next page to explain that behavior), loss of analytic rigor and reification of high level abstractions, and the tendency to ignore limited, midrange explanations that are open to testing and incremental improvement in explanatory power.

One way to handle the problems is to argue that "culture" is a necessary background concept, one that is part of the fundamentals of any inquiry into a society other than one's own, or to comparison of any two societies (another background concept), but that it is so broad as to be not useful for most focused study or closely reasoned argument. If one is analyzing the forces acting on a bridge, or comparing the design of two bridges one does not devote much time to arguing about gravity or mass, so long as one accepts them as basic concepts. When attempting anthropological or historical explanation, going directly from minute particulars to the overarching culture is usually a poor method.

In an echo of Robert Merton and the sociology of the 1950s I would like to offer the modest suggestion that midrange inquiries and theorizing about aspects of Chinese or East Asian social and economic organization may offer more productive avenues than further discussion or argument about "the Confucian paradigm" or the relation between Confucian values and modernization. We still lack complete descriptions or adequate models of many aspects of commonplace Chinese social practices that might be thought to have some bearing on the major themes of economic development and growth, or on the effectiveness of state intervention in the economy, assuming those to be topics worth focusing on. Where, for instance, is the monograph on rotating credit societies, or on variations in family economic strategies? Where is the study that shows how such attitudes or orientations as those for industry, perseverance, or long-term perspectives are actually taught to children? Where is the study of traditional forms of contract or of accounting techniques? Where are the detailed occupational and business histories of successful and unsuccessful business ventures?

With this sort of knowledge in hand it should be possible to move beyond the unproductive wrestling with hopelessly vague and global categories that I see as, in the last analysis, vitiating most of the discussion of "the Confucian paradigm." I would argue that relations of credit, business networks, and long-term economic strategizing are after all as much elements of traditional Chinese civilization as are discussions of the proper rituals of mourning or the details of the referential nomenclature of distant agnates, that they can be brought into the ambit of what we understand by such terms as "Chinese civilization" and that they should be. What is needed is economic history, sociology of business, and accounts of the ways economic activity is situated within particular configurations of social relations and forms of community. Detailed monographic accounts of some particular aspects of the interactions between governmental bodies and private enterprises in contemporary Taiwan or Hong Kong or Guangdong would also be useful. In every case, the goal would be to move away from "Confucianism" or "Chinese culture" to more productive midrange generalizations.

Lessons from Lukang

My initial inquiry into social life in Lukang was motivated by what I saw as some intellectual puzzles generated by the manifest inadequacy of the native Chinese model of society—that provided by Confucianism—for describing that society. I still feel that attempting to work out the model of society contained in the most prestigious and explicit texts of Chinese civilization was a useful exercise, and one that provided a stock of productive questions to ask in the field. Experience in the field and subsequent reflection on that experience, however, should serve to help reformulate the questions, the intellectual puzzles, that initially motivated the field research.

In retrospect, my sojourn in Lukang represented a quest for "the native model," which is of course but a variant of "the culture" or the "pattern of culture." Beneath all the references to the literature and awareness of what seemed illuminating and productive modes of anthropological inquiry in non-Chinese societies, lay the attempt to either discern the whole pattern, or, more modestly, to at least illuminate a few pieces of the puzzle and show where they fit in with the other assembled bits. The effort began with Confucianism and the translation of that into the language of Western sociology, the better to point out what struck me as lacunae in the Confucian model. The next step was to look for "the native model" on the ground, in an actual Chinese community. There I found not a single "model" but a complex set of contrasting emphases or partial models, summed up by such contrasts as li/ch'ing or temple/faction/ administrative unit. Although I have generally restrained myself from discussing this point, each of the various and partial "folk models" used by the people of Lukang could in turn be translated into the terms of Western social-scientific theories, ranging from social exchange theory to ethnomethodology to classical microeconomics to classical functionalism. Further, each of the major models could, under further analysis, be broken down yet further into midrange or minor models. Images that come to mind are Chinese boxes, or molecules—atoms—particles—quarks.

Furthermore, the various models of society and social life that I derived from the speech and actions of the people of Lukang were not abstractions intended for debate in seminar rooms or learned journals. They were employed or deployed in concrete situations, by actors with their own purposes, which did not include being internally consistent social theorists. And the actors of course were not uniform and interchangeable "Lukang people" or carriers of the local culture; they were men or women; young, middle-aged, or old; well-off or poor; educated or semiliterate, and so on. People's conception of their own society can clearly be expected to be shaped, if not wholly determined, by their position in that society.

By this point, plainly, we seem to have too many models. Attempting to discuss relations between the models introduces yet another dimension of complexity and multiplicity. What began as a way to raise interesting questions and to guide inquiry now threatens to metastasize into a classificatory apparatus so unwieldy as to bring exposition and discussion to a halt. Either we must return to the assumption that, in some Platonic way or other, there is an overarching and integrated culture or model that lies behind the shifting surface of social life alluded to in the previous paragraph, or we may restrict discussion to a narrow range of social phenomena, or we may try to reformulate the question.

There is another way to put it. What we see in Lukang is overlapping frameworks; multiple, partial, and inconsistent "models" and ideals; sets of structural poses; situational interpretations. I think of a stack of transparencies, or, to continue the Platonic imagery, overlapping slides projected onto the same screen by many projectors. Or, in an island full of noises, we have a large room full of voices and echoes. As observers we can use our scholarly theories and research methods to pick out certain conversations, as with a directional microphone or software that looks for key words. We can define certain sounds as signals, others as noise. Most analysis, almost of necessity, does this. Differing or rival schools of thought will disagree on what is signal and what noise. The wider the scope of our inquiry, the broader our questions, the more likely we are to pick up what appears to be cacophony, mutual interference, or disjointed utterances. On the other hand, a broad approach may enable us to realize that what appear to be distinct monologues or the conversation of a small circle are in fact responses to or comments on other pronouncements and conversations. Although the people in the room are certainly not singing in harmony and there is no score or script for them to follow, each speaker is aware of the earlier conversations and of what the other people will probably regard as appropriate examples, stories, or references.

Hence the culture of the people in the room can be thought of as the aggregate of examples, stories, maxims, and references that they recognize and employ to persuade or dissuade each other in particular circumstances.[16] In Lukang the aggregate common culture includes elements that we may, if we choose to, identify as "Confucian" or "Taoist" or "Republic of China primary school textbook" or "Hollywood stereotype." Most of these elements would be recognizable in other Taiwanese communities; many of them would be meaningful in communities on the Chinese mainland; a different subset would be meaningful in Singapore. From year to year the content will change slightly as people learn new things or find that citation of some examples or references no longer seems useful or appropriate to their current circumstances.

Such a way of thinking of culture offers several advantages. By downplaying the element of integration or internal consistency that is one element of that complex notion, it makes room for both the echoes of the Classics and the statements of shopkeepers, as it does for the same shopkeepers' descriptions of Lukang both as an undifferentiated community and as the backdrop for the contention of smiling villains. It permits analysis that includes both the Confucian Classics and the "Things the Master Did Not Speak Of" such as commerce and factional rivalry as aspects of a common fund of references, examples, and taken-for-granted definitions. It offers a way to recognize the significance and commonplace quality of a range of Chinese institutions, such as rotating credit associations and business networks that have seemed to fall outside the ambit of conscious Chinese categories and of much anthropological theorizing. This should enlarge our understanding of the nature of that society and help to obviate the depressing phenomenon of fieldworkers repeatedly and apparently independently rediscovering the significance of such matters as *hsin-yung* or *jen-ch'ing*.[17]

Once that is done, it should be more possible to listen to the full range of conversations, arguments, and special pleadings that makes up so much of the ongoing life of a Chinese community such as Lukang. By knowing what to expect, one could better apprehend not only those formal statements beginning "We Lukang people," but the variety of less formal, less self-conscious statements beginning "I don't know if it's true or not, but some people say . . ." or "Do you know old Huang who has the drug-store . . ." By recognizing that it is the very same actors standing before their ancestral altars, bargaining in the marketplace, conspiring in back rooms, and idly gossiping with the neighbors in the street on hot summer nights, one could more closely approach the ideal anthropological goal of presenting alien culture in a way that obviates the puzzles and paradoxes that our own misapprehensions generate.

Notes

1. The sociologist Ambrose Yeo-chi King argues that the concept of *kuan-hsi* is "deeply embedded in Confucian social theory," in that, in his reading of Confucianism, the Confucian individual is an active self, who defines roles and builds networks of relationships. See Ambrose Yeo-chi King, "Kuan-hsi and Network Building: a Sociological Interpretation," *Daedalus: Journal of the American Academy of Arts and Sciences* 120, 2 (Spring 1991), pp. 63–84.

2. For a discussion of the "narrow-heartedness" of women, see Margery Wolf, *Women and the Family in Rural Taiwan.* (Stanford: Stanford University Press, 1972).

3. Nathan Sivin, "On the Word 'Taoist' as a Source of Perplexity, With Special Reference to the Relations of Science and Religion in Traditional China," *History of Religions* 17, 3 and 4 (February–May 1978), pp. 303–330; Tu Weiming, Milan Hejtmanek, Alan Wachtman, eds., *The Confucian World Observed* (Honolulu: Program for Cultural Studies, East-West Center, 1992).

4. Abner Cohen, *Custom and Politics in Urban Africa.* (Berkeley: University of California Press, 1969), pp. 188–189.

5. Indeed, according to the classical Great Treatise of the Book of Changes, after the mythical sage-ruler Shen Nung made plows and taught the people agriculture, he next taught them to trade. Subsequently his successors taught transportation, defense, processing of grain, weapon production, burial and mourning, and, last, writing. Commerce is a fundamental component of civilization. The actions of Shen Nung are discussed in Wang

Gungwu, "The Chinese Urge to Civilize: Reflections on Change" (1982), in his collection of essays *The Chineseness of China* (Hong Kong: Oxford University Press, 1991), pp. 150–151.

6. See Mark Edward Lewis, *Sanctioned Violence in Early China* (Albany: State University of New York Press, 1991).

7. See *inter alia* Wong Siu-lun, "The Applicability of Asian Family Values to Other Sociocultural Settings," in Peter L. Berger and Hsin-Huang Michael Hsiao, eds., *In Search of an East Asian Development Model* (New Brunswick, N.J.: Transaction Publishers, 1988); Justin T. Niehoff, "The Villager as Industrialist: Ideologies of Household Manufacturing in Rural Taiwan," *Modern China* 13, 3 (1987), pp. 278–309; and Myron L. Cohen, "Family Management and Division in Rural China," *China Quarterly* 130 (June 1992), pp. 357–377.

8. Joanna Handlin Smith in Tu Weiming et al., 1992, p. 87.

9. Maurice Freedman, "The Politics of an Old State: A View from the Chinese Lineage," in John H. R. Davis, ed., *Choice and Change: Essays in Honour of Lucy Mair* (London: Athlone Press, 1974) (LSE Monographs on Social Anthroplogy, No. 50).

10. William Theodore de Bary, *The Trouble with Confucianism* (Cambridge: Harvard University Press, 1991), pp. 97–102. de Bary cites the work of Tu Wei-ming, *Centrality and Commonality: An Essay on Confucian Religiousness* (Albany: State University of New York Press, 1988).

11. Thomas A. Metzger, *The Internal Organization of Ch'ing Bureaucracy.* (Cambridge, Harvard University Press, 1973); *Escape from Predicament: Neo-Confucianism and China's Evolving Political Culture* (New York: Colombia University Press, 1977), esp. pp. 200–202, 234–235.

12. Ronald P. Dore, *Taking Japan Seriously: A Confucian Perspective on Leading Economic Issues* (Stanford: Stanford University Press, 1987). See chapter 9, "Goodwill and the Spirit of Market Capitalism," pp. 169–192.

13. B. Schwartz in Tu Weiming et al., 1992, pp. 16, 83.

14. Robert Weller, *Unities and Diversities in Chinese Religion* (Seattle: University of Washington Press, 1987).

15. For one example from many, see Wu Yu-shan's review of *The East Asian Region: Confucian Heritage and Its Modern Adap-*

tation (Princeton: Princeton University Press, 1991), a collection of essays edited by Gilbert Rozman, in *The China Quarterly* 129 (March 1992) pp. 258–259.

16. This way of considering a shared culture owes some inspiration to the views of Fredrik Barth, as set out in the concluding chapters of *Balinese Worlds* (Chicago: University of Chicago Press, 1993).

17. A partial list would include DeGlopper, 1972; Silin, 1972; Barton, 1977 and 1983; Kao Cheng-shu, "'Personal Trust' in the Large Businesses in Taiwan: A Traditional Foundation for Contemporary Economic Activities," and Wong Siu-lun, "Chinese Entrepreneurs and Business Trust," both in Gary Hamilton, ed., *Business Networks and Economic Development in East and Southeast Asia* (Hong Kong: Centre of Asian Studies, University of Hong Kong, 1991); Thomas Menkhoff, "Xinyong or How to Trust Trust?" *Internationales Asienforum* 23–4 (November 1992).

Bibliography

English Language Sources

Admiralty, Lords Commissioners of the. *China Sea Directory.* London: Admiralty, 1884.

Ahern, Emily Martin and Gates, Hill, eds. *The Anthropology of Taiwanese Society.* Stanford: Stanford University Press, 1981.

Amyot, Jacques. *The Chinese Community of Manila: A Study of the Adaptation of Chinese Familism to the Philippine Environment.* Unpublished Ph.D. Dissertation, University of Chicago, 1960.

Appleton, William. *A Cycle of Cathay.* New York: Columbia University Press, 1951.

B. B. "Life Saving and Other Benevolent Associations at Wuhu." *The China Review* 6 (1878).

Baker, Hugh. *A Chinese Lineage Village: Sheung Shui.* Stanford: Stanford University Press, 1968.

Baller, F. W. *The Sacred Edict (With a Translation of the Colloquial Rendering, Notes and Vocabulary).* Shanghai: American Presbyterian Mission Press, 1892.

Barclay, George. *Colonial Development and Population in Taiwan.* Princeton: Princeton University Press, 1954.

Barth, Fredrik. *Balinese Worlds.* Chicago: University of Chicago Press, 1993.

Barton, Clifton G. *Credit and Commercial Control: The Strategies and Methods of Chinese Businessmen in South Vietnam.* Unpublished Ph.D. Dissertation, Cornell University, 1977.

————. "Trust and Credit: Some Observations Regarding Business Strategies of Overseas Chinese Traders in South Vietnam" in L. A. Peter Gosling and Linda Y. C. Lim, eds., *The Chinese in Southeast Asia, Volume One: Ethnicity and Economic Activity*. Singapore: Maruzen Asia, 1983.

Benet, Francisco. "Sociology Uncertain: The Ideology of the Rural-Urban Continuum." *Comparative Studies in Society and History* 6,1 (1963).

Blok, Anton. *The Mafia of a Sicilian Village: 1860–1960*. New York: Harper and Row, 1974.

Brockman, Rosser H. "Commercial Contract Law in Late Nineteenth Century Taiwan" in Jerome A. Cohen, R. Randle Edwards and Fu-mei Chang Chen, eds., *Essays on China's Legal Tradition*. Princeton: Princeton University Press, 1980.

Burgess, John S. *The Guilds of Peking*. New York: Colombia University Press, 1928 (reprinted Taipei: Cheng-wen, 1966).

Chen Cheng-chih. "The Police and *Hoko* System in Taiwan under Japanese Administration." *Papers on Japan*. Vol. 4, Cambridge: Harvard University, 1967.

Chen Cheng-hsiang. *Taiwan: An Economic and Social Geography*. Taipei: Fu-min Institute of Economic Development, 1963.

Chen Ta. *Chinese Migrations*. Washington: U.S. Bureau of Labor Statistics, 1923.

Cheng, Lim-keak. *Social Change and the Chinese in Singapore*. Singapore: Singapore University Press, 1985.

Cheng, Lucie and Arthur Rosset. "Contract With a Chinese Face: Socially Embedded Factors in the Transformation from Hierarchy to Market, 1978–1989." *Journal of Chinese Law* 5, 2 (Fall 1991).

Cheng Tien-hsi. *China, Moulded by Confucius*. London: Stevens and Sons, 1946.

Chesneaux, Jean. *Popular Movements and Secret Societies in China, 1840–1950*. Stanford: Stanford University Press, 1972.

Clark, J. D. *Formosa*. Shanghai: 1896.

Cohen, Abner. *Custom and Politics in Urban Africa*. Berkeley: University of California Press, 1969.

Cohen, Myron H. "Family Management and Family Division in Contemporary Rural China." *The China Quarterly* 130 (June 1992).

————. "Cultural and Political Inventions in Modern China: The Case of the Chinese 'Peasant'." *Daedalus* 122, 2 (Spring 1993).

Colquhoun, A. R. and J. E. Steward-Lockhart. "A Sketch of Formosa." *The China Review* 13,3 (1885).

Crissman, Lawrence W. "The Structure of Local and Regional Systems" in Ahern, E. and Gates, H., eds., *The Anthropology of Taiwanese Society*. Stanford: Stanford University Press, 1981.

Davidson, James W. *The Island of Formosa*. New York: Macmillan, 1903 (Reprinted Taipei: Cheng-wen, nd.).

Dawson, Raymond. *The Chinese Chameleon*, London: Oxford University Press, 1967.

de Bary, William Theodore. *The Trouble With Confucianism*. Cambridge: Harvard University Press, 1991.

DeGlopper, Donald R. "Doing Business in Lukang" in W. E. Willmott, ed., *Economic Organization in Chinese Society*. Stanford: Stanford University Press, 1972.

————. "Religion and Ritual in Lukang" in A. P. Wolf ed., *Ritual and Religion in Chinese Society*. Stanford: Stanford University Press, 1974.

————. "Social Structure in a Nineteenth Century Taiwanese Port City" in G. W. Skinner, ed. *The City in Late Imperial China*. Stanford: Stanford University Press, 1977.

————. "Artisan Life and Work in Taiwan." *Modern China* 5,3 (July 1979)

————. "Lu-kang: A City and Its Trading System" in R.W. Knapp, ed. *China's Island Frontier: Studies in the Historical Geography of Taiwan*. Honolulu: University of Hawaii Press, 1980.

De Korne, J. C. *The Fellowship of Goodness (T'ung Shan She)*. Grand Rapids, Michigan, 1941.

Diamond, Norma. *K'un-shen: A Taiwanese Fishing Village*. New York: Holt Rhinehart and Winston, 1969.

Dore, Ronald P. *Taking Japan Seriously: A Confucian Perspective on Leading Economic Issues*. Stanford: Stanford University Press, 1987.

Dundes, Alan and Alessandro Falassi. *La Terra in Piazza: An Interpretation of the Palio of Siena.* Berkeley: University of California Press, 1975.

Edwardes, Michael. *East-West Passage,* New York: Taplinger, 1971.

Elvin, Mark. *The Pattern of the Chinese Past.* Stanford: Stanford University Press, 1973.

Evans-Pritchard, E. E. *The Nuer.* Oxford: Oxford University Press, 1940.

Fei Hsiao-tung. *Peasant Life in China.* London: Routledge and Kegan Paul, 1939.

Feuchtwang, Stephan. "Domestic and Communal Worship in Taiwan" in A.P. Wolf, ed., *Ritual and Religion in Chinese Society.* Stanford: Stanford University Press, 1974.

Firth, Raymond. "Social Organization and Social Change" *Journal of the Royal Anthropological Institute* 84, 1954. Reprinted in Firth, *Essays in Social Organization and Values.* London: Athlone Press, 1964.

Freedman, Maurice. *Lineage Organization in Southeastern China.* London: Athlone Press, 1958.

———. "Immigrants and Associations: Chinese in Nineteenth Century Singapore." *Comparative Studies in Society and History* 3,3 (April 1961).

———. *Chinese Lineage and Society: Fukien and Kwangtung.* London: Athlone Press, 1966.

———. "The Politics of an Old State: A View From the Chinese Lineage" in John H. R. Davis, ed. *Choice and Change: Essays in Honour of Lucy Mair.* London: Athlone Press, 1974.

Fried, Morton H. *Fabric of Chinese Society: A Study of the Social Life of a Chinese County Seat.* New York: Praeger, 1953. Reprinted, New York: Octagon Press, 1969.

Gallin, Bernard. *Hsin Hsing, Taiwan: A Chinese Village in Change.* Berkeley: University of California Press, 1966.

———, and Rita S. Gallin. "The Integration of Village Migrants in Taipei" in Mark Elvin and G. W. Skinner, eds., *The Chinese City Between Two Worlds.* Stanford: Stanford University Press, 1974.

Gearing, Frederick O. *Priests and Warriors: Social Structures for Cherokee Politics in the Eighteenth Century.* American Anthropological Association, Memoir 93, (Vol. 64, no.5, part 2, October 1962).

Gearing, Frederick O. *The Face of the Fox*, Chicago: Aldine, 1970.

Geertz, Clifford. "Religion as a Cultural System" in Michael Banton, ed., *Anthropological Approaches to the Study of Religion.* (Association of Social Anthroplogists Monograph No. 3) London: Tavistock, 1968.

———. "Deep Play: Notes on the Balinese Cock Fight" *Daedalus*, Winter 1972, reprinted in Geertz, *The Interpretation of Cultures.* New York: Basic Books, 1973.

Gladney, Dru C. *Muslim Chinese: Ethnic Nationalism in the People's Republic.* Cambridge: Harvard University Press, 1991.

Graham, A. C. *Two Chinese Philosophers: Ch'eng Ming-tao and Ch'eng Yi-ch'uan.* London: Lund Humphries, 1958.

Gutzlaff, Charles. "Journal of a Residence in Siam and of a Voyage along the Coast of China to Mantchou Tartary." *The Chinese Repository* (Canton) 1, 3 (1832).

Hamilton, Gary, ed., *Business Networks and Economic Development in East and Southeast Asia.* Hong Kong: Centre of Asian Studies, University of Hong Kong, 1991.

Hirsch, Fred. *Social Limits to Growth.* Cambridge: Harvard University Press, 1976.

Hu Hsien-chin. "The Chinese Concepts of Face." *American Anthropologist* 46, 1 (1944).

———. *The Common Descent Group in China and Its Functions.* New York: Viking Fund Publications in Anthropology, No. 10, 1948.

Hughes, George. *Amoy and the Surrounding Districts.* Hong Kong: Desouza, 1872.

Jacobs, J. Bruce. "The Cultural Bases of Factional Alignment and Division in a Rural Taiwanese Township." *Journal of Asian Studies* 36 (1976).

———. "A Preliminary Model of Particularistic Ties in Chinese Political Alliances: Kan-ch'ing and Kuan-hsi in a Rural Taiwanese Township." *China Quarterly* 78 (1979)

————. *Local Politics in a Rural Chinese Cultural Setting: A Field Study of Mazu Township, Taiwan.* Canberra: Contemporary China Centre, Australian National University, 1980.

Jordan, David K. *Gods, Ghosts and Ancestors: Folk Religion in a Taiwanese Village.* Berkeley: University of California Press, 1972.

Kao Cheng-shu. "'Personal Trust' in the Large Businesses in Taiwan: A Traditional Foundation for Contemporary Economic Activities," in Gary Hamilton, ed., *Business Networks and Economic Development in East and Southeast Asia.* Hong Kong: University of Hong Kong, 1991.

Kaufman-Winn, Jane. "Decriminalizing Bad Checks Should Help to Rationalize Taiwan's Financial System." *East Asian Executive Reports* 8,8 (August 1986)

King, Ambrose Y. "The Development and Death of Chinese Academic Sociology." *Modern Asian Studies* 12, 1 (Feb. 1978).

————. "Kuan-hsi and Network Building: A Sociological Interpretation." *Daedalus: Journal of the American Academy of Arts and Sciences* 120, 2 (Spring 1991).

King, Frank H. *Money and Monetary Policy in China, 1845–1895.* Cambridge: Harvard University Press, 1965.

Kuhn, Philip A. *Rebellion and Its Enemies in Late Imperial China.* Cambridge: Harvard University Press, 1970.

Kulp, Daniel. *Country Life in South China.* New York: Teachers' College (Colombia University), 1925.

Lamley, Harry J. *The Taiwan Literati and Early Japanese Rule.* Unpublished Ph.D. Dissertation, University of Washington, 1964.

————. "The Formation of Cities: Initiative and Motivation in Building Three Walled Cities in Taiwan" in G. W. Skinner, ed., *The City in Late Imperial China.* Stanford: Stanford University Press, 1977.

————. "Subethnic Rivalry in the Ch'ing Period" in Emily M. Ahern and Hill Gates, eds., *The Anthropology of Taiwanese Society.* Stanford: Stanford University Press, 1981.

Lapidus, Ira M. "Hierarchies and Networks: A Comparison of Chinese and Islamic Societies" in Frederic Wakeman and Carolyn

Grant, eds., *Conflict and Control in Late Imperial China*. Berkeley: University of California Press, 1975.

Lewis, Mark E. *Sanctioned Violence in Early China*. Albany: State University of New York Press, 1991.

Li Ang (pseud). See Shih Shu-tuan.

Lindsay, Hugh. *A Voyage to the Northern Ports of China in the Ship Lord Amherst*. London: B. Fellowes, 1834.

Link, Carol A. *Japanese Cabinetmaking: A Dynamic System of Decision and Interactions in a Technical Context*. Unpublished Ph.D. Dissertation, University of Illinois, 1975.

McGowan, D. J. "Chinese Chambers of Commerce and Trades Union." *Journal of the North China Branch of the Royal Asiatic Society* 21 (1886).

March, Andrew. *The Idea of China*. New York: Praeger, 1974.

Menkhoff, Thomas. "Xinyong or How to Trust Trust? Chinese Non-Contractual Business Relations and Social Structure: The Singapore Case." *Internationales Asienforum*. Hamburg, 23–24 (November 1992).

Meskill, Johanna M. *A Chinese Pioneer Family: the Lins of Wufeng, Taiwan, 1729–1895*. Princeton: Princeton University Press, 1979.

Metzger, Thomas A. *The Internal Organization of Ch'ing Bureaucracy*. Cambridge: Harvard University Press, 1973.

———. *Escape From Predicament: Neo-Confucianism and China's Evolving Political Culture*. New York: Colombia University Press, 1977.

Morse, Hosea B. *The Guilds of China*. London: Longmans Green, 1909 (reprinted Taipei: Cheng-wen, 1966).

Newell, William H. *Treacherous River: A Study of Rural Chinese in North Malaya*. Kuala Lumpur: University of Malaya Press, 1962.

Ng, Chin-Keong. *Trade and Society: The Amoy Network on the China Coast, 1683–1735*. Singapore: Singapore University Press, 1983.

Niehoff, Justin T. "The Villager as Industrialist: Ideologies of Household Manufacturing in Rural Taiwan." *Modern China* 13, 3 (1987).

Olson, Mancur. *The Logic of Collective Action: Public Goods and the Theory of Groups*. Cambridge: Harvard University Press, 1965.

———, Anthony Downs, Fred Hirsch, and David Reisman. *Theories of Collective Action*. New York: St. Martin's Press, 1990.

Oxfeld, Ellen, "Individualism, Holism, and the Market Mentality: Notes on the Recollections of a Chinese Entrepreneur." *Cultural Anthropology* 7,3 (August 1992).

Pickering, W.(illiam) A. *Pioneering in Formosa*. London: Hurst & Blackett, 1898.

Pillsbury, Barbara. *Cohesion and Conflict in a Chinese Muslim Minority*. Unpublished Ph.D. Dissertation, Colombia University, 1973.

Radcliffe-Brown, A. R. "On Social Structure" in *Structure and Function in Primitive Society*. London: Cohen and West, 1952.

Rawski, Evelyn S. *Agricultural Change and the Peasant Economy of South China*. Cambridge: Harvard University Press, 1972.

Redfield, Robert. *The Little Community* and *Peasant Society and Culture*. Chicago: University of Chicago Press, 1960.

Rowe, William T. *Hankow: Commerce and Society in a Chinese City, 1796–1889*. Stanford: Stanford University Press, 1984.

———. *Hankow: Conflict and Community in a Chinese City, 1796–1895*. Stanford: Stanford University Press, 1989.

Ryan, Edward. *The Value System of a Chinese Community in Java*. Unpublished Ph.D. Dissertation, Harvard University, 1961.

Schneider, David M. "Some Muddles in the Models: or How the System Really Works" in Michael Banton, ed., *The Relevance of Models for Social Anthropology*. (Association of Social Anthropologists Monograph No. 1) London: Tavistock, 1965.

Schneider, Jane and Peter. *Culture and Political Economy in Western Sicily*. New York: Academic Press, 1976.

Shepherd, John Robert. *Statecraft and Political Economy on the Taiwan Frontier 1600–1800*. Stanford: Stanford University Press, 1993.

Shih Shu-tuan [Li Ang, pseud.]. *The Butcher's Wife*. San Fransisco: North Point Press, 1986. (Translated from the Chinese *Sha Fu* (Taipei: 1983) by Howard Goldblatt and Ellen Yeung).

Silin, Robert. *Trust and Confidence in a Hong Kong Wholesale Vegetable Market.* Unpublished M.A. Dissertation, University of Hawaii, 1964.

————. "Marketing and Credit in a Hong Kong Wholesale Market" in W. E. Willmott, ed., *Economic Organization in Chinese Society.* Stanford: Stanford University Press, 1972.

————. *Leadership and Values: The Organization of Taiwanese Large-Scale Enterprises.* Cambridge: Harvard University Press, 1976.

Simmel, Georg. *Conflict and the Web of Group Affiliations.* (Translated from *Soziologie* (1908) by Kurt H. Wolf and Reinhard Bendix) Glencoe, Ill.: The Free Press, 1953.

Sivin, Nathan. "On the Word 'Taoist' as a Source of Perplexity, With Specual Reference to the Relations of Science and Religion in Traditional China." *History of Religions* 17, 3 and 4 (February, May 1978).

Skinner, G. W. *Chinese Society in Thailand: An Analytical History.* Ithaca: Cornell University Press, 1957.

————. *Leadership and Power in the Chinese Community of Thailand.* Ithaca: Cornell University Press, 1958.

————. "Overseas Chinese Leadership: Paradigm for a Paradox" in Gehan Wijeyewardena, ed., *Leadership and Authority.* Singapore: Singapore University Press, 1968.

————. "Mobility Strategies in Late Imperial China: A Regional Systems Analysis" in Carol A. Smith, ed., *Regional Analysis: Volume One: Economic Systems.* New York: Academic Press, 1976.

————, ed., *The City in Late Imperial China.* Stanford: Stanford University Press, 1977.

Smith. Arthur H. *Chinese Characteristics.* New York: Fleming E. Revell, 1894.

Sneider, Vern. *A Pail of Oysters.* New York: G. P. Putnam's, 1953.

Stein, Maurice R. *The Eclipse of Community: An Interpretation of American Studies.* Princeton: Princeton University Press, 1960.

Tenenbaum, Edward. *Taiwan's Turning Point.* Washington: Continental-Allied, 1963.

Thompson, Laurence G. "The Junk Passage Across the Taiwan

Straits: Two Early Chinese Accounts." *Harvard Journal of Asiatic Studies* 28 (1968).

T'ien Ju-kang. *The Chinese of Sarawak*. London: Athlone Press, 1953.

Topley, Marjorie. "The Great Way of Former Heaven." *Bulletin of the School of Oriental and African Studies* (1963).

Wang, Gungwu. *The Chineseness of China*. Hong Kong: Oxford University Press, 1991.

Ward, Barbara E. "Cash or Credit Crops? An Examination of Some Implications of Peasant Commercial Production with Special Reference to the Multiplicity of Traders and Middlemen." *Economic Development and Cultural Change* 8, 2 (January 1960).

————. "Varieties of the Conscious Model: The Fishermen of South China" *in* M. E. Banton, ed., *The Relevance of Models for Social Anthropology*. London: Tavistock Press, 1968.

Watson, James L. *Emigration and the Chinese Lineage: The Mans in Hong Kong and London*. Berkeley: University of California Press, 1975.

Watt, John R. *The District Magistrate in Late Imperial China*. New York: Colombia University Press, 1972.

————. "The Yamen and Urban Administration" in G. W. Skinner, ed., *The City in Late Imperial China*. Stanford: Stanford University Press, 1977.

Weller, Robert P. *Unities and Diversities in Chinese Religion*. Seattle: University of Washington Press, 1987.

Williams, Frederick W. "Chinese and Medieval Guilds." *Yale Review* (August 1892).

Willmott, Donald E. *The Chinese of Semarang*. Ithaca: Cornell University Press, 1960.

Willmott, William E. *The Political Structure of the Chinese Community in Cambodia*. London: Athlone Press, 1970.

Winkler, Edwin A. "Roles Linking State and Society" in Ahern, E. and Gates, H., eds., *The Anthropology of Taiwanese Society*. Stanford: Stanford University Press, 1981.

Williams, Raymond. *The Country and the City*. London: Oxford University Press, 1973.